RADICAL EQUATIONS

Radical Equations

Math Literacy and Civil Rights

ROBERT P. MOSES

AND CHARLES E. COBB, JR.

Beacon Press

BOSTON

Beacon Press
25 Beacon Street
Boston, Massachusetts 02108-2892
www.beacon.org

Beacon Press books
are published under the auspices of
the Unitarian Universalist Association of Congregations.

05 04 03 02 01   8 7 6 5 4 3

This book is printed on acid-free paper that meets the uncoated paper
ANSI/NISO specifications for permanence as revised in 1992.

Composition by Wilsted & Taylor Publishing Services

Library of Congress Cataloging-in-Publication Data
Moses, Robert P.
    Radical equations : math literacy and civil rights /
Robert P. Moses and Charles E. Cobb, Jr.
            p.   cm.
Includes index.
        ISBN 0-8070-3126-7 (acid-free paper)
    1. Minorities—Civil rights—United States.   2. Minorities—
Education—United States.   3. Algebra—Study and teaching (Middle
school)—United States.   4. Mathematics—Study and teaching (Middle
school)—United States.   5. Literacy—United States.   6. United States—
Social conditions—1980–   7. United States—Race relations.   8. Social
justice—United States.   9. Afro-Americans—Southern States—History—
20th century.   10. Civil rights movements—Southern States—History—
20th century.   I. Cobb, Charles E., Jr.   II. Title.
        E184.A1   M7   2001
        512'.071'073—dc21

                                            00-010364

CONTENTS

David Dennis

Poor Bob, I thought, disheartened. He's lost his mind, "flipped out." I was married then and I told my wife, Carolyn, "He's out here comparing math to the civil rights movement, saying algebra is some kind of 'gatekeeper' course." Carolyn asked me if I understood what Bob meant by that. I told her I was afraid he had lost me when he said that if our kids were going to gain access to a first-class education and first-class citizenship, algebra was the necessary first step. He was trying to make a connection between his work with kids in getting them math literate and what we were doing in the sixties getting people registered to vote. "The young people today are the sharecroppers," Bob said. "The sharecroppers today are the young people. Kids are being tracked out." They're being told early that algebra is not for them just as sharecroppers and Black people were told voting was not for them. "Testing was put in place for both," he explained in that quiet, insistent way of his.

Bob and I had not talked in years, had not seen each other in over two decades, so for a few days we had been catching up in early-morning conversation while sitting beside the pool of the Edison Wathall Hotel in Jackson, Mississippi. Outrage over the 1988 Hollywood movie *Mississippi Burning* had brought us together again. Set in Philadelphia, Mississippi, it focuses on the murders of James Chaney, Mickey Schwerner, and Andy Goodman, who were killed at the start of the 1964 Summer Project when I was Mississippi director for the Congress of Racial Equality (CORE). Mickey was a CORE field secretary, James was a local volunteer, and Andy was a summer volunteer who had just arrived from New York. The movie was a wrongheaded attempt at a sympathetic portrayal of the movement. It removed Blacks from the center of Mississippi's civil rights struggle, portraying the African-American community as not just weak, but spineless as white power rampaged. In an especially galling falsification of history, the heroes of the film were the FBI. So some of us from the movement, especially those who had been in Mississippi's movement, decided to meet. Bob had come down from Cambridge, Massachusetts, and I came up from New Orleans for the gathering. Although the movie triggered the get-together, all of us were drawn by the need to come to grips with movement history. We were concerned about how it would be viewed and understood by future generations. Now here I was in this conversation with Bob about his new effort, the Algebra Project. For two days I listened to him talk about it, trying to understand what he was doing. I didn't. I felt like everybody else: this so-called target population he was working with didn't want to learn. I didn't know public schools. As a successful lawyer, I'd sent my kids to private and Catholic schools. I was happy to see Bob again and to catch up with his life. But, his conversation . . . well, it just seemed weird.

It wasn't the first time I'd raised my eyebrows at Bob's plans. As I pondered his ideas my mind went back to my early civil rights movement days. The movement was what first brought us together. In 1961, I was a Dillard University student until I joined the freedom riders and landed in jail in Jackson, Mississippi. Then Dillard asked me to leave and I based in Shreveport, Louisiana, as a field secretary for CORE. I was coming home again. I'd spent the first eight years of my life on plantations, and one of them was the Miles plantation near Shreveport, before my family moved into town to a house that my grandfather built. I am named after my grandfather—David. People called my grandmother "Miss Bessie"; my grandfather always called her "friend." But that's another story.

It was while living in that Shreveport house that I first became aware of both the patience and the direct action required for effective Black struggle. We had no sewage line or electricity.

Both stopped at the end of the white neighborhood a couple of blocks away. My grandmother asked the city for electricity and an extension of the sewage line and the city said it would if people in our neighborhood dug a ditch and postholes. So after working all day, the men came home and then worked some more digging. My grandmother organized the women to feed the men. It took months. When it was finished the city came out and inspected it, then said the ditch and postholes were on the wrong side of the road. "Do them over if you want the sewer line and electricity," they said. The men gave up. Quit. Every evening after that my grandmother dragged a chair to the side of the road, sat in it, and sang. Day after day she did that. Kids teased her. Neighbors shook their heads and said she'd gone crazy. But then one day, Mr. Jack from across the street stopped in front of her and asked, "If I start digging, will you stop sitting here singing?" She said yes. He started digging. She stopped sitting and singing. Soon other men joined Mr. Jack. When they finished, instead of my grandmother going down to ask for electric power and the sewer line, they all went down. And they got it. And later, got the dirt road paved. Throughout the South, what is now known as the 1960s civil rights movement has roots in these kinds of direct action.

When the students at Southern University in Baton Rouge began demonstrating I started working with them. These protests led the students into voter registration work and Bob came to Louisiana with the idea of recruiting some of us to come into McComb, Mississippi. I wasn't very impressed with the idea of going to McComb. The way I saw it, to get people out of the middle of Louisiana to go to Mississippi just didn't make a whole lot of sense. Also, at the time although I recognized the importance of voter registration, I was more committed to direct action as the best way to build the movement. So, I stayed in Louisiana. But slowly, with the help and guidance of other people like Jim McCain, a South Carolinian and CORE program coordinator, my interest in the kind of work Bob was doing grew. Specifically I began asking myself: If you don't control the money, what does it mean to sit in at a lunch counter for integration? What is power?

was the underlying question . . . *was* my question. I began to think that maybe going to Mississippi, where organizing seemed central to civil rights work, would help answer the question.

CORE's Mississippi field secretary Tom Gaither was leaving the state and the organization was looking for a replacement in the winter of 1962. I said I wanted to take his place. CORE saw its main role in Mississippi as supervising freedom riders; by then I had something different in mind.

That fall Bob had been assisting the campaign of Reverend R. L. T. Smith for the United States Congress. Smith was the first African American to run for that office since Reconstruction. (Up in the Delta, Jim Bevel had managed Reverend Theodore Trammell in a similar campaign for a congressional seat.) Bob was thinking about a statewide voter registration drive. He and Tom had already written a memo to SNCC and CORE expressing the need for a coordinated effort by the various organizations working in Mississippi. The memo also suggested concentrating in those areas of the state where Black people made up at least 45 percent of the population.

In February, Mississippi leaders of the Council of Federated Organizations (COFO), which brought together all of Mississippi's civil rights organizations, agreed and reorganized, electing Aaron Henry, state president of the NAACP, as its head, and launched a new statewide voter registration effort. SNCC and CORE field secretaries formed COFO's staff. Bob was director; I was assistant director. Bob tells the story of what happened then in this book. Our work transformed the politics of a state. And, it changed our lives.

With so much history connecting us I couldn't just shrug off Bob's new effort to organize around math literacy. Our conversation around *Mississippi Burning* turned to what might be done around documenting the movement—finding ways to tell our own stories. It had been an issue of deep concern to me for some time but I had buried it as I pursued my law career. Now, talking with Bob and being back in Mississippi brought it back to the surface again.

Phil Alden Robinson, a filmmaker who had directed *Field of Dreams,* contacted Bob about doing a story built around his work in McComb. He had some money from Universal Studios to begin this. I had gone back to Louisiana and Bob contacted me there. Bob thought that this film project opened a way to begin some of the documentary work we had talked about. I agreed to work with him. Carolyn and I had put together an organization in Louisiana called Positive Innovations with the idea being to document Louisiana's civil rights movement history. Bob wanted to set up a corporation controlled by movement people in Mississippi to do this. The story of the movement belonged to the people, Bob felt. *This* was the Bob I remembered. He was getting my attention again.

History has a way of repeating itself. As I worked on the film, Bob and his wife, Janet, visited with me and my family at our home in Lafayette, Louisiana, and continued his conversations with me about the Algebra Project. Although the project had begun in Cambridge, Massachusetts, where he was living, and had spread to several other cities in the North, Bob was interested in developing the project in the South, especially in Mississippi. He had begun developing the project in Atlanta. Then in 1991 Bob received a grant from the Ford Foundation by way of the Southern Regional Council to introduce the Algebra Project to the Mississippi Delta. He asked me to work with him on that because I knew this terrain and with so much pulling on him now he could hardly devote all of his time to the Delta. Although I still had not come to any clear conclusions about the project in my own mind, I was beginning to sense its importance. So I agreed.

A three-day visit to Chicago, where an Algebra Project teacher training was under way, led me into some public schools in that city. And that experience gave me a good push toward understanding why the project was so necessary. I had not been involved with public schools for years and while visiting them in that city it seemed as if I had traveled to another world. In one school I saw a mother come in and jump on a teacher in the hallway, pushing her to the wall while actually beginning to throw punches. One day while I was talking to a kid, another kid walked up behind him and hit him in the head with a brick or something. On another occasion I saw a teacher I'd met earlier standing by a wall with his back to me. Not understanding the way things were, I walked up to him and sort of slapped him on the back to say hello. I almost had to peel him off the wall; I had frightened him that much.

Rather than places of learning, some Chicago schools seemed to be places where everybody was trying just to survive. And it wasn't just one "bad" school. Most of the schools I visited seemed like this. I remember overhearing a young Latina tell a group of kids about a trip downtown and the "moving stairs." She'd lived in Chicago all of her life and never seen an escalator, something I might have expected from a kid from rural Mississippi or Louisiana, but not a kid from the big city. What Bob was talking about really hit me and began to sink in. I could see that masses of our children were not being educated. How could they be in an environment like what I was witnessing in Chicago? There was a definite disconnect between schools and communities, teachers and students. It wasn't that students didn't care about learning; they had an attitude: "Who cares?" they asked, and then concluded, "I just do what I want, no one else really cares about it."

Teachers, many of whom do care, react to the attitude in different ways—some by abandoning the kids; some by sighing and understanding that something really needs to be done but who feel powerless to do anything themselves; some by throwing up their hands in hopelessness, feeling that the kids don't want to learn or that they cannot learn. Many are frustrated, underpaid, overwhelmed by "quick fix" programs and feel that they are in the middle being blamed by politicians, school officials, parents, and students for the failure of "broken education" systems that they have no control over. Many feel that they do not have anyplace to turn.

Dysfunctional schools, lack of community involvement, and the sight of our young people being flung into the future's wastebaskets are of course not unique to Chicago, but enormous educational systems like that seem to require hacking through an impossibly thick jungle of difficulties. With relief, I returned to the job of tackling problems below the Mason-Dixon line.

Going back into the Delta after all my years practicing law was like getting religion. I could hear Mrs. Fannie Lou Hamer's voice, Amzie Moore's voice, two of the many Black Mississippians who had struggled so forcefully for the civil rights many young people take for granted today. I felt, too, something was owed Mississippi. In a real way I had come of age here—through the work, through the people, through the pain. Only illness—bronchitis—had kept me from joining Jimmy Chaney, Mickey Schwerner, and Andy Goodman when they drove my car into Neshoba County to investigate a burned-out church on June 21, 1964. Something was owed them, and all the others flung into Mississippi rivers and swamps. Dave Dennis, you have unfinished business with this state, I thought as I began to reconnect with it. At the same meeting where Bob and I were reunited after twenty-four years, another Mississippi movement stalwart's words, Mrs. Annie Devine's, had flayed me: "You gave birth and you left, and you haven't done anything to support your children."

I began spending more time in the state, continuing my conversations with Bob and traveling from Layfayette to the Delta twice monthly for the Algebra Project as well as assisting with Phil's film. One day, I realized I just couldn't leave Mississippi again. So, in August of 1992, I moved myself and my family to Jackson and accepted the position of director of the Southern Initiative of the Algebra Project. That decision caused startled friends and colleagues to react to me as I had reacted to Bob at the Edison Wathall Hotel. *Mississippi! Has he lost his mind?*

I had organized in Mississippi in the 1960s. Now, with the Algebra Project I was organizing again. The fundamentals are the same. The movement depended on our being able to tap into community and family. So too does the Algebra Project, especially the Southern Initiative of the Algebra Project. In the years since the civil rights movement of the 1960s the customary role of adults to look out for children and offer role models to help guide them to adulthood has weakened. The Southern Initiative has developed a program aimed at bringing students together with adults—teachers, parents, and community leaders—around educational reform. If the educational system is going to change, the important customary role of adults being there for the young needs to be reinstated at all levels. And the educational system must be responsive to the needs and interests of the community. That is what we do.

We started with the kids. The kids then pulled in their parents, who began attending meetings and backing up their kids' concerns. Then the adults began to raise their own concerns about the school system. I remembered a reply Bob once made to a reporter when he was asked, "How do you organize?" "By bouncing a ball," he replied. "What?" asked the puzzled reporter. "You bounce a ball," Bob explained quietly. "You stand on a street and bounce a ball. Soon all the children come around. You keep on bouncing the ball. Before long it runs under someone's porch and then you meet the adults."

The Algebra Project has spread across the country with varied impact since its start twenty years ago in Cambridge, Massachusetts. In particular, it has taken root in the South. As director of the Southern Initiative of the Algebra Project I take great pride in that fact. I am also compelled to point out that the project has deep roots in the southern civil rights movement, which perhaps gives us a head start. Bob will describe those roots in this book.

But, you are perhaps asking yourself now, what's this got to do with your life? The short answer is, the civil rights struggle—which began long before the 1960s—has led the way to every important and progressive change in this nation. That is not a boast, that is a fact. You live better because of every fight for civil rights that has been waged. Math literacy, Bob argues in this book, is a civil rights struggle. And the story of the Algebra Project told in these pages begins with the civil rights movement as Bob experienced it. In my mind, this book is worth reading as much because Bob Moses has decided to begin it by telling his story as it is because of its insights into the Algebra Project.

Part I of *Radical Equations* portrays the Algebra Project's southern civil rights movement roots. Even admirers of our efforts still struggle, as I did, to grasp how math connects to civil rights and citizenship. So this section of the book also discusses the high-tech "revolution" that has so radically changed the workplace since World War II, making the case for the linkage between algebra and citizenship. Leadership is needed for this challenge. In painting a portrait of key parts of his movement experience, Bob shows how leadership emerges from movement and movement emerges from organizing around issues on which there is consensus. Consensus on the importance of math literacy may be emerging.

Part II focuses on the Algebra Project today. It is largely set in the South, partly to reinforce understanding of the project's civil rights roots. Here Bob elaborates on what makes the AP special and necessary, offers stories from the classroom, and considers how schools and communities can begin to transform math education. He explores the conflict between old traditions and new changes that slows, and in some cases prevents, embrace of the Algebra Project. The book begins and ends optimistically, foreseeing the emergence of a cadre of young people who are starting to impact the culture of teenagers in school.

The book, like the Algebra Project, is special to me. In a real sense the project saved my life by recommitting me to the movement and ideas of meaningful social change. And no, I haven't lost my mind either.

PART ONE

In the Spirit of Ella

*The Algebra Project and
the Organizing Tradition
of the Civil Rights Movement*

CHAPTER I

Algebra and Civil Rights?

In order for us as poor and oppressed people to become a part of a society that is meaningful, the system under which we now exist has to be radically changed. This means that we are going to have to learn to think in radical terms. I use the term *radical* in its original meaning—getting down to and understanding the root cause. It means facing a system that does not lend itself to your needs and devising means by which you change that system. That is easier said than done. But one of the things that has to be faced is, in the process of wanting to change that system, how much have we got to do to find out who we are, where we have come from and where we are going. . . . I am saying as you must say, too, that in order to see where we are going, we not only must *remember* where we have been, but we must *understand* where we have been.

Ella Baker

The sit-ins woke me up.

Until then, my Black life was conflicted. I was a twenty-six-year-old teacher at Horace Mann, an elite private school in the Bronx, moving back and forth between the sharply contrasting worlds of Hamilton College, Harvard University, Horace Mann, and Harlem.

The sit-ins hit me powerfully, in the soul as well as the brain. I was mesmerized by the pictures I saw almost every day on the front pages of the *New York Times*—young committed Black faces seated at lunch counters or picketing, directly and with great dignity, challenging white supremacy in the South. They looked like I felt.

It was the sit-in movement that led me to Mississippi for the first time in 1960. And that trip changed my life. I returned to the state a year later and over the next four years, was transformed as I took part in the voter registration movement there. The great campaigns of protest so identified with Dr. Martin Luther King, Jr., were swirling around us, inspiring immense crowds in vast public spaces. But along with students from the sit-in movement, in Mississippi I became immersed in and committed to the older but less well-known tradition of community organizing. In my mind, Ella Baker, who helped to found Dr. King's organization, symbolizes this organizing tradition—quiet work in out-of-the-way places and the commitment of organizers digging into local communities.

She was our "*fundi.*" In Tanzania, where I lived for a time in the 1970s, the Swahili word *fundi* refers to a concept of passing on knowledge through direct contact with people who are *fundis*—skilled craftsmen and instructors. Ella Baker, as well as others, was our *fundi* in the tradition of community organizing. Borrowing from another African tradition, I feel the need to speak the names of at least some of these important adult Black grassroots leaders who quietly shaped not only Mississippi's civil rights movement, but the southern civil rights movement as a whole: Amzie Moore, Fannie Lou Hamer, Hartman Turnbow, Irene Johnson, Victoria Gray, Vernon Dahmer, Unita Blackwell, Henry Sias, Aylene Quin, C. O. Chinn, C. C. Bryant, Webb Owens, E. W. Steptoe, Annie Devine, and Hazel Palmer. Their work, which also educated me and other young people, changed the political terrain of a state, and of the nation. What they were is who we are now.

In those days, of course, the issue was the right to vote, and the question was political access. Voter registration was by no means the only issue one could have fought for, but it was crucial and urgent: Black people had no real control over their political lives, and the time was right to organize a movement to change this. There existed a powerful consensus on the issue of gaining the political franchise, and the drive for voter registration—especially where it took place deep in the Black belt of the South—captured the imaginations of Americans, particularly of African Americans. So, for a short period of time, because there was agreement among all of the people acting to change Mississippi, we were able to get resources and people from around the country to come and work with us on a common program to get the vote. There was consensus providing a base for strategy and action.

Today, I want to argue, the most urgent social issue affecting poor people and people of color is economic access. In today's world, economic access and full citizenship depend crucially on math and science literacy. I believe that the absence of math literacy in urban and rural communities throughout this country is an issue as urgent as the lack of registered Black voters in Mississippi was in 1961. I believe we can get the same kind of consensus we had in the 1960s for the effort of repairing this. And I believe that solving the problem requires exactly the kind of community organizing that changed the South in the 1960s. This has been my work—and that of the Algebra Project—for the past twenty years.

I know how strange it can sound to say that math literacy—and algebra in particular—is the key to the future of disenfranchised communities, but that's what I think, and believe with all of my heart. Let me tell you how and why.

HOW MATHEMATICS BECAME
A CIVIL RIGHTS BATTLEGROUND

When I first came to Mississippi, most Black people living in the rich cotton-growing land of the Delta, where they were a majority of the population, were living in serfdom on plantations. They had no control over their lives—their political lives, their economic lives, their educational lives. Within industrialized U.S. society, a microcosm of serfdom had been allowed to grow. The civil rights movement used the vote and political access to try to break that up.

We are growing similar serflike communities within our cities today. This began to become apparent as the southern civil rights movement was gaining some of its most important breakthroughs.

In 1965, Los Angeles and other urban areas exploded for a brief second and everyone got concerned. Those of us who live in these neighborhoods today are watching them *implode* all of the time. The violence and the criminalization make people eat each other up. Most of what is proposed in response are Band-Aid solutions—build more jails, put more police on the street. That is working at the problem from the back end.

What is central now is the need for economic access; the political process has been opened—there are no formal barriers to voting, for example—but economic access, taking advantage of new technologies and economic opportunity, demands as much effort as political struggle required in the 1960s.

A great technological shift has occurred that places the need for math literacy front and center. Consider two epochal machines from the middle of the twentieth century, and how much our society has changed since they were introduced.

The Hopson plantation, a few miles south of Clarksdale on Highway 49, is one of the largest and oldest in Mississippi. In our work we passed it often in the 1960s, unaware of its significance. On a piece of the plantation's land, just off the main highway by the banks of a small creek and a hog farm, there's an old rusted-out machine, one of the first cotton-picking machines used in the state of Mississippi. A nearby marker reports that on October 2, 1944, the Hopson plantation was the site of the first demonstration of a reliable mechanical cotton picker. On that day, a crowd of almost three thousand sharecroppers, landowners, and townspeople gathered to watch eight bright red machines pick a field of cotton.

Each machine picked about one thousand pounds in an hour. A good human cotton picker could pick about twenty to thirty pounds an hour. On that first day the machines picked all of the cotton in the field, about sixty-two bales. In dollars and cents, according to the remarkably precise calculations of plantation owner Howell Hopson, the cost of picking by machine was $5.26; the cost of picking by hand was $39.41.

Afterward, in a memo, Hopson compared the introduction of

the new harvester to the introduction of the cotton gin more than two centuries earlier. But Hopson understated the social implications of the machine. By speeding up the processing of raw cotton, the cotton gin had created the demand for cheap labor that was met by the enslavement of Africans. Sharecropping continued the fundamental relations of slavery: Black labor, white power. Although slavery was abolished, in the decades after the Civil War all of the laws and the police powers of the state were aimed at ensuring that Black economic life be confined to labor in the cotton fields; that no other arena of opportunity be envisioned. Segregation in this sense of dependency on Black labor was a matter of economic survival for whites in states like Mississippi. With the mechanical cotton picker, this was no longer true. And this fact would not only slowly begin to change the economics of Mississippi, but its politics as well. Put simply, Black manual labor became far less necessary. The mechanical cotton picker was perhaps the single most important reason why the White Citizens Council could mount a drive to "export" Black people out of the state after the 1954 Supreme Court decision with so little objection from the powerful planters. Economic necessity no longer acted as a constraint on the virulence of white racism.

The cotton-picking machine was part of a larger technological transformation affecting the entire nation. The year before cotton was first picked by machine in Mississippi, at the University of Pennsylvania the United States Army had contracted some of the school's best engineers to develop an electronic machine for calculating artillery-firing tables. The result was the Electronic Numerical Integrator and Computer (ENIAC), the world's first programmable computer. It was a monster of a machine, weighing thirty tons, standing ten feet high and eighty feet wide with over eighteen thousand vacuum tubes and rewirable control panels. Although it had far less power than today's typical portable computer, ENIAC ushered in the computer era. And just as automation and the mechanical cotton picker were changing cotton fields and southern agriculture, so, inexorably, would the computer push us from the assembly line by shifting work away from industrially based technology to computer-based technology. In field and factory, the twentieth century was being uprooted.

With the joining of science, "high" technology, and commerce, something very different from the smokestack industries that arose in the last century began to dominate production and the economy. Among the offspring of the new technology were fiber optics, computers and electronics, polymers, "research and development," and a range of information technologies. Almost anyone driving a car today is driving a wheeled computer. Detroit automakers now spend more money putting onboard computers and microprocessors in cars than they spend on steel. In industrial zones like the Chicago area, steel plants and slaughterhouses closed or began moving away around the same time the mechanized South began pushing people out. The industrial corridor of great factory cities lying between the Great Lakes and the Atlantic that once powered the economy acquired a new name: the rust belt.

And as the need for assembly line workers diminished, the need for what economists have begun to call the "knowledge worker" grew. Such workers have technical skills related to computers and automated machinery, and interpersonal skills such as the ability to communicate effectively and work as part of a team. The need for such workers continues to grow along with their salaries. The American Electronics Association (AEA) defines high-tech workers as those working in computers, consumer electronics, communications equipment, electronic components, semiconductors, industrial electronics, photonics, software services, data processing, and defense electronics. This industry paid a total of $280 billion in wages between 1997 and 1999 according to the AEA. During that same period the group says, high-tech workers earned 82 percent more than people in other industries earned.

Sixty percent of new jobs will require skills possessed by only 22 percent of the young people entering the job market now. These jobs require use of a computer and pay about 15 percent more than jobs that do not. And those jobs that do not are dwindling. Right now, the Department of Labor says, 70 percent of all jobs require technology literacy; by the year 2010 *all* jobs will require significant technical skills. And if that seems unimaginable, consider this: the Department of Labor says that 80 percent of those future jobs *do not yet exist*. The demand for high-tech workers is now, however. "If there is a dark cloud," former AEA chairman Ed Bersoff told a reporter, "it's that if the trend continues [and the tech industry keeps growing], we better find more workers." Next year, 1.3 million available high-tech jobs are expected to go unfilled and the demand for workers with high-tech skills is expected to double by 2006.

These trends impose new requirements on education and highlight an old problem. "The most important factor affecting the long-term production of scientists is the tragic inadequacy of our primary and secondary science and mathematics education program," National Science Foundation chairman James J. Duderstadt told the *Washington Post*. The traditional function of math education was to identify bright young potential mathematicians and steer them into math programs based on university campuses. The process was almost self-selecting. Before you could get to anything interesting you had to absorb a lot of abstract math, unlike, say, social studies or even English, which in the hands of creative teachers could be presented effectively and interestingly through literature, stories, and events. These subjects didn't have to be boring; math was expected to be.

And in the culture itself—our culture—illiteracy in math is acceptable the way illiteracy in reading and writing is unacceptable. Failure is tolerated in math but not in English. Your parent may well lean over your shoulder as you struggle with the term paper your English class requires, or the book report that is due, making sure that you write it, checking the spelling and the grammar. But if you're struggling with an equation while doing your algebra homework, more likely your parent will look over your shoulder, wrinkle a brow in puzzlement, then say something like "I never got that stuff either; do the best you can and try not to fail." This is an old problem. In effect, math instruction weeds out people and you wind up with what amounts to a priesthood, masters of the arcane secrets of math through what appears to be some God-given talent or magic. Forty percent of students taking freshman calculus in U.S. universities fail it; but not being "good" in math does not in any way imply inferiority, rather, it confirms that you're just like most everyone else.

The love-hate relationship Black people have with technology as well as poor schools concentrated in poor Black communities compound the problem. While technological innovation has deep roots in the overall history of African people—there's ancient Egypt and devices like the shadoof; there's a whole lineage of African-American inventors; even the cotton gin, some say, was first sketched on the ground by an African slave—for most of the last five hundred years Black encounters with technology have been destructive, crushing of aspirations. Compasses led Portuguese explorers to Africa, firearms helped conquer the continent. The Atlantic slave trade was facilitated by innovation in ship design. Human field workers were displaced by machines and moved north, and their children were displaced by newer high-tech machinery.

It is of course a gross oversimplification to say that Black oppression exists because of technology, because the three-masted caravel, the cotton gin, or the cotton picker or the computer was invented. Or that high-tech sneakers advertised by basketball players are the cause of juvenile delinquency. Coming to grips with technology *is* a need; that Black people have not done so for the most part *is* a problem. In inner cities or the rural South there's no tinkering in the garage, with the ambition of designing something better than Microsoft Windows. There's no equivalent in computer programming to the determined practice seen every day on basketball courts or the daily honing of rap style by groups of teenagers. Countless young Blacks envision becoming the next Michael Jordan, or Whitney Houston, or Master P. Few aim at being the next Steve Jobs, or another George Washington Carver, for that matter. Blacks make up perhaps 15 percent of this country's population, yet in 1995 they earned 1.8 percent of the Ph.D.s in computer science, 2.1 percent of those in engineering, 1.5 percent in the physical sciences, and 0.6 percent in mathematics.

Recently I heard from a woman who teaches mathematics at the University of Arkansas at Monticello. She told me that about 80 percent of freshman must take remedial math, for which they cannot get college credit. Another person, the head of a center for academic advising for minority students at the University of Kentucky at Louisville, told me that close to 90 percent of entering minority students had to take remedial algebra during their freshman year, for which they did not get credit. A faculty member in experimental physics at Rutgers recently lamented the absence of minority students in his classes. He said, "They're all across campus in the remedial sections."

Industrial technology created schools that educated an elite to run society, while the rest were prepared for factory work by performing repetitive tasks that mimicked factories. New technology demands a new literacy—higher math skills for everyone, urban and rural. At the warehouse of a large Mississippi Delta shipping service, the area's largest employer, for example, all the dollies have computers on them. The company needs workers who understand those computers and can tell them what to do to better organize the work.

Math illiteracy is not unique to Blacks the way the denial of the right to vote in Mississippi was. But it affects Blacks and other minorities much, much more intensely, making them the designated serfs of the information age just as the people that we worked with in the 1960s on the plantations were Mississippi's serfs then.

There is urgency to this. Consider prisons, these days the fastest-growing public sector industry in this country. The ranks of prisoners grow enough each year to fill New York's Yankee Stadium to overflowing. A young man born this year has a one in twenty chance of living some part of his life in jail . . . unless he is Black, then his chances jump to one in four. In their paper on "incarcerated children," Washington, D.C., attorneys Joseph B. Tulman and Mary G. Hynes write of young people in prisons: "In overwhelming percentages, they are poor children, and they are children of color." They cite a relationship between literacy and prison as well as poverty and prison. "Large percentages of children in the delinquency system and adults in the criminal system are severely undereducated, and literacy skills in these populations are strikingly low."

So today, as when the Mississippi Freedom Democratic Party (MFDP) made its challenge to Mississippi Democrats in Atlantic City in 1964, the question remains: How do the people at the bottom get into the mix? In the 1960s, in Mississippi, it was the sharecroppers. In our time, across the country, it is Black, Latino, and poor white students who are trapped at the bottom with prisons as their plantations.

Are we going to have a society where only a small group of people are prepared for the future, where there's a huge knowledge gap? How does such a society stabilize itself?

MATHEMATICS AS A TOOL OF LIBERATION

Math literacy and economic access are how we are going to give hope to the young generation. The lesson I draw from the history and the statistics I have just recounted is that the idea of citizenship now requires not only literacy in reading and writing but literacy in math and science. And the way we guarantee this necessary literacy is through education conceived of much more broadly than what goes on in classrooms.

The new technologies process information at unprecedented speed and quantities, filtering into unanticipated nooks and crannies of society's (indeed, the world's) economic arrangements—think of the relative suddenness with which computers have become personal, popular, and cheap—thereby creating demand for competent workers who understand these new technological tools. "Business" is forced to pressure "education" to produce students with the requisite understandings and competencies.

But this technological shift and the attention it brings also create some crawl space for those concerned about things other than the needs of corporations. Within this crawl space the Algebra

Project has staked out the goal of establishing math literacy for freedom and citizenship.

And why focus, as we do, on algebra, of all things?

The computer, of course, is the symbol of the great technological shift that has occurred since World War II. Everybody knows that there's something going on with computers out there; *E-mail, the Internet, memory, bits,* and *bytes* have entered into common usage. In the time between ENIAC and Windows 2000, the computer has become a cultural force as well as an instrument of work. (The only equivalent to this impact that I can think of is the automobile.) Strictly speaking, "culture" is not visible; what we see are the ways culture manifests itself. Everybody is willing to accept that what is powering these now-indispensable computers is a mathematical, symbolic language. So, while the visible manifestation of the technological shift is the computer, the hidden culture of computers is math.

That sets the stage; you have something in there that you can organize around if you're concerned about math literacy.

Algebra was assigned a certain role, a certain place in the education system. Students learned how to manipulate abstract symbolic representations for underlying mathematical concepts. Now here comes history, which brings in a technology that places abstract symbolic representations front and center. These representations are the tools to control the technology, and in order to use this technology to organize work you have to understand these symbolic representations and the place that society has assigned for young people to learn this symbolism—this is algebra. So, now algebra becomes an enormous barrier.

Before, in the old system, it was a barrier in the sense that along with foreign languages algebra acted as one of the gates through which you entered college. If you didn't take algebra, you had to take a language and do well in that. Algebra could not stop you from going to college—not having it could hinder you but it couldn't stop you. And it was okay to be in college unable to do math. People boasted like the parent I discussed earlier: "Never could do that stuff," they said, on the college campus then.

But those days are over. It's not so cool or hip to be completely illiterate in math. The older generation may be able to get away with it, but the younger generation coming up now can't—not if they're going to function in the society, have economic viability, be in a position to meaningfully participate, and have some say-so in the decision making that affects their lives. They cannot afford to be completely ignorant of these technological tools and languages.

So algebra, once solely in place as the gatekeeper for higher math and the priesthood who gained access to it, now is the gatekeeper for citizenship; and people who don't have it are like the people who couldn't read and write in the industrial age. But because of how access to—the learning of—algebra was organized in the industrial era, its place in society under the old jurisdiction, it has become not a barrier to college entrance, but a barrier to citizenship. That's the importance of algebra that has emerged with the new higher technology. It didn't have to be algebra; that's the decision the mathematical community made over the years. In France, geometry is the driving force of the math and technology education. So, there's nothing that says that it has to be algebra. There's nothing that says it has to be geometry. It could be a mix of a number of things—and some people would argue that it should be. There are educators and people who are driving math reform who want to make it a mix, but they're dealing with teachers and parents who understand that geometry is one subject, and algebra is another. They don't understand unified math. So I don't think there will be cultural change around that anytime soon. For the time being, it's going to be algebra.

ORGANIZING ALGEBRA:
THE NEED TO MAKE A DEMAND

The Algebra Project is founded on the idea that the ongoing struggle for citizenship and equality for minority people is now linked to an issue of math and science literacy. This idea determines strategies and choices made about the organization, dissemination, and content of the curriculum. It's important to make it clear that even the development of some sterling new curriculum—a real breakthrough—would not make us happy if it did not deeply and seriously address the issue of access to literacy for everyone. That is what is driving the project. The Algebra Project is not about simply transferring a body of knowledge to children. It is about using that knowledge as a tool to a much larger end.

One of the implications of this position has been that we have not spent a major portion of our time developing a full curriculum for any grade level. What we have done is take what we thought was a minimum intervention and try to maximize its effects. In that process we began to define what we're calling a "floor"—an acceptable goal or standard for the mathematics component of math-science literacy at the middle school level. The floor is this: you have all the middle school students ready to do the college prep math sequence when they get to high school.

There are two things to clarify about this floor. First, it's the floor, not the ceiling. We're not trying to put constraints or limits on what any group of children might learn. Second, in many ways the college prep math curriculum is a moving target. It differs from place to place, and it's changing. So for each school, there's a local target. My metaphor is that you're running to get on board the bus. The bus is moving, and you can't get on it from a standstill position. As your speed begins to approach the speed of the bus, you have a chance of hopping on.

In terms of curriculum, this means that for each middle school student there is a standard curriculum out there, which is the college prep sequence in high school. What you want for Algebra Project students is this: whatever is out there, they engage it. In *their* school system, whatever is in place as the standard college prep curriculum, you want them to engage that. It's important, however, that whatever else is coming in to supplement or replace that curriculum has to be a bona fide college preparation. It can't be something that is put in place to continue a tradition of separate tracks for some students.

It is not clear that the expression "standard college prep math curriculum" means something coherent in terms of mathematical content. It certainly does mean, however, something in terms of what colleges are going to accept as admissions requirements. It must mean, at a minimum, that when you finish it you arrive at college ready to do college mathematics. That's another floor that we have to be concerned about, although our work is largely with middle schools. Our aim is to change the situation that currently exists, where large percentages of minority students who get through a high school and get admitted to a college have to take remedial math in order to get to the place where they can even get college credit mathematics courses.

Part of the literacy standard, then, the floor for all students, must be this: when you leave middle school, you are ready to engage with the college preparatory sequence in high school. It's a moving target, but however it's defined, it must then be seen as another floor: when you leave high school, you must be ready to engage college curricula in math and science, for full college credit.

Consider the role of mathematicians here. There is nothing in the training of mathematicians that prepares them to lead in such a literacy effort. Yet the literacy effort really cannot succeed unless it enlists the active participation of some critical mass of the mathematical community. The question of how we all learn to work across several arenas is unsolved. Those arenas are large and complicated. They include the curriculum itself, instructional philosophy, schools, school systems, and individual classrooms. Communities and their processes of social change must also be centrally involved, and in some broad sense, national and local politics. Really working in all these arenas will require that many people adopt a more holistic outlook than they have ever done before.

Organizing around algebra has the potential to open a doorway that's been locked. Math literacy and economic access are the Algebra Project's foci for giving hope to the young generation. That's a new problem for educators. It's a new problem for the country. The traditional role of science and math education has been to train an elite, create a priesthood, find a few bright students and bring them into university research. It hasn't been a literacy effort. We are putting literacy, math literacy, on the table.

Instead of weeding all but the best students out of advanced math, schools must commit to everyone gaining this literacy as they have committed to everyone having a reading-writing literacy.

This is a cultural struggle, the creation of a culture of mathematical literacy that's going to operate within the black community as church culture does. And that means that math won't be just school-based, but available as reading and writing are. Kids now routinely assume that someone will be able to explain some word to them, or teach them how to read a sentence if they don't understand it. They also take it as a matter of course that no one can help them with their "higher" math studies. Projecting several generations down the road we can see a youngster who has grown up in a black neighborhood being able to get his or her questions about mathematics as easily answered in the neighborhood.

It is a little bit like guerrilla warfare. You're striking. You're pulling back. You're looking at where you are. You're striking again. You're looking for an opening. You're looking for a soft spot, trying to find out where you can penetrate. And you are working with and against various structures. You're in them, but you're working against them at various levels.

In several Algebra Project sites students have formed the Young People's Project (YPP). The beauty of the YPP is that its members are in the schools, but organizationally it is not part of the school system. YPP members have carved out their own crawl space in the schools that allows them to operate and get some presence, some visibility there, some legitimacy. That's a big step for young people, to get a piece of turf in school. They're not going to be easy to dislodge.

Many people will see our vision as impossible. There's a sense in which most people are not going to believe or accept any of this agenda until they are confronted with the products of such an effort: students who come out of classrooms armed with a new understanding of mathematics and with a new understanding of themselves as leaders, participants, and learners. As I said before, in the sixties everyone said sharecroppers were apathetic until we got them demanding to vote. That finally got attention. Here, where kids are falling wholesale through the cracks—or chasms—dropping out of sight, becoming fodder for jails, people say they do not want to learn. The only ones who can dispel that notion are the kids themselves. They, like Mrs. Hamer, Mrs. Devine, E.W. Steptoe, and others who changed the political face of Mississippi in the 1960s, have to demand what everyone says they don't want.

DRAWING ON THE PAST: THE ROOTS OF OUR MOVEMENT

The Algebra Project is first and foremost an organizing project— a community organizing project—rather than a traditional program of school reform. It draws its inspiration and its methods from the organizing tradition of the civil rights movement. Like the civil rights movement, the Algebra Project is a process, not an event.

Two key aspects of the Mississippi organizing tradition underlie the Algebra Project: the centrality of families to the work of organizing, and organizing in the context of the community in which one lives and works. As civil rights workers in Mississippi, we were absorbed into families as we moved from place to place with scarcely a dollar in our pockets, and this credential—being one of the community's children—negated the white power structure's efforts to label us "outside agitators." In this way we were able to sink deep roots into the community, enlarging and strengthening connections in and among different communities, absorbing into our consciousness the community's memories of "where we have been," forcing us to our own understanding of our collective experience.

We are struggling to frame some important questions: Is there a way to talk with young people today as Amzie Moore and Ella Baker did with us in the 1960s? Is there a consensus for young Blacks, Latinos, and poor whites to tap into that will drive such a literacy effort? What price must they pay to wage such a struggle?

Like Ella Baker, we believe in these young people, that they have the energy, the courage, the hope to devise means to change their condition. Although much concern about the education of African-American young people is voiced today, I am frequently asked why I have turned to teaching school and developing curriculum—teaching middle school and high school no less. There is a hint of criticism in the question, the suggestion that I am wasting my time, have abandoned efforts at attempting real, meaningful social change. After all, in the end, such work "merely" leads to youngsters finding a comfortable place in the system with a good job. Nothing "radical" about that, I am told. This is a failure to understand what actually is "radical," so it might be useful to repeat what Ella Baker posits as necessary to the struggle of poor and oppressed people: "It means facing a system that does not lend itself to your needs and devising means by which you change that system."

The key word here is *you*. Our efforts with our target population is what defines the radical nature of the Algebra Project, not program specifics. To make myself very, very clear, even the development of some sterling new curriculum—a real breakthrough— would not make us happy if it did not deeply and seriously empower the target population to demand access to literacy for everyone. That is what is driving the project. What is radical about the Algebra Project is the students we are trying to reach and the people we work with to drive a broad math literacy effort— the Black and poor students and the communities in which they live, the usually excluded. Ella's words finally mean, whether for voting rights or economic access, "You who are poor and oppressed: your need, you must make change. You must fashion a struggle." Young people finding their voice instead of being spoken for is a crucial part of the process. Then and now those designated as serfs are expected to remain paralyzed, unable to take an action and unable to voice a demand—their lives dependent on the goodwill and good works of others. We believe the kind of systemic change necessary to prepare our young people for the demands of the twenty-first century requires young people to take the lead in changing it.

These are radical ideas the way that forty years ago constructing the MFDP so that sharecroppers and day workers could have a voice was radical. What made it radical was the work, the effort, at encouraging this group to empower itself. This was Ella Baker's great lesson, and still a touchstone for us today: that the target population should also make a demand instead of just having their needs advocated by well-intentioned "radical" reformers. You might say that it radicalizes radicalism. That's what we learned in Mississippi, that it is getting people at the bottom to make demands, on themselves first, then on the system, that leads to some of the most important changes. They have to find their voices. No matter how great Martin Luther King, Jr., was he could not go and challenge the seating of the Mississippi Democrats at Atlantic City. He could advocate for them and support them, but he could not lead the challenge. The only people who could do that were the people from Mississippi. And people will not organize that kind of seminal effort around somebody else's agenda. It's got to be internalized—this is our agenda.

There had been advocates for civil rights long before SNCC and CORE field secretaries arrived in Mississippi. Indeed, the 1954 Supreme Court decision was one important victory won by civil rights advocates. And perhaps because it was primarily won by advocates, it proceeded "with all deliberate speed." No one disputes the importance of such victories, but, nonetheless, it was when sharecroppers, day laborers, and domestic workers found their voice, stood up, and demanded change, that the Mississippi political game was really over. When these folk, people for whom others traditionally had spoken and advocated, stood up and said, "We demand the right to vote!" refuting by their voices and actions the idea that they were uninterested in doing so, they could not be refused, and the century-long game of oppression through denial of the political franchise ended.

So to understand the Algebra Project you must begin with the idea of our targeted young people finding their voice as sharecroppers and day laborers, maids, farmers, and workers of all sorts found theirs in the 1960s. Of course there are differences between the 1960s and what the AP is doing now. For one, the time span between the start of the sit-in movement and the challenge by the MFDP in Atlantic City was incredibly brief, sandwiched between two presidential elections (Kennedy-Nixon and Johnson-Goldwater). When I look back it feels like twenty years folded into four; I still can hardly believe how short a time period that was. Math literacy, however, will require a longer time frame. There is a steep learning curve and what we're looking at with the AP is something evolving over generations as math literacy workers/organizers acquire the skills and training through study and practice and begin tackling the system. Young people, however, may speed this up as youth clearly did in the civil rights movement. And, whereas the right to vote campaign took place in the Deep South, the math literacy problem is throughout the entire nation.

Yet to understand the Algebra Project, you need to understand the spirit and the crucial lessons of the organizing tradition of the civil rights movement. In Mississippi, the voiceless found their voice, and once raised, it could not be ignored. Organizers learned to locate the vast resources in communities that seemed impoverished and paralyzed at first glance. The lessons of the movement in Mississippi are exactly the lessons we need to learn and put into practice in order to transform the education of our children and their prospects for the future. As with voting rights four decades ago, we have to flesh out a consensus on math literacy. Without it, moving the country into systemic change around math education becomes almost impossible. You cannot move this country unless you have consensus. The country's too big, too huge, too diverse, too confused. That's part of what we learned in Mississippi. We learned it on the ground, running.

In this book I present other people's voices as well as my own. Voices from the movement: Ella Baker's, for one. Voices of my colleagues: Dave Dennis's, especially. And voices of kids: the young people's of the Algebra Project. Part of what happened in Mississippi was the creation of a culture of change—a change in the climate of the consciousness of Black people in that state. It is the establishing of this climate and change of consciousness about

mathematics in the larger community that will go a long way toward making it possible to change the classrooms—really change
the classrooms; for we are talking about systemic change and as a
country we don't yet know how to do systemic change. We can't
point to any school system where we have put through systemic
change around math education.

This is a very personal book. The stories and lessons I recount
from Mississippi are stories and lessons of transformation in the
white heat of struggle for change. The story I tell about how the
Algebra Project started continues that story of struggle and transformation, in my family and my community. We see in this book
the new needs of the twenty-first century, and that meeting these
new needs will take us into new territory the way that need for
voter registration took us into rural Mississippi. There's even a
politics: Who's going to gain access to the new technology? Who's
going to control it? What do we have to demand of the educational system to prepare for the new technological era? What opportunities will be available for our children? These are questions
that ultimately challenge power as the civil rights movement did,
for that earlier movement was about more than lunch counters
and ballots.

CHAPTER 2

Learning from Ella

Lessons from Mississippi, ca. 1961

We are smuggling this note from the drunk tank of the county jail in Magnolia, Mississippi. Twelve of us are here, sprawled out along the concrete bunker: Curtis Hayes, Hollis Watkins, Ike Lewis and Robert Talbert, four veterans of the bunker are sitting up talking— mostly about girls—Chuck McDew ("Tell the Story") is curled into the concrete and the wall; Harold Robinson, Stephen Ashley, James Wells, Lee Chester Vick, Leotus Eubanks, and Ivory Diggs lie cramped on the cold Bunker; I'm sitting with smuggled pen and paper thinking a little, writing a little; Myrtis Bennet and Janie Campbell are across the way wedded to a different icy cubicle.

In the words of Judge Brumfield who sentenced us, we are "cold calculators" who design to disrupt the racial harmony (harmonious since 1619) of McComb into racial strife and rioting; we, he said, are the leaders who are causing young children to be led like sheep to the pen and be slaughtered (in a legal manner). "Robert," he was addressing me, "haven't some of the people from your school been able to go down and register without violence here in Pike County?" I thought to myself that Southerners are most exposed when they boast. . . .

This is Mississippi, the middle of the iceberg. Hollis is leading off with his tenor, "Michael, row the boat ashore, Alleluia! Christian brothers don't be slow, Alleluia! Mississippi's next to go, Alleluia!" This is a tremor from the middle of the iceberg—from a stone the builders rejected.

> my letter delivered by hand to SNCC,
> November 1, 1961

Mississippi. Say the name. Even the sibilants conjure the hiss before a sudden strike from nowhere. And "back in the day" as the kids say nowadays, no place seemed more deadly to Black America. Mississippi. It had maintained a rep for a long time: worse slavery to be sold into; greatest number of lynchings; a place where the blues sank its deepest roots. In the state, local folks make their own distinctions related to danger and hard times: "hill country," "the Delta"; folks from one place often speak of another section of the state as far worse than where they are. Since I came from Harlem, New York, it all felt like Mississippi to me.

With a population of almost fifteen thousand, McComb was the urban center of southwest Mississippi when I arrived in the summer of 1961. Just 250 of the Black residents were registered to vote but that put it way ahead of the surrounding counties. Outside of McComb heading south toward the Louisiana border you hit the red clay countryside that hardly seemed a part of America. Rural, impoverished, brutal; in counties like Amite and Wathall very few of the Black homes had heat or indoor toilets. Hand-dug wells supplied the water. This is the Klan country of poor whites defined by subsistence farming. Of Amite County one writer said, "It has not only missed the civil rights revolution, but the Industrial Revolution as well." In Amite, only one Black person was registered to vote. In Wathall, none.

But in this hostile corner of a state that many considered the most hostile to civil rights, the NAACP had established some of its strongest bases. The branch in Wathall County was the first to file a school desegregation suit. After the 1954 Supreme Court decision as NAACP chapters around the state came under assaults that resulted in declining membership and participation, meetings in McComb were getting larger and the state's NAACP field secretary, Medgar Evers, had even managed to set up a youth chapter that was specifically concerned with police brutality. Members from the Pike County branch of the NAACP came to Washington, D.C., to testify in support of the 1957 civil rights act.

August 29, 1961, was one of those hot Mississippi mornings when the sun starts lashing you early. I'd been staying at the farm of fifty-three-year-old E. W. Steptoe. He was head of the Amite County NAACP and a Black man who owned land—he raised cows and planted cotton. His father had owned land before him. Steptoe was a small man with an easy smile that hid a shrewd mind. He could almost be called tiny, but every ounce of his wiry frame was muscle toughened by farming and determined political effort. Steptoe had begun the Amite County NAACP branch in 1953 after learning about the organization during a trip to New Orleans. It had grown to almost two hundred by 1954 when Sheriff Ira Jenkins walked into a meeting one night with fifteen or twenty white men including a school board member and seized the membership lists as well as other records. Not surprisingly, after that raid the branch's numbers dropped sharply, but Steptoe kept the chapter alive by buying some memberships himself. He had welcomed me over from McComb and for almost two weeks I'd been holding voter registration workshops in a little church building that belonged to the Steptoe family. On August 15, I had already brought three people who wanted to register to vote to the Amite County courthouse—the first Black people to make this effort in anyone's memory. This morning two more people were going to try. One of them, Curtis Dawson, swung by Steptoe's farm and picked me up, then we went to pick up Reverend Alfred Knox—everybody called him Preacher Knox—at his place, negotiating a long, winding drive on a rutted road to reach his house. But Preacher Knox had already gone into town, so we went on to the courthouse, where we asked for him. If that seems strange, it isn't, because although these courthouses are bastions of white power and good-ol'-boy fraternity, in these small, majority-Black towns there are plenty of Black folk around these courthouses too. Absent political challenge—Black political challenge—there is an intimacy, an air of easy familiarity. Seemingly comfortable master-servant relationships prevail between Black and white with the capacity for the sanctioned eruption of ugly Klan violence understood but kept well hidden until needed.

Preacher Knox wasn't at the courthouse either, so we left the car there and began walking down Liberty's main street toward the cotton gin to look for him. Finding Preacher Knox didn't take long, and when we did we started walking back toward the court-house. For a moment a funeral blocked our way. A highway pa-trolman was directing the procession traffic. We continued walk-ing. We paused at another corner for a moment, then suddenly some white men walked up, and without a word, one of them swung, hitting me in the temple with the handle of a knife. It was Billy Jack Caston, the sheriff's cousin and the son-in-law of then state representative E. H. Hurst. He swung again and again, hit-ting me in the head as I tried to shield myself by stooping with my head between my knees. Preacher Knox tried to pull Billy Jack off but was warned away by other whites. Two other white men joined in the pummeling. Finally they stopped, leaving me in a semiconscious heap on the street.

"We've got to go on to the registrar," Dawson recalls me saying as I got up; I don't remember saying anything. It is remarkable that the two men didn't flee and I still find it difficult to know what they reached into for the courage. But Dawson and Preacher Knox helped me to my feet and we began heading back to the courthouse. I spoke to the highway patrolman we had seen earlier: "Those guys up there jumped me," I told him, pointing back up the street. You could still see them standing there. He didn't say anything and didn't do anything. Nothing. Strangely I didn't feel dizzy or nauseous and I didn't know I was bleeding until I got to the courthouse, where people gave me startled, even shocked stares, and I noticed that my once white T-shirt was red with blood. The registrar quickly closed the office and told us to leave. Dawson then drove me back to Steptoe's farm, where Steptoe's son Charles examined my head and found deep gashes. There was no Black doctor in the county and they had to drive me to McComb, where nine stitches were sewn into my head. Dr. James Anderson, who tended me, offered the use of his car to the project.

And so I met the Mississippi of Harlem nightmares, but also the Mississippi of unexpected Black strength. My journey here had begun almost two years before.

ELLA BAKER

The time was 1960, the place the U.S.A.,
that February first became a history-making day,
from Greensboro all across the land
the news spread far and wide
that quietly and bravely
youth took a giant stride.

Heed the call
Americans all,
side by equal side,
brother, sit in dignity
sister sit in pride
in pride in pride, in pride in pride, in pride.

Guy Carawan, Eve Merriam, and Norman Curtis

On February 1, 1960, four freshmen at North Carolina A&T College in Greensboro refused to leave the lunch counter of the local Woolworth until they were served. They "sat in" without getting service until the store closed. Within days their action was being repeated by other students across the South. During my spring break from Horace Mann that year I decided I wanted to go see the sit-ins firsthand. My uncle Bill—an architect—was teaching at Hampton Institute in Hampton, Virginia, and I wrote him asking if I could come down. Of course you can, he replied. Uncle Bill was active with the NAACP. Hampton students were sitting in and demonstrating in nearby Newport News. I joined their picket lines and discovered a genuine feeling of release.

I had been almost totally immersed in white society since 1952, first at Hamilton College in New York, where I was an undergraduate, then at Harvard, where I was a graduate student, and then at Horace Mann, where I was working as a teacher. One of the things I had taught myself to do was repress my feelings or at least expression of my feelings whenever I felt humiliated—to hide them. I think many African Americans becoming deeply involved with white society for the first time do this. You don't

demonstrate your feelings, you put yourself in the role of an observer. That's pretty much what I did for four years at Hamilton:
developed a way of watching as opposed to engaging, a sort of self-
repression. And, finally finding a way to personally take on preju-
dice and racism—to engage—creates a feeling of great release. It
is what I felt participating in my first demonstration in Newport
News, Virginia—release.

One night there was a mass rally and one of Martin Luther
King, Jr.'s key associates, Reverend Wyatt T. Walker, who lived
in St. Petersburg then, was the main speaker. In his speech he
announced that the Southern Christian Leadership Conference
(SCLC), the organization Dr. King had created in the wake of the
Montgomery bus boycott, would be opening a fund-raising office
in Harlem. After he finished I went up to ask about this office. I
also questioned Reverend Walker about a remark he had made in
his speech. "We all need to get behind one leader," he had said.
That struck me as strange, but this was my first contact with the
movement. "Don't you think we need a lot of leaders?" I wanted
to know. His response was a quizzical look before offering the
general and inarguable explanation of the need to support Dr.
King. That hardly meant that other organizations had no legitimacy, he claimed. We did not talk long. This would be a recurring
issue within the civil rights movement, manifesting itself not so
much in verbal debate as in styles of working in communities. Indeed, the formation of SNCC, in the end, turned on this issue—
students creating and controlling their own organization. As to
the main reason I had approached Wyatt, he told me that Bayard
Rustin would run the Harlem SCLC office and gave me the date,
time, and place of its organizational meeting. I decided I would
attend.

At that meeting Bayard asked for volunteers and I became one
at the Harlem office—the Committee to Defend Martin Luther
King, I think it was called—going there to work after leaving
Horace Mann at the end of the school day. As just a young guy, a
student face showing up wanting to do something like licking
stamps or stuffing envelopes, I was invisible to Bayard for a while.

He had no recollection of our meeting on conscientious objection to the draft seven years before when I was at Hamilton College and Channing B. Richardson, a Quaker professor, had put me in touch with him. But in showing up I became somebody because I was the only Black kid coming in.

I expressed an interest in going deeper into the South. My thought was to visit Montgomery, Alabama, but not much was happening there, Bayard said, and suggested Atlanta instead. He wrote a letter of introduction to Ella Baker and later in the summer I got on a bus and went to Atlanta as a volunteer worker at the SCLC headquarters. I was hoping to see "the movement" as I idealized it, rooms of energetic volunteers getting out mailings, bold campaigners preparing to hit the streets and rural roads with a message of change, and strategies for political struggle being conceived behind closed doors. But I found none of that. The office on Auburn Avenue—"Sweet Auburn," a street called by *Forbes* magazine, in 1956, "The Richest Negro Street in the World"—consisted of three small rooms at the top of a short flight of stairs. It was occupied by just three full-time people: Ella Baker, who was being eased out as SCLC executive director, in one room; sharing the main space, SCLC's secretary/office manager and Jane Stembridge, first executive director of the newly formed SNCC, who inhabited a tight corner given to them by Ella Baker; and Dr. King in another room he rarely used. Miss Baker was out of town when I arrived. No one else directed me toward work that first day in the office but I saw Jane stuffing envelopes and joined her, startling her a bit she told me later because I didn't even ask if it was all right for me to help.

Jane Stembridge, the daughter of a white Baptist minister from Virginia, was a twenty-four-year-old student from Union Theological Seminary. Martin Luther King, Jr., had spoken at Jane's school that spring and afterward she had walked up to him and asked about returning to the South and becoming involved with the student movement. "I feel like I'm in a ivory tower up here," she told him. Dr. King told her to write to Ella Baker.

Through Jane, I soon met Julian Bond, Ruby Doris Smith, and others involved in Atlanta's student movement. There was so little to do at the SCLC office that I regularly manned their picket line protesting discriminatory hiring policies at the local A&P. They were suspicious of me, wondering what the intentions of this northerner were. ("We thought he was a Communist because he was from New York," recalled Julian Bond years later. "He wore glasses, picketed *for hours* by himself. His views and concerns were much broader than ours. We thought he was smarter than we were.")

One day I was picked up by police while getting out of a car intending to picket in support of a planned sit-in at Rich's department store in downtown Atlanta. This protest was organized by the Southern Conference Educational Fund (SCEF), a mostly white southern organization campaigning against segregation. Mississippi senator James O. Eastland had been investigating SCEF for Communist ties since 1954. One of Atlanta's newspapers identified me specifically as "Robert Moses of SCLC," and the students from the Atlanta movement wanted to know how I had come to be involved with SCEF. I told them I had heard of the demonstration while attending a mathematics lecture on the "Ramifications of Gödel's Theorem" at Atlanta University by Lonnie Cross who had recently graduated from MIT. That hardly reduced their suspicion of me and because I was officially an SCLC volunteer they asked Dr. King to question me.

He spoke with me in his study at Ebeneezer Baptist Church down the street from the SCLC office. Dr. King wasn't particularly worried about the presence of Communists in the Communism-is-evil-and-going-to-take-over sense. And in this, ironically, he was ahead of many of the students. I even learned later that he was on friendly terms with some of the SCEF leadership. Dr. King explained that SCEF was an outgrowth of one of Eleanor Roosevelt's interracial groups. It was part of a larger southern white liberal and left tradition that included the Highlander Folk Center in Knoxville, Tennessee, which King and others had used for workshops. But SCLC was in the midst of a major fund-raising campaign. I sat silently as he got to the heart of his concern. It's amazing. I think there was never a time when Dr. King was without melody in his voice.

"Robert, I am not saying that SCEF is Communist, but some people think it's Communist and that's what matters. We have to be careful."

The tones seemed to roll slowly across his desk and look at me. "You understand that, don't you, Robert?" Dr. King then advised me—he didn't order me—not to participate in other SCEF demonstrations. I was hardly going to argue with him, however. This was Martin Luther King, Jr., and here I was in Atlanta, just a young guy come down from Harlem as a summer volunteer.

I did take advantage of our brief meeting to get him to step into a dispute I'd been having at SCLC about its fund-raising effort. Every day we were licking and stuffing envelopes trying to get out this enormous mailing to thousands of people around the country. I'd been saying to let me take over this job New York–style, round up some people, and get the mailing out in a couple of days. I wanted to do it at the Butler Street YMCA where I was staying. But I kept being told that leaving the office to do the mailing was against the rules. So when Dr. King finished I asked him if it would be all right for me to take the mailing out of the office over to the Y, and that I thought I could find volunteers to get it out. He agreed, and that's what I did. Jane Stembridge got students; some of the folks at the Y helped. After two or three days it was done—the mail was gone. And that was my real work for the SCLC in the summer of 1960.

Jane, who understood better than I the political crosscurrrents buffeting SCLC, explained later that Dr. King and his organization were torn between the need for mainstream acceptance and continuing some of the political relationships on the left that had been important to them early on. Bayard Rustin, for example, had provided critical organizational assistance and Dr. King had insisted on his employment as publicist over the objections of his own board which was nervous about it because Rustin was homosexual and a Socialist. The internal pressure against Bayard never

abated and ultimately he chose to resign rather than risk embar-
rassing Dr. King.

Ella Baker, on the way out too, had a relationship with SCLC
far more complex than where she was on a left-right political
scale. Shortly after my session with Dr. King, Ella Baker, back in
Atlanta, made time for me to come in, sit down, and talk with her.
She asked me about my upbringing, my thoughts on Harlem, my
entrance into the movement. Her interest in me was what struck
me; it was in marked contrast to that of Dr. King, who had met
with me because of controversy over my involvement with people
who were considered radicals. Miss Baker was actually talking to
me. I felt that this first conversation had seemed important enough
to her that she had made time for it; it was not something that she
had just squeezed into her busy schedule. She was frank as well as
intelligent. Her interest in me, I think, was something I needed
because reaching out to really probe into personal things isn't a
particularly strong point of mine. This style that was so much a
part of her would be important to the future shape of my work and
SNCC's work, and is important to the Algebra Project today. It
was part of what we learned from Ella Baker: if you really want to
do something with somebody else, really want to work with that
person, the first thing you have to do is make a personal connection. You have to find out who it is you are working with. All
across the South you could see that in grassroots rural people. That
was their style. Miss Baker took this style to a sophisticated level of
political work.

And we discovered a connection. I used to sell milk when I
was in elementary school. My mother, brothers, and I had run a
little milk station for a Harlem-based milk co-op. Every morning
the co-op delivered two cartons holding twenty one-quart con-
tainers of milk to a doorway in the projects on 151st Street, right
across from Resurrection Church near McCombs Dam Place. We
would get up early and open up the basement doorway and stand
there inside of it. People would line up and we sold the milk for
nineteen cents a quart. We kept one penny; the rest went to the
co-op. If we sold both cartons we could pay for two quarts of milk

ourselves and that's how we made our milk money, how we got milk for the house. Miss Baker had been deeply involved in Harlem's cooperative movement; in a sense, I used to joke with her, she helped put the milk on our table.

Miss Baker also had deep roots in the southern civil rights movement. In 1943 she was NAACP director of branches. Rosa Parks had attended one of her training workshops in 1946. That same year, "the frustrations of coping with the general NAACP tendency to treat the membership in terms of numbers and dollars rather than as a mass organization" caused her to resign her NAACP position, writes her biographer Joanne Grant. In 1955 she joined with Bayard Rustin and others to form In Friendship, a group that offered economic support for Blacks suffering reprisals for political activism. The group also began discussing the possibility of a southwide grassroots organization. She had hoped that such an organization would grow out of the Montgomery bus boycott and in 1957 edited the working papers that were presented at the founding meeting of the Southern Christian Leadership Conference.

As executive director of SCLC, a position she took reluctantly, Miss Baker had hoped to steer the ministers who formed its membership into grassroots community organizing for civil rights. She was doubtful and doubts and dissatisfaction with the organization deepened with her involvement. Southern ministers, she felt, weren't inclined toward grassroots organizing because of the hierarchical structures of their churches. And more broadly she felt, as she put it, that it "[handicaps] oppressed people to depend so largely on a [single] leader, because unfortunately in our culture, the charismatic leader usually becomes a leader because he has found a spot in the public limelight. It usually means that the media made him and the media may undo him. . . . My basic sense of it has always been to get people to understand that in the long run they themselves are the only protection they have against violence or injustice. . . . People have to be made to understand that they cannot look for salvation anywhere but to themselves."

Her style strained an already uncomfortable political relationship and finally made it impossible for Miss Baker to continue with SCLC. "She wasn't church," one SCLC minister said. She wasn't deferential. She wasn't a man in an organization that was patriarchal as well as hierarchical. And what I think was probably the most critical tension: her concept of leadership, that it should emerge from the community and be helped in its growth by grass-roots organizers, clashed with SCLC's idea of projecting and pro-tecting a single charismatic national leader.

In the protesting students, however, Miss Baker found reason for renewed hopes of vigorous and effective grassroots struggle in the South. The sit-in movement had quickly spread in the weeks after it began in February. Miss Baker wrangled eight hundred dollars from the SCLC to gather students for an Easter weekend meeting at Shaw University, her alma mater in Raleigh, North Carolina. She expected about 100 students; 175 showed up. "Just as the sit-ins had skyrocketed or escalated without rhyme or rea-son," she commented years later, "so too the response to the con-cept of a conference escalated beyond our expectations." The students were finding their voice. Miss Baker immediately recog-nized this and in a speech called "Bigger Than a Hamburger" warned the gathering of the need to avoid co-optation by adults. Find your own way, she urged the students. Jim Lawson, spiritual father and adviser to the Nashville student movement, one of the strongest student bodies at the Shaw meeting, echoed both Ella Baker's and the students' sentiments by calling the sit-ins "a judg-ment upon middle-class conventional, halfway efforts to deal with radical social evil." Although representatives of the SCLC and NAACP, attending as observers, had hoped to fold the students into their organizations, the meeting ended with the founding of the Student Nonviolent Coordinating Committee (SNCC). "The students . . . ," Miss Baker commented afterward, "are seeking to rid America of the scourge of racial segregation and discrimination—not only at the lunch counters but in every aspect of life."

SNCC

Look at that gal shake that thing
We can't all be Martin Luther King

I too hear America singing
   But from where I stand
I can only hear Little Richard
   and Fats Domino
But sometimes
I hear Ray Charles
   Drowning in his own tears
   or Bird
Relaxing at Camarillo
   or Horace Silver doodling
Then I don't mind standing a little longer.

                        Julian Bond

Two months before I arrived in Atlanta eleven students had met in the city for the first official meeting of SNCC. They voted to hire a temporary worker who with the help of volunteers would put out a small newsletter—*The Student Voice*—and act as a clearinghouse, coordinating information about student protests. The other task was the planning of an October conference to clarify the goals and principles of the new organization. Ella Baker had given them the corner of the SCLC office, an ancient desk, an equally ancient typewriter, one ream of paper, and a roll of stamps.

Although I'd come to Atlanta with the intention of working for SCLC, I had little to do and found myself gradually moving in a direction I couldn't have anticipated—toward SNCC. There'd been no mention of SNCC in the New York SCLC office. The students may have been uncertain about their long-range plans then, but at least I could involve myself in their protests. In SNCC's corner of the office, where I helped Jane with her press releases and mailings, we carried on long conversations. She had read what I had read and often Jane and I got into deep discussion and argument about philosophers and thinkers like Tillich, Camus, Kant, Buber, and Gandhi. From the office our discussions flowed into the back room of B. B. Beamon's soul food restaurant, sometimes continuing late into the night. Discussing plans for SNCC's October conference, Jane raised a particular concern. Although there were strong student movements in Nashville, Atlanta, and other cities and towns of the upper South, the sit-in movement was just stirring in the deeper South of Alabama, Mississippi, and Louisiana. Participation by activists from these areas in the fall conference would be vital but few of their names were known. I had come to the conclusion that SCLC had very little work for me to do, no program, and I had come down thinking there was one. So when Jane suggested that I consider traveling and collecting names for SNCC's fall conference, I was open to the idea. Soon Ella Baker was drawn into our conversation around this notion and she agreed that I should go. She drew up a list of NAACP contact people to build the trip around and Jane began writing them. Gradually an itinerary took shape.

SNCC didn't have any staff except for Jane, and it didn't have any funds, so I used my own money to buy a bus ticket. Jane, Miss Baker, and Connie Curry, then working for the National Student Association and who had a car, took me down to the bus station. And because I was now representing the sit-in movement I was expected to sit right in the front of the bus. Ella, Jane, and Connie stood there watching to see where I would sit. I sat in the front until the bus neared the Alabama line. Then some kind of instinct made me move to the back. It was lucky I did because the highway patrol stopped the bus at the Alabama line; someone had alerted them that a Black passenger was riding in the front. The patrolman, however, couldn't tell who; in the back mine was just another indistinguishable face among the Black folk. The distance between rhetoric and reality is so great that even now it's difficult to find a real way to write about it—but I didn't mind shifting gears when I left Atlanta. I had no intention of flaunting anything, and had no need to. I was sure about myself in that way, because of the capacity I had developed to pass through unobtrusively while

at Hamilton. I understood where Jane and SNCC folk were coming from and I didn't want to try to argue with them. And I knew
this job I was going out to do needed someone who was going to
merge with the people. I was going to figure out how to do that,
how to move around and get the names and come back out. I sat in
the back of the bus as we crossed into Alabama.

AMZIE

> Come 1956, we decided to start trying to get people to vote. Our
> first effort was to try in the East Cleveland [Mississippi] precinct.
> Fourteen Negroes went to the East Cleveland precinct with their
> poll tax receipts in their hands, to try to register in the first Demo-
> cratic primary. . . . When they came into the polling place, there
> were ten burly [white] men sitting behind a counter. At the box,
> where they were to drop our ballots, a man stood with a .38 Smith
> and Wesson on his side. We marked our ballots and came to the box
> to drop them in. We were informed by the man standing at the bal-
> lot box that we could not put the ballots in the box. There was a
> brown envelope there on the table by the box. He suggested that
> we put the ballots in the brown envelope.
>
> Amzie Moore

My itinerary took me to Talladega, Birmingham, Clarksdale,
Cleveland, Jackson, Shreveport, Alexandria, New Orleans, Gulf-
port, Biloxi, Mobile, and back to Atlanta. There was another bus
incident on this trip. When I left Jackson going to Shreveport,
there weren't many seats on the bus and there was a Black guy sitting near the front. In fact he was sitting in front of a white man.
So I sat down in the only available seat, one near the front and next
to a white guy. When the bus reached Monroe, Louisiana, it was
stopped by police and we were asked to get off. It turned out the
other Black guy was an African and had been on the bus since
Washington, D.C. He had a passport, an African passport. When
they came to me, as it happened the only official documentation I
had was an American passport. This totally confused them. For
some time they did not know what to do. Finally, after making all

the passengers shift around on the completely full bus so that no
Black folks were riding in front of or next to any white folks, they
put us back on the bus and sent us on our way.

Although I was now traveling in the much-feared Deep South
I didn't know enough to be afraid. The Hamilton habit was at play
again. I was in the role of observer, listening and watching, learning how the dominant society feels. As I moved through it, I could
see that the South was not the same everywhere. Birmingham,
Alabama, belching smoke and fire from surrounding steel plants,
matched no image of the South we held in Harlem. Low hills dot-
ted with pine and hardscrabble farms rolled through southern
Mississippi, then north along the Mississippi River the land flat-
tened dramatically presenting an expansive vista of cotton fields,
big plantations, and sharecropper's shacks. Everywhere, white
power was clearly the dominant power, but every day was not
roiled with lynchings. Black folks had a life and I began learning
how to enter into it.

One of my most important contacts on the trip was forty-
nine-year-old Amzie Moore, president of the Cleveland, Mississippi, branch of the NAACP and vice president of the state's conference of NAACP branches. He was the only adult I met on this
trip who had clearly fixed the students in his sights. It was as if he
had been sitting there in Cleveland watching the student movement unfold, waiting for it to come his way, knowing it had to
eventually come, and planning ways to use it in light of his fifteen-
year effort, since World War II, at making change in the cotton
plantation land of the Mississippi Delta. He saw in the students
what had been lacking in adults with their more obligated lives—
some kind of deep commitment that no matter what it cost they
were going to go out and get the job done. As I wrote to Jane
shortly after meeting him, Amzie was dug into the Mississippi
Delta countryside like a tree that's planted by the water.

He'd been branch president since 1955 and was a still-walking
witness to the reign of terror directed at grassroots leaders like
himself. After the 1954 Supreme Court decision, the White Citizens Council had formed in nearby Indianola. NAACP colleagues around the state, such as Reverend George W. Lee in Bel-

zoni and Jack Smith in Brookhaven, had been ambushed and killed. Others, such as Gus Coates or T. R. M. Howard, president of the Regional Council of Negro Leadership, which Amzie had helped organize, were driven from the state. But Amzie persevered, setting up a citizenship school in 1957 after the state legislature passed a new law requiring applicants for voter registration to interpret a section of the state constitution to the satisfaction of the circuit clerk. He once wanted to get rich, Amzie told a reporter in 1977. Then one winter he was taken to a sharecropper's shack. "There was a woman in there with about fourteen kids, naked from the waist down. Had an old barrel, metal barrel that they were burning cotton stalks in to keep warm. Not a single bed in the house. A few old raggedy quilts were used to wrap the kids up to keep 'em warm as possible, an *no food*. . . . I kinda figured it was a sin to think in terms of trying to get rich."

Still, Amzie had some independence, more than most Delta Blacks. He worked part-time at the post office—a federal job— and owned an Amoco gas station on Highway 61 when I met him. There was a restaurant and beauty salon attached to the gas station and he refused to put up "white" and "colored" signs segregating its entrances, or services like toilets. This was a significant refusal, for then Highway 61, running right through the heart of the Mississippi Delta, was the main artery between Memphis and New Orleans. Whites walked in expecting segregation.

This highly visible challenge to the customary way of life was unacceptable and Delta whites tried to mount a boycott against Amzie, who was certain that any night he could expect white mob violence. Often when I fell asleep at his home, Amzie, a World War II veteran, was still sitting and watching in his rear bedroom window, rifle at the ready and floodlights washing across his backyard.

He was ready for me when I showed up, especially since I was coming to him through Ella Baker, whom Amzie knew and respected. Her group, In Friendship, had given him some assistance. His only issue with me was whether I was ready for Mississippi, and whether I was reliable. Amzie and all the others like him— Hartman Turnbow in Holmes County, Steptoe in Amite, C. C.

Bryant and Webb Owens in McComb, Henry Sias in Issaquena, Hazel Palmer and Annie Devine—survived by learning how to read people. It is a characteristic of people who are living on the margins and are not beat-up or debilitated. In places like the Mississippi Delta, indeed, in the entire Black belt South, your life depends on being able to read people—not just white people; you've got to be able to read the Black people around you too. Amzie could.

I recognized his personality as being akin to that of my father, who could also read people and who moved around the way Amzie moved. Growing up, whenever I could I went with Pop as he made his rounds talking to people, visiting them. I liked hanging out with my father listening to adult conversations and exchanges. At my grandmother's house Pop might get up and say, "Well, I think I'm going to go now and holler at [my aunt] Lucia." In her kitchen there was always this running conversation about the state of the country. Even when my aunts talked about big names like Lena Horne or Duke Ellington whom they had worked with, they were engaged in what was really political dialogue about other Black talent they knew who were unable to emerge. Their discussions were like one long discussion on the larger issue of race. Inevitably they would turn to me. "You're going to be whatever you want to be. There's things that are opening up."

Pop also analytically mapped out for me what was going on. So-and-so said this because . . . So-and-so said that because . . . And that's how Amzie took me around the Delta. But Amzie was engaged and tested in the roughest of political waters where there was a level of danger that did not exist in Harlem. My father lacked this exposure to a sustained struggle on a large canvas that involves a large network of people, not just the struggle of your family and your own personal life and your own personal surroundings. He didn't have that. Amzie did.

So unlike Pop, Amzie rarely told me where we were going until we were well on our way, protecting himself by keeping to himself crucial information about how he planned to move. As we traveled, Amzie schooled me, giving me a detailed oral history of the state, explaining motives and politics . . . and possibilities. He had all the records; he had been keeping all the data. He had got the information that was then available because of the 1957 civil rights act and he laid out the state county by county. I became conversant with the details of Mississippi's complex voter registration law. Amzie also stood me up in front of church audiences, introducing me as a "visitor" who might have a few words to say. He wanted to see how I was going to talk about this movement I was representing, how I was going to relate to people and how they were going to relate to me. I developed kind of a stock message: "There's something coming. Get ready. It's inevitably coming your way whether you like it or not. It sent me to tell you that." I got a few "amens" too.

Amzie's range of contacts was wider than Pop's; he was more at ease with political ideas. Like Pop, Amzie had no college education, so I wasn't dealing with any affectation, nor was there any trace of political arrogance. But Amzie had no sense of being incapacitated intellectually or unable to understand and explore any concept in the broad world of politics, culture, history, and race. Ideas simply didn't intimidate him and I found conversation with him invigorating and liberating. Amzie was the first one to really speak to me about the potential in Mississippi of the students' energy to blow open the issues of racial discrimination and white supremacy. And their energy had to be applied in the right way, Amzie insisted. He was not interested in sit-ins to desegregate Mississippi's public accommodations. This is before the freedom riders and only a few sit-ins had occurred in the Deep South anyway—nothing major. He favored school integration but the NAACP's legal battles for it were not his priority. He had concluded that at the heart of Mississippi's race problem was denial of the right to vote. Amzie wanted a grassroots movement to get it, and in his view getting that right was the key to unlocking Mississippi and gaining some power to initiate real change. I had not given that idea any thought at all; I didn't know before I began talking to Amzie that the Mississippi Delta where he lived was a congressional district that was two thirds Black. I had been sitting up hearing about oppression behind the *iron* curtain and the meaning of the vote for freedom all through my college years and graduate years without knowing about the Delta and its congressional district with a Black majority. I had not made the connection to the denial of the right to vote behind the *cotton* curtain. Like the sit-ins, Amzie's words slammed into me powerfully.

Amzie also had a plan. For the summer of 1961 he envisioned students spearheading a Delta voter registration campaign. He felt that the students would push hard instead of taking the cautious legalistic approach of groups like the NAACP or of grown-ups in general. He was tired of the slow legal procedures that he had been going through for years. "Amzie thinks, and I concur, the adults here will back the young folks but will never initiate a program strong enough to do what needs to be done," I wrote Jane. Amzie was turning myself and SNCC around, leading us into grassroots organizing. He thought it fine for young folks from Mississippi to go to the October conference in Atlanta, but more important, he thought, young people—"SNCCers" from other parts of the South—needed to begin planning to come *into* Mississippi. I must have passed Amzie's tests because he encouraged me to work with him. I wanted to stay but I still had one more year on my teaching contract at Horace Mann as well as obligations to my father. I bid a reluctant good-bye to Amzie, promising to return the following year.

C. C. BRYANT

> Lord, guide my feet while I run this race.
> Lord, guide my feet while I run this race.
> Lord, guide my feet while I run this race.
> 'Cause I don't want to run this race in vain.
>
> traditional

Amzie attended the October 14 conference in Atlanta; I did not. His voter registration proposal attracted only lukewarm interest as the more dramatically militant idea of "jail without bail"— a campaign to get arrested for civil disobedience and refuse bail —was discussed and embraced. But undoubtedly the roots of SNCC's first commitment to Mississippi were sunk at that meeting. Unlike the Shaw meeting, the Atlanta gathering was completely organized by the students, and while it was smaller in size, some were considering a deeper commitment than campus-based part-time activism. It was also the conference in which the students left their first imprint on national electoral politics. After the meeting Atlanta students persuaded Dr. King to participate in a downtown protest at Rich's department store they had been planning, and on October 19 he was arrested. Dr. King refused bail and in a few days was transferred, first to the De Kalb County jail, and then to the maximum-security prison in Reidsville—Ku Klux Klan heartland—miles away from Atlanta. While Dr. King was still in jail, John F. Kennedy, then campaigning for president against Richard Nixon, telephoned a very worried Mrs. King and expressed his sympathy. The call was widely reported by the press; it also committed King's father, a staunch Black Republican leader, to Kennedy, and swung significant numbers of Black votes to Kennedy in that close election. (In the 1956 presidential election 60 percent of Black voters voted Republican. In the 1960 election just 30 percent voted Republican.) Nixon had chosen not to call.

Meanwhile, as protests continued drawing students into what amounted to full-time activism, I had returned to teaching at Horace Mann. In the spring of 1961 CORE launched the freedom rides. SNCC soon joined this effort. Fearing a political backlash from the southerners who dominated Congress, the new Kennedy administration was becoming increasingly alarmed over student-led direct action. It had unsuccessfully tried to halt the freedom rides by calling for a "cooling-off" period. Now it offered money, beginning discussions with foundations and political allies that led to the creation of the Voter Education Project (VEP). In a calculation striking for how far off the mark it was, the Kennedys believed that voter registration drives would not trigger the kind of violent white response that sit-ins and freedom rides did. But the prospect of this money and the pressure to turn from direct action to voter registration fueled intense debate inside SNCC. Some charged that the Kennedy administration was trying to restrain the movement's radical ardor by sucking it into a corrupting politics of expediency. Others argued that voter registration was a natural evolution of the protest movement, leading to change through expansion of participation in the political process. I was happy not to be involved in this debate. Amzie Moore had already convinced me that in hard-core areas of the Deep South, voter registration *was* "direct action." And nowhere did this become clearer than in Mississippi.

I had originally planned to make my base in Cleveland when I returned to the state, but Amzie was having trouble acquiring a bus and securing a site for voter registration workshops. He'd been looking for a place along Highway 61 to hold the workshop sessions and hadn't found one yet. Father John LaBauve, a Catholic priest in Mound Bayou whose parish house Amzie had used for voter registration workshops before, had been transferred out of the Delta. "We're not quite ready yet," he told me. I felt, too, there were perhaps other layers of meaning in this statement. With the freedom rides racial tension in the state was rising dramatically. Membership in the Ku Klux Klan as well as in the White Citizens Council was growing. Amzie wanted to be well prepared.

Meanwhile SNCC, meeting at the Highlander Folk Center as I was getting established in Mississippi, continued its internal debate and partially resolved it under prodding by Ella Baker. Two cooperating wings were established: one, a direct action wing headed by Diane Nash of the Nashville student movement; the other, a voter registration wing headed by Charles Jones from the Charlotte, North Carolina, student movement. Also at that meeting a core group of students decided to drop out of school and become full-time civil rights organizers—"field secretaries." Charles Sherrod, a sit-in leader and divinity student from Virginia Union, was the first to do this. After talking to Amzie, he concluded that SNCC should send volunteers into the Delta. Because I was already in Mississippi, SNCC sent out a press release announcing a voter registration drive in Mississippi and that resulted in a story that appeared in *Jet* magazine saying that SNCC had sent a "voter registration team" into the Delta. C. C. Bryant, head of the Pike County NAACP, wrote Amzie asking him to send some of these voter registration workers down to McComb. I was the entire "team" and Amzie put me on the bus.

Like Amzie, C. C. Bryant had some independence. He worked for the Illinois Central Railroad; his paycheck came from Chicago. He was a church deacon, Boy Scout leader, and Sunday school teacher as well as NAACP branch president. He barbered in his front yard, and kept a small "library" of Black newspapers, books, and NAACP material there. C.C. was also an official with the Freemasons and arranged for me to use the second floor of the Masonic temple as a voter registration school. A butcher shop occupied the ground floor of the unpainted wood and cinder block structure.

Although C.C. brought me into town, Webb Owens took me around. He was a retired railroad porter and in charge of membership for the Pike County NAACP. Webb was grand in style; "Super Cool Daddy," as everyone called him, was a smart, slim, cigar-smoking, cane-carrying, sharp-dressing gregarious man liked and trusted by all. Every day for about two weeks he picked me up in a taxi driven by George Head, who also owned a juke joint where liquor flowed. George was illegal in the dry state of Mississippi. But George, who paid off white officials to keep his illegality in good working order, and who also packed a pistol, said, "I don't give a damn." George was one of Webb Owens's Black people of "standing"—folks who were making their living off the Black community in an era of racial segregation, like Aylene Quin, a big woman who actively supported us and fed us at her restaurant, South of the Border. There was Mr. Bates, who like Amzie had a filling station. Because it's *when* it is, in towns of any size like McComb you have independent Black businesses. Somebody is a tailor. Somebody is a barber, has a store, runs a café or juke, is the butcher below our office. And Webb and C.C. were asking them for fives and tens to bring in and support two of SNCC's new field secretaries. In what turned out to be essential to building and sustaining a movement in Mississippi—the connection between young folks and adults—Webb Owens also introduced me to students from the local high school; he'd known them all their lives. They agreed to help with canvassing for voter registration. They helped quickly spread the word that the "movement" had arrived in McComb.

Finally I began hitting the town's hot, dusty streets, knocking on doors. Whenever one opened, I introduced myself: "C. C. Bryant brought me here. I'm C. C. Bryant's voter registration man." I carried mimeographed reproductions of the official voter registration form with me (a local church allowed us to run them off) and found that the best approach was a straightforward one. "Have you ever tried to fill out this form?" I would ask. "Would you like to sit down now and try to fill it out?" Often the response was negative: "Don't want none of that mess here, boy." Or, "Now ya'll be careful foolin' around with that white folks' business." But I liked to think I got anyone I spoke with imagining himself or herself at the registrar's office. Getting someone to make this kind of mental leap, even for a moment, had to be considered an achievement in the Black Mississippi of those days where even the idea of citizenship barely existed. In McComb, as in the rest of the state, there was a deeply entrenched habit of deference to as well as genuine fear of white power, accumulated over years of living in a society that not only denied, but enforced through reprisal, any effort by Blacks to participate in the political process.

And fear of reprisal wasn't the only thing operating against attempts to register. The literacy test was intimidating in a community where few had much formal education. A section of the long form read "Write and copy in the space below Section_____of the Constitution of Mississippi." The registrar was empowered to choose any one of 285 sections and have the applicant write a "reasonable interpretation" of it. An illiterate white, if asked at all, might get a short, easy section like the one-sentence, "There shall be no imprisonment for debt." A Black person was likely to be given one of the many dense, complex, legalistic sections containing multiple paragraphs. Already deemed inferior by whites,

few black folks wanted to risk humiliation and even further ero-
sion of their sense of self-worth by taking a test designed for them
to fail. So, not surprisingly, the pace of the work was slow, even te-
dious, with few people attempting to register. But the few who
tried represented a significant breakthrough that can't be mea-
sured by numbers. They were early predictors of a time, coming
sooner rather than later, when Blacks would register and vote in
significant numbers.

The work was invisible for a while, but not a long while. Some
of the handful of people I brought to try to register actually succeeded: three of the four people in the first group I brought to the
county seat in Magnolia, and two of the three people I brought a
couple of days later. These small successes resulted in articles in the
McComb Enterprise-Journal newspaper that got the attention of one
old man and two middle-aged women from Amite County: Ernest Issac, Bertha Lee Hughes, and Matilda Schoby. They came to
the office in McComb and asked if I would accompany them to
Liberty, the county seat of Amite, where they would try to register
to vote. And on the morning of August 15—almost two weeks before I was beaten in Liberty—I brought them—the first Blacks in
memory to attempt to register at the Amite County courthouse
in Liberty.

"What y'all want?" growled the registrar.

They froze in terror and I spoke up. "They want to try to register to vote," I answered him.

"Y'all have to wait," he said.

In the crowd of white courthouse employees milling about us
during the six-hour wait before, one by one, the folks I'd brought
were permitted to fill out registration forms, there was a highway
patrolman who sat watching us. After we left the courthouse he
followed us down the highway. He waited until we crossed the
county line from Amite into Pike. Finally, he forced us to a halt on
the side of the highway. I got out of the car. It was dusk, a time
when rural Mississippi seems especially defined by shadows. The
patrolman stepped out of them and spoke to me.

"You the nigger that came down from New York to stir up a lot of trouble?" he drawled, the lazy sound not hiding the menace in his voice.

"I'm the Negro who came down from New York to instruct people in voter registration," I replied.

"Get in the [police] car, nigger!" he ordered when I began jotting his badge number down. He angrily slammed the door behind me. I was taken to jail in Magnolia and charged with interfering with an officer in the discharge of his duties. Just a few weeks before, SNCC's new chairman, Chuck McDew, had given me the private telephone number of John Doar at the Department of Justice's Civil Rights Division. I had written Doar outlining my plans to work on voter registration in Mississippi. He had written back asking me to call him directly with any reports of harassment or reprisal. So at the Magnolia jail I did, placing a collect call to Doar, which was accepted, and in a loud voice I demanded a federal investigation. The call may have intimidated the local authorities a bit; they surely had never before met a Black person able to call a federal agency collect. I was given a ninety-day suspended sentence and fined five dollars for court costs. I refused to pay the fine, explaining to the justice of the peace that the fine was part of an unjust prosecution. I stayed in jail for two days, coming out reluctantly when an NAACP lawyer arrived from Jackson and posted a bond.

E. W. STEPTOE

> Oh, oh freedom
> Oh, oh freedom
> Oh, oh freedom over me,
> and before I'll be a slave
> I'll be buried in my grave
> And go home to my Lord and be free.

traditional

The incident was written up in the *Enterprise-Journal* and widely broadcast on local radio. It was then that C. C. Bryant decided that he should take me to Amite County and introduce me to E. W. Steptoe, the head of the NAACP there. We arrived at night and Steptoe greeted me at the door. "I've been expecting you" were the first words he spoke to me. Inside the small farmhouse were his wife, Sing, and the two youngest of their nine children, Charlie and Shirley Jean. We sat and talked and I agreed to return immediately and stay for at least two weeks. George Head drove me back to Amite County two days later and we began canvassing.

Steptoe didn't have a car but his good friend, neighbor, and fellow NAACP member Herbert Lee had a vintage pickup truck. The three of us squeezed into the front seat to move about the county. We held nightly meetings at a little church on Steptoe's land. Two or three people showed up for them each night.

Our voter registration work began triggering angry white reaction almost immediately. And whites began to organize. Steptoe's network in the Black community reported regular meetings by whites at the county courthouse. The Black janitor there told us that many of the cars parked at the courthouse for these meetings were from surrounding counties. My arrest after bringing the first group of Blacks to the courthouse, and my beating on the streets of Liberty that followed two weeks afterward, were certainly connected to this white opposition that was organizing to halt our activities.

After the assault on me, violence escalated throughout the fall in the rural counties. When SNCC field secretary John Hardy, for the fourth time attempting to get potential Black voters registered, brought two farmers to the courthouse in Tylertown, the county seat of Wathall County, Registrar John Q. Wood said he wasn't registering voters that day. When John leaned forward to ask why, the registrar pulled a gun from his desk and smashed it across the side of John's head. John staggered out onto the street intending to report the attack; the sheriff placed *him* under arrest for disturbing the peace. Rumors flew that a lynch mob was forming and John was whisked off to the Pike County jail in Magnolia for safety.

The white fury now blistering southwest Mississippi culminated in murder. Herbert Lee, a boyhood friend of E.W. Steptoe and a founding member of the Amite County NAACP, was a key supporter of our voter registration efforts. On the evening of September 25 he pulled into the local cotton gin. E. H. Hurst, a state legislator and father-in-law of the Billy Jack who had beaten me in Liberty the month before, pulled in behind him and jumped out of his pickup truck holding a .38 pistol. The two men had played together as young boys but now Hurst was bitterly opposed to Lee's civil rights activities.

"I'm not going to talk to you until you put the gun down," Lee told him, according to reports.

Hurst put it back under his coat. But as Lee stepped out of his truck, Hurst whipped out the pistol and shot Herbert Lee just above the ear. There were a dozen people at the gin but Lee's body, dying and then finally dead, lay on the ground for two hours with Blacks afraid to touch it and whites refusing to. Hurst claimed that Lee attacked him with a tire iron and was never charged with the murder.

Medgar Evers spoke at Lee's funeral, but more weight pressed down on me there when a distraught Mrs. Lee walked up to Chuck McDew and myself. Looking into our faces, she spit out in bitter accusing tones, "You killed my husband! You killed my husband!" I had no answer. It is one thing to get beaten, quite another to be responsible, even indirectly, for a death. If we hadn't gone into Amite to organize, Herbert Lee wouldn't have been killed. I was sure of that.

Lee's killing paralyzed the voter registration movement, stopped it cold, with no Black person in all of rural southwest Mississippi willing to make an attempt at registering. Amzie Moore came down from the Delta and for several nights the two of us began investigating, moving from farm to farm, talking to fearful Black residents. Neither of us knew the county and it's a wonder we didn't pull into the drive of a white farm and get ourselves lynched, for the land wasn't sharply segregated in Amite County (Hurst's farm, in fact, was right across the road from Steptoe's). We managed to track down Louis Allen, a witness to Lee's killing. Allen said he was willing to testify that Lee had no tire iron in his hand if the federal government guaranteed protection for himself and his family. The government refused and fear deepened as both the request and the refusal leaked out. (Six months later a deputy sheriff told Allen that he knew Allen had tried to get FBI help, and smashed his jaw with a flashlight. Almost two years later Allen was ambushed and killed in the driveway of his farmhouse.)

Now, second thoughts seemed about to immobilize me. Can we do this? I couldn't help wondering. Can we really keep doing this? I asked myself, knowing that the price could get higher. But staying with this work in Mississippi was more important than ever, I concluded. It was the only way to make any sense out of Herbert Lee's death. Still, I wasn't sure what to do next. Because of the amount of activity going on around us, McComb offered some breathing room, a place to sort out my thoughts. The student movement was heating up there. Their ground was getting rougher too but they were insistently continuing to traverse it.

HOLLIS AND CURTIS

> Ain't gonna let nobody turn me 'round,
> Turn me 'round, turn me 'round
> Ain't gonna let nobody turn me 'round,
> I'm gonna keep on a walkin', keep on a talkin'
> Marching up to freedom land.
>
> traditional

As an important harbinger of what would happen in county after county that we entered, just as I was getting started in McComb, two nineteen-year-olds, Hollis Watkins and Curtis Hayes, both from rural Pike County, walked into the office one afternoon. It seemed to me they'd come out of nowhere. Later I would understand that the movement itself had called them up as it would call forth and commit other young people wherever we worked. A "friend-girl," Hollis said had told him that Martin Luther King, Jr., was in town.

"Are you Martin Luther King?" Hollis asked me.

"No," I replied.

"We heard he was here."

"I don't know anything about that. I'm here to teach Negroes how to vote. I'm working with C. C. Bryant."

I described our voter registration effort. Both Hollis and Curtis had vague plans for further schooling, but nothing definite. Both were still living at home. They had time as well as interest and the very next day Hollis and Curtis began distributing leaflets announcing voter registration classes. They were SNCC's first student volunteers in Mississippi.

Shortly after Curis and Hollis began work, Reggie Robinson from the Civic Interest Group, a SNCC affiliate in Baltimore, Maryland, and John Hardy, a member of the Nashville student movement, arrived. Reggie took over the voter registration work in McComb; John did the same in Wathall County as I began working in Amite. With the arrival of Reggie and John, an office, and a community willing to provide support, McComb and southwest Mississippi were now bright on SNCC's radar screen. Diane Nash, Jim Bevel, Marion Barry, all members of SNCC's direct action wing, showed up in early August, and after their release from Parchman prison in the Delta some of the freedom riders drifted in. For Hollis and Curtis and other McComb students who were too young to vote themselves—voting age was twenty-one then—and impatient with the slow, frustrating work of convincing reluctant elders to attempt registration, the incoming "freedom riders" (an identity given to any civil rights worker) and their nonviolent direct action workshops generated great excitement. This exposure to the SNCC activists soon had the students eager to launch some direct action themselves.

I didn't encourage sit-ins in McComb, even though such protests the year before had inspired me to journey into the South. Here in McComb, I was C. C. Bryant's voter registration man. That, however, mattered little to the McComb students who had their own ideas, not mine. On the same day I was assaulted in Liberty, Hollis and Curtis sat in at the lunch counter of McComb's Woolworth and were arrested for breach of the peace. Two hundred people held a mass meeting that night. I was whisked to it after Dr. Anderson finished bandaging my head at his office. At the mass meeting, a young girl kept staring at me, and late the next day that young girl—fifteen-year-old Brenda Travis—was arrested along with four other students she had led in a sit-in at the Greyhound bus station. I think the sight of my battered and bandaged head triggered some great outrage in Brenda. In any case, McComb now had a student movement—the Pike County Nonviolent Movement. Hollis was president and Curtis was vice president. The two streams of civil rights activity—direct action protests and voter registration—were beginning to converge as both Blacks and whites responded and reacted.

Brenda Travis and the students who had joined her sit-in at the McComb bus station remained in jail. They were finally released October 3, one week after Lee's murder, and when the principal of Burgland High School, Commodore Dewy Higgins, refused to readmit Brenda, about one hundred students walked out. Their protest washed into our McComb headquarters, engulfing us like a sudden tidal surge. At first we heard only the faint sound of singing in the distance, the sound of freedom songs that gradually became louder and then thunderous as the marching students, still singing, came up the stairs and entered our headquarters. To protest Lee's killing and the denial of voting rights they wanted to march on the county courthouse in Magnolia, some eight miles away.

Their very presence in our office was a demand for support and there was no way we could ignore it or refuse it. But we urged them to reconsider going to Magnolia. It was already late in the afternoon, and it would be dark and dangerous before they reached the town. We suggested McComb's city hall instead. They agreed to that and set out, with more warnings from us chasing them: "Stay off the grass." "Keep to the sidewalk." "Don't go against the light." "You don't want to get arrested for no jive reason," Chuck McDew yelled out at one point. "I thought about Gandhi when he saw his people massed for protest," McDew said later. " 'There go our people,' he said. 'We have to hurry and catch up with them.' "

On the steps of city hall, Curtis knelt in prayer and was arrested. Then Hollis was arrested too. Then a student tried to pray on the steps and was arrested. Finally the police arrested everybody including Bob Zellner, SNCC's one white field secretary, a southerner from Alabama. He, of course, stood out, and was a special target of enraged whites who attacked him while he was being held by the police. He was kicked in the face, gouged in the eyes, and knocked to the ground by a rain of blows. The police weren't protecting him, so Chuck McDew and I rushed over and grabbed him, trying to shield him, and pushing through the police we hustled him inside.

Everyone was bailed out in a few days but when the principal of the high school told the students that as a condition of being allowed to return to classes they would have to accept a reduction in their grades and sign a statement promising no further demonstrations, more than 100 students promptly walked out of school again. Return or be expelled, the principal ordered. A day later 103 students returned to school, handed in their books, and walked back out. We opened a "nonviolent high school" with 50 to 75 kids in one big room. This ended as McDew, Zellner, myself, and nine others who were not minors were sentenced to four months in jail. In sentencing us, Judge Robert W. Brumfield blamed us for the mob scene at city hall and made clear with bloodcurdling words that, in Mississippi, the state apparatus would be used to stop us by any means necessary. "Every effort you make to stir up violence will be met," the judge said, staring sternly at me. "Some of you are local residents, some are outsiders. Those of you who are local residents are like sheep being led to the slaughter. If you continue to follow the advice of outside agitators you will be like sheep and slaughtered." Some of the students then went back to school; others went to the high school section of Campbell College, a church school in Jackson. Nonetheless, the students had fashioned a movement that no one in town could have anticipated and that no one could ignore. Amzie had been prescient.

As organizers, we were just getting our feet wet, but in personal as well as political terms we were beginning to see the outlines of what organizing in the state required. I learned to live with my fears. Organizing myself was a necessary first step. When you're out there in a really rural area with no electricity, no radio, no running water, everything moves very slowly and you really have time to go into yourself. I used to think, Pick one foot up and step forward, put it down and pick the next one up. You get down to that level of reality if you're doing canvassing in these dangerous areas. What you learn is the importance of a daily routine carrying you through, and in the midst of routine, you can dissipate a lot of fears.

It was clear that sustaining the work would require a consensus that linked student, parent, and community. Such a consensus could override specific points of disagreement. Thus even C. C. Bryant, who did not foresee the McComb student protests and would have disapproved of them if he had, was drawn into a position of support, although it was not completely of his own volition. When the students marched downtown, local authorities were certain that C.C. must have had a hand in organizing their protest. A warrant was issued and he was arrested at the railroad yards of the Illinois Central. In the final analysis, he concluded as he saw parental support of their children, increased interest in voter registration, and white power at least momentarily uncertain, that the students had empowered his efforts and were even opening a way toward change. So speaking at an NAACP meeting after his release on bail, C.C. proclaimed, "Where the students lead, we will follow." And Webb Owens—Super Cool Daddy— continued to offer unwavering support: "I'm with the NAACP, SCLC, CORE, SNCC, anything that will bring us freedom," he said, articulating an idea of unity that anticipated formation of the Council of Federated Organizations (COFO).

The energy of the students in McComb was confirming the accuracy of Amzie Moore's judgment that young people could be the cutting edge of meaningful change in Mississippi. And if the whole question of the possibility of change in Mississippi depended upon finding agents to produce that change, as I thought it did, McComb seemed to confirm that those agents most likely would be young people. I had thought after first meeting and talking with Amzie that a voter registration campaign would require the importation of SNCC workers. Now, young Mississippians who would spread across the state to work seemed the logical and most likely nucleus. Furthermore, "direct action" had taken on a new character in Mississippi. We did not know yet how far we could go with it, but if McComb was any indicator, young people were prepared to try to go as far as they could.

But what was totally unexpected was the recognition that I had become part of something else besides a civil rights organization in Mississippi. Everywhere we went, I and other civil rights workers were adopted and nurtured, even protected as though we were family. We were the community's children, and that closeness rendered moot the label of "outside agitator." Indeed, if we had any label at all, it was "freedom riders." It did not matter whether we had arrived in that fashion or not. This identity was liberating, conferring respect in every community we worked in. In calling us freedom riders these communities were finding the most defiant image they could to signal their approval of our work, even if they crossed the street when they saw us, or were not yet prepared to brave the dangers of trying to register down at the county courthouse. Importantly, as is always true in close families, our young generation was dynamically linked to a rooted older generation who passed on wisdom, encouragement, and concrete aid when possible. This was empowering, enabling SNCC and CORE field secretaries to move from county to county across a network that provided different levels of support, a network made up of people offering whatever they could within their means. We could show up, as I often did at Steptoe's farm, unannounced, and there were people ready to take care of us. We could be carried to a doctor, as I was after I was beaten in Liberty. Our movement family saw to it that we had something to eat or a place to sleep. Inside this "family" was the true place where the movement's moral authority was anchored. I would not have guessed, in a thousand years of guessing, the impact of this nucleus of young and old, organizer and community leader, that came together in Mississippi.

By the winter of 1961–62, Curtis and Hollis had become the first of SNCC's full-time Mississippi staff drawn from local people in the state. And in the spring of 1962 Amzie drove down to Jackson and said it was time to move into the Delta. We held a meeting and recruited Charles McLaurin, Dorie Ladner, and Colia Lidell to go to Ruleville in Sunflower County, James Jones to go to Clarksdale, Mattie Bivens to work in Cleveland, where Diane Nash and Jim Bevel married and were living with Amzie, and Emma Bell to work in Greenville. Later, Sam Block was recruited in Cleveland to start a project in Greenwood where some months later he was joined by Lawrence Guyot and later still by Willie Peacock. Frank Smith came over from Georgia and went to work in Holly Springs. Dave Dennis arrived at the beginning of 1962 and, after staying in the Jackson "Freedom House" briefly, began working in Hattiesburg. As 1962 drew to a close twenty young people were on SNCC's Mississippi staff. Only myself and three others were from out of the state.

CHAPTER 3

Standin' at the Crossroads

From Voter Registration to Political Party

> We went up to register and it was the first time visiting the court-house in Greenwood, Mississippi, and the sheriff came up to me and he asked me, he said, "Nigger, where you from?" I told him, "Well, I'm a native Mississippian." He said, "Yeh, yeh, I know that, but where you from? I don't know where you from." I said, "Well, around some counties." He said, "Well, I know that, I know you ain't from here, 'cause I know every nigger and his mammy." I said, "You know all the niggers, do you know any colored people?" He got angry. He spat in my face and he walked away. So he came back and turned around and told me, "I don't want to see you in town any more. The best thing you better do is pack your clothes and get out and don't never come back no more." I said, "Well, sheriff, if you don't want to see me here, I think the best thing for you to do is pack your clothes and leave, get out of town, 'cause I'm here to stay, I came here to do a job and this is my intention, I'm going to do this job. . . ."
>
> field report from Sam Block, 23, late summer 1962

Like any Black person living in America I knew racism. What I hadn't encountered before Mississippi was the use of law as an instrument of outright oppression. Mississippi stood out as the state most completely organized in terms of its state apparatus to foster apartheid. In the Delta counties of Leflore and Sunflower, where we began focusing our efforts, state food aid was cut off—reprisal for our voter registration drive. Murderous tension instigated by

Governor Ross Barnett thickened the air in the fall of 1962 when James Meredith became the first African American to enroll in the University of Mississippi. He was escorted onto campus by federal troops as whites rioted. Perceiving that their "way of life" was under assault, whites across the state worked themselves up into a boiling fury and considered all civil rights efforts acts of war. Meanwhile, outside of Mississippi SNCC had grown, and the organization now had a network of northern support groups, the "Friends of SNCC." In late February 1963 I wrote to one in Chicago:

> The voting drives I've experienced in Mississippi have proceeded by steppes instead of slopes and we have been on a deep plateau all winter, shaking off the effects of the violence of August and September and the eruption that was Meredith at Old Miss.
>
> We know this plateau by now; we have had to crawl over it in McComb city, Amite and Wathall counties, Hattiesburg, Greenwood, and Ruleville: You dig into yourself and the community to wage psychological warfare; you combat your own fears about beatings, shootings, and possible mob violence; you stymie, by your mere physical presence, the anxious fear of the Negro community, seeded across town and blown from paneled pine and white sunken sink to windy kitchen floors and rusty old stoves, that you maybe *did* come only to boil and bubble and then burst, out of sight and sound; you organize, pound by pound, small bands of people who gradually focus in the eyes of Negroes and whites as people "tied up in that mess"; you create a small striking force capable of moving out when the time comes, which it must, whether we help it or not.
>
> When a thousand people stand in line for a few cans of food, then it is possible to tell a thousand people that they are poor, that they are trapped in poverty, that *they* must move if they are to escape. In Leflore county there are 14,400 nonwhite workers, 12,000 make less than $1,500 a year and 7,200 of these make less than $500 a year. After more than 600 lined up to receive food in Greenwood on Wednesday, 20 Feb., and Sam's subsequent arrest and weekend in prison on Thurs. 21 Feb., over 100 people overflowed city hall on Mon. 25 Feb. to protest at his trial. Over 250 gathered at a mass meeting that same night

and on Tues. by 10:30 A.M., I had counted over 30 people standing in silent line in the county court house; they say over 200 stood in line across the day.

This is a new dimension for a voting program in Mississippi; Negroes have been herded to the polls before by white people, but have never stood en mass in protest at the seat of power in the iceberg of Mississippi politics. Negroes who couldn't read and write stood in line to tell the registrar they still wanted to vote, that they didn't have the chance to go to school when they were small—and anyway Mr. John Jones can't read and write either and *he* votes.

For almost two years we had been struggling to open up Mississippi. University of Mississippi professor James Silver had described the state as "the closed society" and many of the powers deeply behind the closure—organized and organizing to keep Mississippi closed—were right up there in the Delta. The founding meetings of the White Citizens Council had been held in Indianola, county seat of Sunflower County and the home base of Senator James O. Eastland, one of the most powerful men in the United States Senate. Up the road, the city of Greenwood in Leflore County was one of the hubs of monied cotton plantation society. Nearby Clarksdale and Greenville, on the Mississippi River, were also influential centers of plantation wealth. Despite the declining importance of cotton production, real white power, shaping culture as well as the economy, was here and in many ways the Delta rivaled the capital at Jackson as a power center. And here we were, right in their backyard.

As the state began to churn with new Black political activity, some of the older Black leadership were confounded. They were uncertain about how to respond to the unexpected development of insurgent young people. But we needed to bring them in and with the promise of Voter Education Project (VEP) money, they needed to come in. Despite the misgivings of Roy Wilkins and others in the national headquarters in New York, state NAACP president Aaron "Doc" Henry, a Clarksdale pharmacist, and NAACP state field secretary Medgar Evers quickly embraced the idea of coordination. Meanwhile Dave Dennis, a new state field secretary sent from Louisiana by the Congress of Racial Equality, and I were finding ourselves in sync on the necessity of presenting a united civil rights front. As a result, the Council of Federated Organizations (COFO), an inactive organization formed the year before, was resurrected during a politically intense Clarksdale meeting and Doc Henry became its president. I became its director of voter registration. This was a major development; established local groups were conferring a kind of formal legitimacy on us by opening up to the young people of SNCC and CORE networks they had built up over years of struggle. It clearly established, cutting through age, economic status, and the often bruising rivalries of national civil rights organizations, that, for the time being anyway, wherever it might lead, grassroots organizing for voter registration was the agreed-upon work in Mississippi. Sustained movement, whether for civil rights or for math literacy, requires this kind of consensus.

As the kids say, Dave and I now had each other's back, a relationship that continues today as he directs the Southern Initiative of the Algebra Project. But "back in the day," as the kids also say, with virtually all of COFO's staff provided by SNCC and CORE, Dave and I wrestled with life-and-death questions hard to imagine now. And finding a way to deal with the still-increasing violence was at the top of our concerns. A heavy curtain seemed to have dropped down on the state, making us invisible to the nation. Behind it, an upsurge in shootings, bombings, and arson bloodied much of the summer and fall of 1962. As 1963 began I was targeted in a machine-gun ambush outside of Greenwood. Instead of hitting me, one of the thirteen bullets that penetrated our car smashed into the neck of Tougaloo student Jimmy Travis who was driving and lodged half an inch from his spine. I grabbed the steering wheel, one foot feeling for the brake as the car swerved and Travis's head slumped onto my shoulder; somehow he survived without paralysis. Amzie used to call these shootings Mississippi's modern form of lynching. And that was what was happening. There were disappearances (while searching for the bodies of Schwerner, Chaney, and Goodman in 1964, the FBI found in the Pearl River the bodies of two Alcorn student activists who had vanished the year before).

Still, we could not get the country to pay attention to what was going on in the state. One argument, originating from Mississippi whites and echoed by federal authorities as well as much of the news media, was that Mississippi Black people were apathetic. Mississippi whites were counting on us never being able to involve large numbers of people in our efforts. This pragmatic need was behind much of the violence and economic reprisal in the state. Small numbers meant being able to claim that Black folk were "happy and satisfied" with their lot. This local argument conformed to the national stereotype of southern Black people in particular. It was only when hundreds of people began showing up at the Leflore County courthouse after food aid was shut down that this argument began to erode. They could say people were hungry, but they couldn't say they were apathetic if for a little bit of food they were willing to risk everything and go down and stand at the registrar's office trying to register for voting rights. You could see that there was a point at which people would begin to do *something,* and whatever it was—southern whites now talked about "their niggras" being stirred up by "outside agitators"— you could no longer call them apathetic. And how did this happen?

The winter of 1963 had been an exceptionally cold one in the Delta, and it had been a poor year for cotton pickers. Plantation owners used fewer field hands and paid them even less than usual because labor was less valuable than ever. Machines and automation were coming in. Commodities—surplus cheese, rice, flour, and sugar which were distributed free by the county as a supplement to often meager food supplies—were now crucial to fending off destitution. So when county officials halted the commodities program in reprisal for voter registration efforts, Leflore County Blacks saw what hadn't been clear to them before: a connection between political participation and food on their table. For months Sam Block, Willie Peacock, and Lawrence Guyot had been patiently canvassing with scant success, standing up to mob violence, police intimidation, and repeated jailing. Sam had come first, arriving in Greenwood alone, early in the summer of 1962. For six weeks he had no place to stay and no local support as he initiated the voter registration campaign. He was arrested six times after his arrival. But when he was arrested for the seventh time, Black folks—more than a hundred—filled the courthouse to overflowing for his trial. These were new people, many of whom came off nearby plantations and from the ranks of the unemployed in town; they were angry at the cutoff of commodities. With little to lose now, they protested that Sam Block had done nothing wrong. Even we were surprised by their militancy. Some were drinking from "white" water fountains in the courthouse. Others—plantation workers—were actually talking back to plantation owners, perhaps inspired by Sam. For when the judge offered to suspend Sam's six-month sentence in return for his agreement to abandon the voter registration project, Sam replied in a remark that quickly spread through town, "Judge, I ain't gonna do none of that." Suddenly Greenwood had a mass movement, this time defined by hundreds attempting to register to vote. These circumstances surrounding the shooting of Jimmy Travis for a time made Greenwood the main center of attention of northern liberals and the national civil rights network.

SNCC called in staff from other projects in the state and around the South to demonstrate that violence would not stop the work. It mobilized northern support groups to send down food to Greenwood. VEP director Wiley Branton announced a "saturation campaign to register every qualified Negro in Leflore County." Television crews from the national networks arrived. Responding to appeals for food aid, comedian Dick Gregory announced that he was chartering a plane, filling it with food, and flying down from Chicago. After arriving, Gregory mingled with folks in the long voter registration lines, regularly startling local authorities by hurling taunting words in their faces to the delight of local Blacks who had never seen anything like it. "Look at them!" he shouted at a police squad preventing a group of Blacks from entering the courthouse, "a bunch of illiterate whites who couldn't even pass the test themselves." Before long, it seemed everyone had a favorite Dick Gregory line. "We will march through your dogs!" he declared at a mass meeting one night to applause and stomping feet. "And if you get some elephants, we'll march through them. And bring on your tigers and we'll march through them!"

Even the White House could not ignore events in Greenwood. At a press conference, President Kennedy was asked about the situation and he replied that the Department of Justice had filed a suit aimed at securing federal protections for Blacks attempting to register to vote. It would address two of our main concerns, department officials assured us: prohibit city and county officials from harassing or intimidating prospective Black registrants, and provide federal protection at the courthouse for registrants. Sam, a half dozen others, and I were in jail at the time. During a march from a church to the courthouse we had been arrested and convicted of disorderly conduct, sentenced to four months, and had decided to serve out our time rather than appeal. Our incarceration was more pressure on the federal government, and just a day after Kennedy's press conference Department of Justice officials brought us before a federal judge in Greenville who vacated our sentences. Almost immediately after our release, however, the president and his brother, Attorney General Robert Kennedy, began reneging on their promise of federal protection for Black people trying to register to vote. John Doar of the justice department's Civil Rights Division finally confessed that Washington had cut a deal: our release in exchange for abandoning the lawsuit. The federal government could not police the South, the Kennedys rationalized.

WE HAVE COME THIS FAR BY FAITH . . .

> Tonight the Negro knows from his radio and television what happened today all over the world. He knows what black people are doing and he knows what white people are doing. . . . He knows about the new free nations of Africa and knows that a Congo native

can be a locomotive engineer, but in Jackson he cannot even drive a garbage truck. . . .

Jackson can change if it wills to do so. If there should be resistance, how much better to have turbulence to effect improvement, rather than turbulence to maintain a stand pat policy. . . . But whether Jackson and the state choose change or not, the years of change are upon us.

Medgar Evers, 1963

Greenwood commanded national attention for only a moment before the spotlight swung to another scene on the civil rights stage: Birmingham, Alabama. And Greenwood officialdom had learned what Bull Connor had yet to find out: that you couldn't maintain white power if your reaction to change was so violent and hard-line that it brought angry national attention on yourself. By late spring, Greenwood Mayor Charles Sampson was offering a city bus for Blacks wanting to take the registration test. Most harassment ceased at the courthouse. Still, few Blacks were actually getting registered. Of the more than one thousand five hundred Black people who took the registration test in Leflore County, only about fifty were accepted. It probably seemed to many that little had changed. But anyone looking deeper would have seen one key transformation. Black people had learned how to stand on their feet, look the white man in the eyes, and say this is what we demand. They had found a voice in Greenwood and there was no silencing it, despite the national obscurity Greenwood soon returned to. Even the small concessions wrung out of county officialdom taught Leflore County Blacks that their voices could no longer be ignored. For the first time we had been able to penetrate the heart of the Delta in a significant way; some liberated political space had been created.

And, what was true in McComb had become even more evident in Greenwood: work with people and leadership will emerge. You don't have to know in advance who that leadership will be, but it will emerge from the movement that emerges. After the national figures left Greenwood, after national attention wandered to other places, it was this local leadership that returned to the organizing work that had begun before the national campaign in Greenwood. And there was much more local leadership at the end of the year than there had been at the beginning. Completely ignored by the press was the reactivation of the NAACP in Greenwood. Medgar Evers came up frequently from Jackson until he was assassinated (by Byron de la Beckwith from Greenwood).

Just as important as the development of local leadership in the city, SNCC organizers like Willie Peacock from neighboring Tallahatchie County had come through the fires of Greenwood annealed like steel. Amzie had taken me up to Tallahatchie County to meet Willie in August 1962. Earlier in the year, SNCC field secretaries Dion Diamond, James Bevel (before joining the SCLC staff), and Sam Block had visited the Rust campus where Willie was one of the leaders of a boycott students had mounted against the segregated theater in downtown Holly Springs. He'd also been working on voter registration with SNCC field secretary Frank Smith, who was based in Holly Springs. Now Willie was considering going on to medical school. "We need you," I told Willie as he, Amzie, and I sat and talked in his Charleston, Mississippi, home. On the spot, he agreed to come with us. Willie walked into a bedroom and told his mother he was leaving. Willie's father smiled approvingly. As it turned out, Willie's dad was part of Amzie's network. The two men had known each other for years, going back to the days of the huge mass meetings of the Regional Council of Negro Leadership in the Delta. Both men were also Freemasons.

At the exact moment Amzie and I were talking to Willie at his home in Tallahatchie, whites in Greenwood were making plans to invade the SNCC office there. Late that night a white mob battered in the office door forcing Sam Block, Lawrence Guyot, and Luvaghn Brown to flee by jumping out of a back window and sliding down a television antenna before finally racing down back alleys. The next day Willie joined Sam Block in Greenwood. Willie, who like Sam, Luvaghn, and Guyot was born and raised in Mississippi, did not find this violent assault surprising. And in any case, he was committed now. Recently, he reflected on committing to the movement in a way that reminded me of how the Algebra Project is connected to movement experience. "There was camaraderie; I was really committed by [young] people like me and we kicked up some dust. The papers were talking about how we were going to start something and leave, so although Greenwood was pretty hard to crack, I *couldn't* leave." Fifteen years after arriving in Greenwood, Willie, now "Wazir" Peacock, was one of the organizers who helped Jesse Jackson carry Mississippi in the 1988 presidential primary (Hollis Watkins was another).

Others were called forth by the movement. There was Robert Burns, the World War II veteran who took Sam Block in and stuck with him. Reverend Aaron Johnson, who opened his church to the movement. Lou Emma Allen, a cleaning woman whose strong voice rang out in song at mass meetings and whose strong and honest personality brooked no pretensions from anyone white or Black. As had happened in McComb, a slew of young people had emerged and were playing key roles as leaders and organizers: June Johnson, Dewy, George, and Freddie Greene, Mary Lane, Euvester Simpson from nearby Itta Bena, Silas McGhee—indeed, his entire family. There were others, all thrust up by the movement, enough to fill this page. Church sisters who pushed timid preachers into silence if not active participation. These were people who not only took the lead in challenging white power, but perhaps more important for the movement, challenged themselves and changed themselves. (In an interesting development of local leadership, when the 1964 Public Accommodations Act was passed by Congress, independent of SNCC-COFO, local activists who had emerged because of the voter registration drive began testing compliance with downtown sit-ins.)

We knew more about organizing now. A small dedicated band—even one person—could dig in, establish a beachhead, survive and perhaps get some kind of breakthrough, punch a small hole in the wall of white supremacy by linking everyday issues to political participation. It was dangerous; just a few people would attempt voting registration, and then only if we went down with them. Organizers were acting, in part, as a kind of buffer because the initial violence was often directed at us. It was only when that didn't work to drive us out that you began to get violence directed at the people from the community who were involved with us. The key to surviving all this as an organizer was understanding that sometimes you were in no danger and sometimes you were in very real danger. After all, you can't live as though you're in very real danger every day, every minute; no one can survive like that. The communities we worked in didn't live like that. They knew how to survive, and part of organizing *in* them was learning *from* them how to move in times of real danger and how to take advantage of those times when you were not in real danger. Those were the times when you relaxed and deepened ties and forged bonds that were not directly connected to any specific political act like going to the county courthouse. You went to church. Or perhaps had a beer at the local juke joint. Or just sat on a front porch and talked. Maybe helped with something—and always learned. Doing this, we continued to find that local leadership emerged.

Elsewhere in the state, however, the kind of easing of courthouse intimidation that had occurred in Greenwood didn't exist. For most Blacks, it was still dangerous, even deadly, to make an attempt to register to vote. But the numbers in Greenwood—those attempting registration, those denied after attempting it—made it clear that we were going to have to push to do away with the literacy requirement. Why should there be one to gain the right of political participation at all? Not only did illiterate whites vote, but without question Blacks, regardless of the level of their formal education, knew the people who governed their daily lives and could judge who should be in or out of political office. In all probability, I used to say, they knew their papas and mamas.

What was emerging was the concept of "one person one vote." We were asking some broader questions now: Who can be a citizen? What are the requirements? These questions are still unresolved and part of what we are tackling in the Algebra Project. But in the 1960s we were just discovering them. Buried in the deepest recesses of our thinking, almost invisible to ourselves, were other questions, harder questions, that connected to the larger question of citizenship: What is the vote for? Why do we want it in the first place? What must we do right now to ensure that when we have the vote it will work for us to benefit our communities?

After Greenwood, we began thinking that the Department of Justice needed to incorporate the idea of one person one vote in any suits for voting rights it might file, or else the fight for voter registration—citizenship—would be reduced to a fight for the right of well-educated Blacks to be able to go down and register— perhaps 10 percent of the Black population in Mississippi. In the Delta, especially, education took a backseat to servitude. Even school sessions there—Black school sessions—were halted so that students could join the labor pool of cotton pickers. You can't deny people an educational opportunity and then say that the reason people can't vote is because they can't read, I had argued in my testimony when we were taken from the Greenwood jail and brought before the federal judge in Greenville.

In total at the end of 1963, there were approximately three hundred Black voters and ten thousand white voters in a county that was almost two thirds Black. We were learning, too, that we weren't just up against the Klan, or a mob of ignorant whites, but political arrangements and expediencies that went all the way to Washington, D.C. For neither the federal government, nor the two political parties that dominated the federal government, were prepared to take on the unfairness of the actual process by which citizenship was bestowed or denied. A few new Black voters were acceptable, but neither Democrats nor Republicans were going to cram universal suffrage down the throats of white people. In the Delta and throughout the Black belt South, such suffrage would turn a century of political power upside down by granting voting rights to Black people who outnumbered whites but were without formal education. Even in the north, Black votes were largely ghettoized, so to support us, the government would have to ask Mississippi whites to do something they didn't ask whites any-place else to do. In his speech at the March on Washington, SNCC chairman John Lewis succinctly summed up our dilemma. "The party of Lincoln is the party of Goldwater," he said. "The party of Kennedy is the party of Eastland. Where is our party?" These questions were going to lead us step-by-step to formation of the Mississippi Freedom Democratic Party.

We needed to get Blacks involved with trying to participate in the workings of the political system in greater numbers and at a faster pace than the rigged official process was permitting or would ever permit. We needed to turn the pressure up. That would require a statewide effort.

And quite separately from the arguments we were having with the federal government over the idea of one person one vote or the need for federal protection against continuing white violence, a statewide effort was also a natural outgrowth of Greenwood. When Medgar Evers came up from Jackson to speak, he had gotten fired up by what he saw. I remember, Greenwood made him feel he needed to go back to Jackson and really start working there. He was determined to move Jackson, he said, because if people up in Greenwood could get themselves together and do what they had done—*in the Delta, no less*—then there was just no excuse for Jackson not to be in motion. By June in Jackson, more than six hundred people—mostly students—had been jailed for conducting sit-ins and walking picket lines in front of segregated businesses. Medgar *and* Roy Wilkins got arrested when they picketed Woolworth. It was after these actions that Medgar was assassinated.

We also took a busload of people from Greenwood to Greenville when we appeared before the federal judge there. They went out and started doing voter registration work. June Johnson's mother, Lula Belle, was on that bus and she said that we had really done the right thing getting her out of Greenwood, that, while she would never have canvassed for voter registration among people she grew up with, she had no reluctance at all about walking the streets of Greenville, buttonholing people. Sometimes even working a distance away did not completely protect family and friends from threats and reprisal. CORE's Ann Moody was from Centreville, a small southwest Mississippi town. She became involved in the movement while a Tougaloo student in Jackson. When she did, the sheriff stopped in on her mother and told her it wouldn't be a good idea for Ann to return home unless she changed her ways. A mob of whites beat an uncle. In February 1963 another relative was killed, shot in the face with buckshot. These shared concerns and sorrows, however, became part of what bonded the Mississippi COFO staff—incentive to press on with efforts to change the state.

So we began working to secure and extend this larger sense of identity and organization. It had already begun to happen among young staffers like Curtis, Hollis, Guyot, June, and all the others working under the COFO umbrella. But, the large push in Greenwood notwithstanding, most of our efforts had been concentrated in small Delta projects and the fourth congressional district around Canton, where Dave Dennis and CORE were doing the same kind of grassroots organizing we were. It was still difficult for people in Ruleville to see themselves connected to people in Liberty or Tylertown. Or people in Canton to really identify with people in Clarksdale. We needed some larger unifying force.

GO TELL IT ON THE MOUNTAIN . . .

> They say that freedom is a constant struggle,
> They say that freedom is a constant struggle,
> They say that freedom is a constant struggle,
> O Lord, I've struggled so long,
> I must be free, I must be free.
>
> traditional

So now we decided to run our own candidates for governor and lieutenant governor in a "mock" election that paralleled the state election scheduled for the fall. By registering Black people at our own sites, and setting up polling places in our own precincts, we sought to both establish clearly that there was interest in political participation and make the point that to get it you needed registration and voting sites that weren't dangerous and intimidating. But how were we going to make this a statewide effort? This was a statewide mobilization, not exactly the same as the slower-paced community organizing we had been doing, and we were still relatively few in number. Also, there was a time frame that added to the pressure on us; the election was going to be held the first Tuesday in November. So we accepted his offer when Allard Lowenstein, a white Democratic Party operative who'd come to Jackson after Medgar's assassination, said he was willing to recruit students from Yale, where he was dean of freshmen, and students from Stanford, where he'd been a dean before going to Yale. They'd come and work for the two weeks before election day. With these additional bodies—about one hundred came down—we were able to significantly increase our spread around the state. But it meant that for the first time we would be using significant numbers of white workers.

Lowenstein's students were an important factor in our successfully getting more than eighty thousand Black voters out in that election. This was really a continuation of a tactic that began two years before when we ran Rev. R. L. T. Smith for Congress in the fourth congressional district, even though he didn't have a chance of winning. But we used that campaign as an organizing tool and as a way to raise the consciousness of people to the idea that eventually they would be electing people to office, Black people to office. But when we began Reverend Smith's campaign that thought wasn't anywhere in their minds. Now with the freedom vote we were using the voter registration drive as a way to fix their consciousness around the idea that a Black person would run for governor and lieutenant governor of Mississippi. Independently of getting the candidate elected to office, the vote also made a certain practical sense from an organizer's point of view. Part of being effective has to do with a kind of continual shaping and reshaping of oneself using accumulated experiences and anticipated needs as raw material. We had been trying to build a strong Black movement in Mississippi, so unlike the SNCC project in southwest Georgia where Charles Sherrod consciously introduced whites to help define what integration was to be, we hadn't used whites as organizers in any significant way. SNCC itself had never really resolved what it meant by integration and in Mississippi we more or less left the idea alone, the question open. We talked local leadership instead. The integration question had actually been around for a while in SNCC. There were whites in the Atlanta office pushing to get out into the field. Can you make integration a goal and not live it? they were asking. Could SNCC integrate itself and live as kind of an island of integration in society's sea of separation? How? Of course, it's a still unresolved problem of this country and in the end SNCC foundered on the question.

But in 1963 we realized that a statewide election campaign required more manpower than we had in Mississippi. The Jackson COFO office already had a handful of whites who had trickled in, white SNCC staffers working at desks. Bob Zellner had been involved in McComb. Mickey and Rita Schwerner came to Mississippi in the fall of 1963 to begin working with Dave as CORE's first white staffers in the state. And Mickey had managed to successfully dig in over in Meridian. I think CORE—at least its national organization—had a clearer concept of integration than we did. But our freedom vote ticket was integrated. Aaron Henry and Edwin King, a white chaplain at Tougaloo College, had been selected as our candidates for governor and lieutenant governor respectively. We couldn't answer the question of integration for the long term, but we could agree to use it for the particular purpose of Doc's and Ed's campaigns.

It seemed only natural to do something similar on a larger scale the following summer, to help get some much-needed national focus on Mississippi. I felt that with increasing automation of the cotton fields, and the White Citizens Council campaign to export Blacks out of the state, with the staff we had Blacks were not going to get the vote fast enough to have significant impact as their numbers shrank and the population balance changed in favor of whites. The battle we had been waging would be lost. So Lowenstein, SNCC executive secretary Jim Forman, and I began discussing the possibility of getting as many as a thousand mainly white students to come to Mississippi in the summer of 1964. Bring the nation's children, and the parents will have to focus on Mississippi, our thinking ran. And if the parents raised their voices, the political establishment would be forced to listen. The debate that ensued, both formally in meetings, and informally throughout the fall and early winter of 1964, contains an important lesson about the distinctively different perspectives of organizer and community leader.

The arguments against the summer project came entirely from field organizers, although not all of them opposed it—Lawrence Guyot and Dorie Ladner supported the idea. For the most part our organizers were from Mississippi and were not anxious to introduce large numbers of white volunteers into what they viewed as *their* project, something they had created out of nothing and at great risk to themselves. They had only reluctantly agreed to white volunteers coming in for the freedom vote, and they agreed mainly because it was short term, just two weeks, then they would be gone. Furthermore, Aaron Henry, who commanded their respect, had wanted the volunteers. But the idea of hundreds of such folks generated concern that local leadership just emerging from the grassroots would be drowned in a tidal wave of white volunteers.

On the other hand, in sharp contrast to the organizers, most of the local leadership didn't think that way at all. Like Aaron Henry in his freedom vote campaign, virtually all of the community folk we were working with—established leaders like Amzie Moore, Steptoe down in Amite, as well as new leaders thrust forward by the movement like Mrs. Fannie Lou Hamer in Sunflower County —strongly supported the 1964 summer project idea. "If we're trying to break down this barrier of segregation, we can't segregate ourselves," Mrs. Hamer argued at a heated November 1963 COFO meeting we held in Greenville to discuss the project. In part, what she and others were seeing very clearly was that the summer project would help open up Mississippi some more. And that couldn't do anything but help them, they felt. That was their experience. Exposure was an important part of what defined the movement—had been from the very beginning—exposure to ideas, to people, to places that had been closed to them. Even the simple fact of my physical presence in Mississippi, as well as others from out of state, pried open this "closed society" a little bit and contributed to folks' growth as a result of being exposed to something the state wanted them not to be exposed to; same for McLaurin going up into Sunflower County from Jackson, or Curtis and Hollis going over to Hattiesburg, or someone slipping off the plantation to attend a mass meeting. Who knows how the still-funny taunts and defiance of Dick Gregory on the streets of Greenwood have been handed down in some households. Perhaps someone is laughing in the kitchen while recalling them now. Exposure. The community leaders we were working with wanted more. It didn't matter if white Mississippians refused to integrate, Black communities would, by having whites living in their homes, going to their churches, eating at their tables. You could almost say that, like the freedom vote in the political arena, absorbing incoming student volunteers would be a parallel social arrangement.

Although I favored the 1964 summer project I held back after the Greenville meeting as the Mississippi staff continued to wrestle with the question. I traveled and talked about the need for the project but did not push. I didn't change many minds even though outside of the state talk, even plans, for coming to Mississippi that summer were growing. Medgar's assassination brought some attention to the state. Ministers led by Bob Spike, head of the National Council of Churches, had joined us in a January 1964 "Freedom Day" in Hattiesburg when during a meeting to discuss the summer project the telephone rang and I learned that Louis Allen had been killed in Amite County. He'd been found dead under his truck with two buckshot wounds in his head. A little more than a year before a deputy sheriff had broken his jaw with a flashlight, and I had written Amzie Moore saying that county authorities were out to get him. Allen knew he was a marked man. He'd received death threats and been arrested and jailed twice since the Lee killing. One of those times word reached his sons that a lynch mob was forming and the boys came and stood guard outside jail all night. Allen wanted to leave the state but he had an elderly mother who was ill, and bills to pay off. When his mother died he made plans to leave for Milwaukee on February 1. He was a day away from leaving when he was murdered. On the night of

January 31, while getting out of his truck to open the gate to his property, he was shot.

For me, it was as if everything had come full circle. I had started in Amite County, unable to offer protection or force the federal government to provide it. Herbert Lee had been killed; Louis Allen had witnessed it and now he was dead. Across Mississippi I had watched the growth of white violence that was part of a statewide assault on our efforts. Throughout the fall of 1963 Black churches were being systematically bombed. Louis Allen's death after two years of harassment was the latest in a string of murders—lynchings. There had to be a response, a larger response than we had been able to provide two years before, or would be able to provide with the people we had working now. I spoke up for the summer project, threw all my weight behind it. In my mind, the need for a major gesture outweighed legitimate worries of how the influx of white students would affect Black leadership. Until then, the staff had been deadlocked, at loggerheads with each other; this decided it.

Almost all of the nearly one thousand students who came to Mississippi that summer were white. Within the effort there were a lot of contradictions, some of which only mirrored large, unresolved contradictions within the country. The summer project was able to tackle certain critical things about Mississippi, but it couldn't handle the larger issues that erupted into Black power. A kind of universal consensus had been reached about Mississippi. This small group of young Black people—who had worked in the state over the three years from 1961 to 1963 under extreme danger and exposed themselves—had credibility. They had credibility for other people to come and say, "Well, these are the people I'm going to work with to do something about Mississippi. And I can announce to the world that I'm working with them because, in fact, they have been doing this over the last so-many years."

This is an important part of the legacy inherited by the YPP. We were organizers. Local people—local leadership—was at the center of everything we did. Keeping that in mind—and it wasn't always easy—kept us on course. Local folks might not be paying us, but we were working for them.

It was fortunate that a strong Black group came off the campus of Howard University in Washington, D.C. The small towns and restaurants in nearby Virginia and Maryland were segregated in the early 1960s. Howard's SNCC affiliate, the Nonviolent Action Group (NAG), had led sit-in protests. Stokely Carmichael and other members of NAG had participated in the freedom rides. And while the Nashville, Tennessee, student group was arguably the most theologically influenced of SNCC's member groups— Gandhi and the ideas of "a beloved community" and nonviolence had taken root—Howard's group was ideological and intensely political and in the end took a more nationalist stance. Bayard Rustin had been an important influence on several of NAG's leaders, many of whom belonged to Norman Thomas's Young People's Socialist League (YPSL), as well as NAG. A high school senior considering enrollment at Howard, Stokely Carmichael was introduced to NAG not at a sit-in demonstration against lunch counter segregation, but on a Capitol Hill picket line protesting the House Un-American Activities Committee.

Unlike Stokely, who had been coming to Mississippi regularly after being arrested as a freedom rider and serving forty-nine days in Parchman prison, few of the other NAG members had been down. Though active in SNCC from its beginning, the Howard students adopted nonviolent action strictly as a tactic. It was a way to fight effectively and above all else NAG saw itself fighting for the race. This commitment had been cultivated not only by Bayard, but also by Howard scholars like Sterling Brown. But for all this they were not wholly convinced that voter registration wasn't a ploy to blunt militant action. Some thought that what SNCC really needed was a radical economic program. What did excite the NAG activists was taking on Mississippi, the worst of the Deep South states. Especially because we were now organizing a political party.

AIN'T GONNA LET NOBODY TURN ME 'ROUN . . .

> Senator Humphrey, I been praying about you, and I been thinking
> about you, and you're a good man. The trouble is, you're afraid to
> do what you know is right.
>
> Fannie Lou Hamer to Hubert Humphrey,
> Atlantic City, 1964

The need for some sort of political vehicle for people we worked
with across the state had become increasingly evident. This would
not be an organizer's structure; it wouldn't be another SNCC or
CORE, but an instrument in which communities could shape
and articulate ideas and one that could move into political action.
We had registered thousands for the freedom vote and from this
process the answer leaped out, perfectly obviously—a political
party, a freedom party. We had sent some of the few registered voters willing to try, to local Democratic Party meetings. Their re-
quests to participate in party activities had been denied. So getting
into the state Democratic Party seemed a futile exercise and the
Republican Party was out of the question.

In August 1964 hundreds of people from around the state met
in Jackson, and the Mississippi Freedom Democratic Party elected
sixty-eight delegates to represent the party at the Democratic National Convention. Ella Baker gave the keynote address. Part of
what we wanted to do was challenge the national Democratic
Party to recognize us as its legitimate arm in the state and Miss
Baker spoke directly to the way the Democrats and the entire nation contributed to the sustenance of white supremacy in Mississippi. Southern states were not denied representation in Congress
on the basis of the way they denied Black citizens the right to participate in elections, and they should be, she pointed out. Miss
Baker challenged the delegates to turn off radios and televisions
and read more. Uninformed people can't participate in democracy, she said. Until the killing of Black mothers' sons is as important as the killing of white mothers' sons, she concluded, returning to the primary objective of the summer project, "We
must keep on."

Meeting with James Forman and me earlier that spring, Joseph

Rauh, then counsel for the United Auto Workers and a man who wielded great influence with the Democrats, had promised, "If the Mississippi delegation is challenged, they will be unseated." I told him they would be challenged, thinking, however, that it was doubtful the Mississippi delegation would be unseated. My experience with the Democratic Party so far didn't suggest that they were prepared to challenge their powerful southern wing.

The political prospect of this challenge, and organizing a party to make it, stoked NAG's determination to be present as a group in Mississippi that summer. Clearly, the issue of political power was central to the NAG people and they had been talking it through for some time. And what they wanted to do because they were political people on the left—YPSL, Bayard, those working with unions—was work with people at the bottom. I know that was what Stokely wanted to do and he was more or less NAG's leader. And that matched nicely with concerns of ours that the MFDP be an organization where Mississippi's Black poor, therefore Mississippi's most voiceless, could speak and make decisions.

About twenty NAG folk came down to Mississippi in the summer of 1964. I put them all in the Delta and made Stokely project director for the region. It didn't exactly eliminate staff misgivings over the summer project (part of the local staff's objection to the project was concern about *outsiders,* not just white outsiders, and to some local organizers the NAG folks laid claim to a political correctness that seemed arrogant.) But as Stokely drew on the group for appointments as project directors in various Delta counties, it eased the concern that in expanding into new areas of operation, white students would have to be given leadership roles in the organizing.

People often wonder at the strength of the MFDP delegation in Atlantic City. They stood up to some of the most powerful forces inside the Democratic Party, including then President Lyndon Johnson. "We didn't come here for no two seats," Mrs. Hamer said in words that captured the internal strength of the delegation. The delegation, which had taken shape at the grassroots, reflected not so much our control as our ideals. Mrs. Hamer is a case in point. As a sharecropper and timekeeper on the Marlow plantation in Sunflower County, she had had some contact with Amzie before we ever arrived. In 1962 she was among the first eighteen people we brought to the county courthouse in Indianola. She didn't stand out at first; there was nothing immediately special about her . . . until we needed her. To get to the courthouse we had rented an old school bus usually used for hauling day workers to cotton fields. Trepidation thickened the atmosphere on it as we journeyed to Indianola, birthplace of the White Citizens Council. Then from the back of the bus the voice of a woman who seemed to know every song ever sung in a Black church burst out in song, filling the bus with song after song driving away all fear. That woman was Fannie Lou Hamer. At the Atlantic City convention, her voice would be so powerful in televised testimony about the situation of Black Mississippians that President Johnson was compelled to break in and push her off the air with a hastily called press conference about nothing in particular. What you felt when Mrs. Hamer spoke and when she sang was the presence of someone who was opening up her soul and really telling you what she felt—the pain that she felt and the life that she had lived. Somehow she was able to convey that to people in a way that most of us could not. It was powerful and beautiful and I think that one of the most powerful and beautiful things about the movement was that it enabled people like Mrs. Hamer to emerge.

What we had, which cultivated and protected these voices, was space to organize. The state's response to civil rights organizers was violent and there was virtually no federal protection. To organize you had to take life-threatening risks and very few people were willing to do that. SNCC was. So was CORE. Local grassroots leaders like Amzie Moore were. For a short while we literally had the field to ourselves, access to people that other people and organizations did not have, simply because they were not willing to run the risks we were. This is what gave us the space to create a political organization out of the voter registration. And it was a political organization that we felt would be responsible to the people that we were working with, an organization that they actually controlled. That's what we created with the MFDP. Inside it, people learned how to stand up and speak. The meeting it-self, or the meetings, became tools.

Today's commentary and analysis of the movement often miss the crucial point that, in addition to challenging the white power structure, the movement also demanded that Black people challenge themselves. Small meetings and workshops became the spaces within the Black community where people could stand up and speak, or in groups outline their concerns. In them, folks were feeling themselves out, learning how to use words to articulate what they wanted and needed. In these meetings, they were taking the first step toward gaining control over their lives, and the decision making that affected their lives, by making demands on themselves. This important dimension of the movement has been almost completely lost in the imagery of hand-clapping, song-filled rallies for protest demonstrations that have come to define portrayals of 1960s civil rights meetings: dynamic individual leaders using their powerful voices to inspire listening crowds. Our meetings were conducted so that sharecroppers, farmers, and ordinary working people could participate, so that Mrs. Hamer, Mrs. Devine, Hartman Turnbow, all of them were empowered. They weren't just sitting there. It was the message of empowerment for grassroots people these meetings generated that was delivered to the entire country on national television at the 1964 convention by the sharecroppers, domestic workers, and farmers who formed the rank and file of the MFDP. They were asking the national Democratic Party whether it would be willing to empower people in their meetings in a similar way.

The answer was no. In Atlantic City, the credentials committee delayed making a decision about the MFDP and we went into a "negotiation" session in Hubert Humphrey's suite at the Pageant Motel. Walter Reuther and Bayard Rustin were there as well as Martin Luther King, Jr. Ed King, Aaron Henry, and Fannie Lou Hamer were there representing the MFDP. At the meeting we were told that the Democrats were willing to give the MFDP two symbolic seats at the convention and that Ed and Aaron had been chosen to fill those seats. No one from the MFDP had been consulted, not even Aaron and Ed. We rejected it right there in front of Humphrey and Reuther. We told them there was no way we could accept that decision without the delegation discussing it and deciding whether it was something that it could accept. Suddenly, someone knocked on the door, leaned in, and shouted, "It's over!" and when we looked at the television, there was Walter Mondale announcing that the MFDP had accepted the "compromise." He hadn't approached anyone from the MFDP either. I stomped out of the room, slamming the door in Hubert Humphrey's face. Although Senator Humphrey was probably caught by surprise too, I was furious. I had doubted that our delegation would be seated, and even the pretense at negotiation was not wholly unexpected; but here the Democrats were saying we'll pick your leadership too.

In the years since that convention the MFDP has been attacked for being unwilling to accept the offer of two seats. They've been accused of ignorance, and if you think knowledge is book knowledge, they were. They hadn't been through the schools; they hadn't been processed in the ways in which most of the delegates to the convention were processed. Their knowledge was about life, not books, especially about life in Mississippi. And they understood the relationship of the politics they were trying to challenge to the life they wanted to lead. They were as cognizant of *that* as anyone needed to be. They were relying on this knowledge, plus the ability to speak directly to the truth, to qualify them for admission as the proper delegation.

The issue of seating them was also a moral one that challenged the political expediencies of the national Democratic Party. We were trying in part to bring morality into politics, not politics into our morality. The MFDP was raising an important question with this country, and with the Democratic Party, as one of its major political institutions: Generations of Black people had been denied access to the political process; could they get it now? The sharecroppers and others who made up the constituency of the MFDP were the voice of the real "underclass" of this country and to this day I don't think the Democratic Party, which has primarily organized around the middle class, has confronted the issue of bringing poor people actively into its ranks. We were challenging them not only on racial grounds, obvious racial grounds. We were challenging them to recognize the existence of a whole group of people—white and Black and disenfranchised—who form the underclass of this country. Senator Humphrey was blunt about the party's unwillingness to face up to this when we "negotiated" at the Pageant Motel. Under no circumstances was Mrs. Hamer going to be part of any officially recognized Mississippi delegation. "The President will not allow that illiterate woman to speak from the floor of the convention," he said. No, they weren't prepared to hear *her;* it's not clear that they are now.

Kids today, like many of those I teach, do not know much of this story. A lot of this is the failure of those of us who were involved in it. We have not put down our stories. So imagine this. Every day around 3:30 P.M. there are kids sitting on the steps of Brinkley Middle School in Jackson, Mississippi. The school is not very far from the house where Medgar Evers was killed. Sometimes they are waiting to be picked up by their parents. Sometimes the steps just serve as a good place to hang out for a little while after school. Directly across the street from Brinkley is the Fannie Lou Hamer Public Library. Ask the kids about her. It's easy to start a conversation with them, perhaps because so few adults do.

> Can anybody tell me something about Fannie Lou Hamer?
> *She was doin' some civil rights a long time ago.*
> *Yeah, with Martin Luther King, Jr.*
> Where did she do that?
> *Uhh, I don't know exactly. Mississippi, I think.*
> Yes, but don't you know where? How about the Delta?
> *Yeah.*
> Where in the Delta?
> *We really don't study that.*
> You don't study about the civil rights movement?
> *We learn about Martin Luther King, Jr.*
> *We know about slavery and the Civil War.*

And the March on Washington.

But what about Mississippi? You know Mississippi was really important to the civil rights movement. Medgar Evers's house is just a few streets over. You heard of him?

Didn't he get killed?

What about COFO, SNCC, CORE, you know about them?

No, we just don't study it enough.

Maybe you could start with Miss Hamer; I knew Miss Hamer, and . . .

You did! You was there back then?

Talking to teenagers about the civil rights movement of the 1960s, you sometimes have the sense that in their minds they lump everyone from the first African enslaved in America through Martin Luther King, Jr., as living at the same time. And in their young minds that time is a distant past that can only be read about or perhaps seen in historical footage on television. They are often surprised to be talking to someone who is alive and was an actual participant in the movement, although someone might say something like, "My grandma was in that." In addition to the way time is sometimes collapsed in young minds there is also history's sometimes confusing softness. Who is telling the story defines the historic "truth" and accuracy of the story. So there is a character called Bob Moses in many of the history books that discuss Mississippi's civil rights movement of the 1960s. I read about him. I sympathize with him. Sometimes he seems like me, and then sometimes I am confused by him and want to understand him better. Algebra Project kids know a little about Bob Moses's involvement with the civil rights movement, but there is a great deal they don't understand yet for "our" stories in our words are largely absent from the historical canon. And these stories are more important than just remembering some old times. We need to use them.

Several lessons stand out in my mind as I reflect on those years in Mississippi and on how it shapes my work today.

In the post–Civil War period in Mississippi and other Black communities in the South, Black people had consensus around their need to own land. But in the Mississippi I entered in 1960

Blacks who were acting to try to change the state had consensus to work together on a common program to get the vote. Although such an effort was not in my mind when I first came to Mississippi, I had to respond to this consensus. So did other SNCC and CORE organizers. Community support for this effort was not immediately obvious because it was largely hidden beneath layers of fear, or some expediency thought necessary, or ignorance even, but in the depths of their minds and souls almost all Black people in the state agreed that voting was a right being unfairly denied them. This denial symbolized white power over Black lives and they wanted to end it. Community support emerged as we began working around this consensus. And in the final analysis, we survived violent white reaction because we were embraced by and absorbed into communities, not because of our organizational affiliations or connections.

Effective organizing in 1960s Mississippi meant an organizer had to utilize the everyday issues of the community and frame them for the maximum benefit of the community. Staking out some area of consensus was necessary, but an organizer could not create consensus, an organizer had to find it. And it took time and patience to search out where it was lodged beneath layer after layer of other concerns. Then, if the organizer found it, the question of how to tap into this consensus, how to energize it and use it for mobilization and organization, remained. Organizers—civil rights organizers in the 1960s, math literacy organizers now—work to flesh out consensus: So, Mr. Joe McDonald thinks voter registration is important. Will he try to register? Oh, he doesn't want to go to the courthouse by himself. Can we find other people willing to try? How? Who? What do we need to know in order to get registered anyway? I've got a copy of the form right here on my clipboard; let's try to fill it out now. Do we need to start a voter registration school? How about doing it at the church, William's Chapel? You say the preacher's afraid white people will bomb the church. Well, Mrs. McDonald is really close to the preacher's wife. Can she get her to talk to him? And so on. It helped that this was a movement; not only were individuals in a particular community challenging themselves and the system, but other communities were as well.

We came to see that we had to launch a campaign that was broad enough to reach through to where power was—political power as expressed through political decision making in the state and about the state. At that time in Mississippi this turned out to include, most importantly, the national Democratic Party, some of whose most influential members were Mississippi senators and congressmen. We also had to think about the issue of the actual political party in the state, the party that already existed and represented life in the state as it had gone on for almost a century. And the young who formed the core cadre for doing this, myself included—field secretaries and organizers for SNCC and CORE—were so few as well as so young and inexperienced at any of this we would hardly seem to stand a chance of having any impact at all. There were now about thirty of us on the eve of the 1964 summer project: Curtis Hayes, Hollis Watkins, Emma Bell, James Jones, Mattie Bivens, Dorie and Joyce Ladner, Colia Lidell, Mateo "Flukie" Suarez, Ida Mae "Cat" Holland, Euvester Simpson, Juadine Henderson, Lawrence Guyot, Charles McLaurin, Dave Dennis, James Chaney, George Raymond, Lafayette Surney, Willie Peacock, Sam Block, Mary Lane, June Johnson, Leslie McLemore, Frank Smith, Ivanhoe Donaldson, Charlie Cobb, MacArthur Cotton, Silas McGee, and George and Freddie Green. I was the only one over twenty-five; a few were still teenagers. June was only fourteen.

So here we were, faced with developing a strategy that operated at all of these different levels simultaneously. As we struggled we stumbled across tools to help bring forth a new generation of leadership from among Mississippi's Black sharecroppers, day laborers, domestic workers, and farmers. These were the people who ultimately had to make their own case. They were the ones who had to go try to register to vote. They were the ones who had to challenge the existing political party and say: "We are here with power. We are able to articulate our positions. We are here in such a way that you cannot look us in the face and tell us that we cannot represent ourselves in this process."

One tool that turned out to be critical in the process of establishing this kind of political literacy was understanding how meetings could mobilize the participants. These meetings were training grounds, allowing participants to develop and emerge as political leaders of their state. These were not credentialed people; they did not have high school diplomas for the most part. They were not members of labor unions, or national church associations. Yet through the process, they became leaders. Meetings had to shift their focus from being places where there was a person or panel of people presiding, delivering information that the rest of the participants listened to and accepted, and become places where people actively engaged the problems that were embedded in various political arenas—from local precincts in Mississippi all the way to the federal and congressional environs of Washington, D.C. Sharecroppers and young organizers alike used meetings to figure out approaches to solutions, and ways to organize themselves to effect those solutions.

When the MFDP challenged the seating of the "regular" Mississippi Democrats at the 1964 Atlantic City Democratic Convention, our efforts reached a national audience. However, the national Democratic Party and the institutions surrounding it in government, church, and politics rejected any extension of power into the hands of the black and poor. They were not prepared to risk status quo arrangements. But though the MFDP did not succeed, the issue of empowerment of the poor for meaningful citizenship has not vanished.

PART TWO

Radical Equations

The Story of a Grassroots
Education Movement

CHAPTER 4

Bouncing a Ball

The Early Days of the Algebra Project

I suppose in a way the Algebra Project starts with me. I am the oldest of the four children in our family, and even before we started
school all of us grew up doing math, me first. My mother would do
reading with us and my father, he would do the math. I could not
have been five yet but I remember my dad had this felt board and we
used to have to arrange things on this board and it wasn't just playing games. It was math even though I don't remember exactly what
it was. I liked it when I was young, then when I got older I didn't
like it. It was like I always had to do it, after school, on weekends.
We went to Denver, Colorado, to visit the Hardings and lugged the
math books out there. I started to resent it because I had to do it and
keep doing it. The sessions were kind of hard because my dad would
ask me questions and I just wouldn't answer or I would have an attitude in my voice giving the answer. Interestingly, although I didn't
like doing the math at home, I always liked math in school and it's
because of the work we did at home that I never had a problem with
the math we did in school.

Maisha Moses

The concept of "one person one vote" provided Mississippi sharecroppers and their allies with a *minimum of common conceptual cohesion*. That is, "one person one vote" was a shared goal. It was an organizing slogan; but more than that, it reflected an ideal that
tapped deep traditions in American democracy and that allowed
at the time a consensus to develop around it. The daily grind of
living in Mississippi in 1961 ("if they don't get you in the wash,

they get you in the rinse") gave rise to grassroots demands for political access that in turn gave rise to demands for unity that could use "one person one vote" as an organizing tool.

Organizing, in turn, required space to develop. The "crawl space," as I call it, in which we actually carried out such organizing was the 1957 civil rights bill creating the Civil Rights Division of the Department of Justice. The existence of that new department meant, among other things, that John Doar and his federal lawyers could investigate beatings of potential voters walking up to the courthouse in vicious towns like Liberty, Mississippi, and return an opinion at odds with that of the FBI and local police authorities: that is, that people other than the "usual suspects" anxious to protect local custom were watching; Mississippi could not simply lock up voter registration workers and throw away the keys. This federal involvement—tiny though it was—was important because it was what provided the little crawl space that enabled us to begin working.

Both things were important: the consensus around a minimum of common conceptual cohesion and the crawl space that allowed it to become effective.

The concept that provides minimum common conceptual cohesion for the work of the Algebra Project takes the form of an "if, then" sentence:

If *we* can do *it,* then *we* should.

The "we" refers to a complex configuration of individuals; educational institutions of various kinds; local, regional, and national associations and organizations (both governmental and nongovernmental); actual state governments as well as the national political parties; and the executive, legislative, and judicial branches of the national government. The "it"—the goal of educating all our children well—rests on a complex conceptual consensus that is woven into the cultural fabric of this country: the idea that young people who grow up in the United States are entitled to free public education, from kindergarten through twelfth grade. But there is emerging in U.S. culture something more specific and powerful than that. In recent years a real national consensus, on the political left and on the political right, has begun emerging that holds that all children can learn, and that all children deserve the best education they can get. And that such an education is absolutely necessary. This is actually a new consensus; it did not exist fifty years ago, when, schools were segregated North and South and not finishing high school was much more widely accepted because lacking a high school diploma was not the handicap to putting food on the table that it is today. Of course, this expressed belief in the capacity of all children to learn, and commitment to making the effort to provide them the opportunity, is an ideal that's often given lip service more than real action. And it drives wrongheaded as well as constructive "school reform" efforts. But it is a widespread public viewpoint. Compare the national consensus in favor of educating all children well with the absence of such a consensus on health care. It is clearly not true that Americans as a whole believe (yet) that "if we can provide universal access to quality health care, we should." They do believe it about education.

Obviously, the work of the Algebra Project has to do with math in particular. The consensus on education—like the "one person one vote" consensus forty years ago—provides the necessary foundation for a more specific agenda, in this case the concept that every student will complete a college preparatory mathematics curriculum in high school. (It is clearly not sufficient since only 11 percent of students in the United States do so now.) The work of the Algebra Project is to help close the gap between universal free public education and universal completion of a college preparatory math sequence in high school. Specifically, our work is to build a consensus—and organize a movement—around another hypothetical that gives the required minimum conceptual cohesion:

If *we* can teach students algebra in the middle school years,
then *we* should do it.

Like the effort to bridge the gap between the ideal of "one person one vote" and the reality of registering every Black voter in

Mississippi, this work of the Algebra Project is ambitious and can be realized. Like our work in the 1960s, it requires organizing, and organizing requires some crawl space.

What, then, is *our* crawl space? Like the crawl space created by the 1957 Civil Rights Act, it is a space created in the larger political and social world that we can use to our advantage. The space for algebra as a civil rights issue is created by nations and institutions now making a global transition from reliance upon technology that primarily organizes physical labor to technologies that directly organize mental labor. I see history's broom sweeping us all along a common corridor. As organizers, we can make use of that corridor as a crawl space toward liberation.

My wife, Janet, and I first entered this crawl space in the late 1970s as parents intent on having our four children, Maisha, Omowale, Tabasuri, and Malaika, attend public schools, and equally intent on having the school they enrolled in, the Martin Luther King, Jr., School in Cambridge, Massachusetts, *work* for them. The King school is a large, relatively modern facility for kindergarten through eighth grade, built on the site of a school that had served Cambridge's Black community for many years. In the 1970s it housed five programs: a "regular" program staffed by teachers from the former school, a magnet "open" program, a program for Chinese students, plus small bilingual and small "special needs" programs. Our children enrolled in the open program.

Since our children's elementary school years Janet and I had been thinking through what we wanted in terms of their education. As parents, we had concluded that math literacy was fundamental for this generation, different from ours, where reading and writing were fundamental. Janet and I felt that when the kids arrived at college they should be ready to take any course. Their curriculum choices should not be restricted because they did not have their math. So, the Algebra Project in a profound way has its beginnings in a mix of family, movement, and work. Africa, too, which is where the movement led Janet and me in the late 1960s, played a role. We taught at Same Secondary School in Tanzania, East Africa, and it was there, in a nation far poorer than the United

States, that for the first time I saw what it meant for a school *system* to be committed to its children. After returning from Africa I was searching for something that I could feel comfortable with. King Open seemed consistent with my needs in terms of family, work, and movement.

For two reasons, 1982 became the crucial year: I received a MacArthur Foundation "genius" award (primarily recognizing my civil rights work in Mississippi) and the income it provided freed me at exactly the time I needed freedom. Maisha, my oldest child, was entering the eighth grade at the Martin Luther King School. I had been doing math exercises at home with Maisha for years. Now I felt she was ready for algebra, but the school didn't offer it to eighth graders. I kept talking to Maisha about working with an algebra textbook at home, but she was rebelling against doing "two maths" and she was old enough now to really argue about it. *We complained [said Maisha]. "Why do we have to do this? No one else has to do this." Dad would say, "It's important. I want you to do it. You need to do it." But we wouldn't be satisfied. I didn't really want to do it. Dad would have to sit there and force answers out of me. Finally he decided that the only way to get me to do algebra was to go into school.* I told her, there is no way I'm just going to let you sit in eighth grade and do the eighth-grade math offered by the school. It would be repeating what you've done already, I said, wasting your time.

"How about letting Maisha sit by herself so that she could do *my* algebra assignments," I suggested to her teacher, Mary Lou Mehrling, who taught seventh and eighth graders. After all, the open program at King was an innovative, flexible program within a school. Why not try this experiment? Well, how about coming into school to teach Maisha and some other students who have also requested algebra—three to be exact—Mary Lou responded. In her own training she was weakest in math and was pleased that I was willing to step into the classroom. I agreed to take on the additional three students and thus began the Algebra Project.

I began a seminar-style course with them in a corner of Mary Lou's room. We could have that space because there wasn't a lot of lecturing in Mary Lou's class; she moved about tutoring, helping kids. That spring, Maisha and two others of these four students became the first students in the history of the King school to take and pass the citywide algebra test and to take, as ninth graders, geometry at Cambridge's only high school, Cambridge Rindge and Latin. The fourth student entered a private high school.

During that first year of teaching in the open program I began to look around, trying to see who was doing what kind of mathematics in Maisha's classroom. I saw three distinct groupings: mostly upper-middle-class white kids above grade level; a better racial mix of kids at grade level, mostly middle-class; and kids below grade level who were primarily minority students and working-class whites. This skewing of math along racial and class lines had the effect of sending the message to students of color that little was expected of them. Gender didn't seem to matter; there were two girls and two boys in the group I had. So I began thinking about who takes math, and what kind of math they take. Clearly it wasn't enough to just say generally, "Well, we're going to have a progressive program," a commitment the open program already made. I felt there had to be very specific goals and supports to see that minority students did not fall through the cracks. Although still working on my doctoral degree at Harvard, I was beginning to think I had found my work. I agreed to continue in the 1983–84 school year after Maisha graduated.

The next year, 1984–85, Omo was entering seventh grade and Mary Lou wanted me back to take a few more students. She had begun to study math herself; her previous training had been in music. She assigned nine eighth graders to me, and then later on in the year seven seventh graders were added to the group. With these students I was committed; I was back teaching school after having been away from it since teaching math in Tanzania. I settled on Saxon's *Algebra 1* because I liked the way it reviewed concepts and processes through questions at the end of each chapter. The questions always included problems introduced in previous lessons. This helped ease my worries about how to get at fundamental concepts from the material.

I was really a parent-organizer as much as a teacher, and I found myself drawing on my Mississippi experience, raising broader questions around a specific issue: Can a culture be created in King's open program where every child is expected to get ready for and do algebra in the eighth grade? What should the content of such a program be? What curricular processes make that content available to all students? Some things leaped out at me almost immediately—symbols and language, for instance. In math books you get symbolic forms like a minus sign for subtraction. You do not get the conceptual mathematical language that undergirds these symbolic forms.

As I moved toward the idea of algebra for all I began to zero in on the learning curve that arcs between thinking about or reflecting on a problem and making abstract conceptualizations of it. My Harvard studies in the philosophy of mathematics led me in that direction. As a student there I had been impressed by the ideas of one of my professors, Willard Van Orman Quine. Professor Quine argued that arithmetic, elementary logic, and elementary set theory got off the ground by regimenting natural language, by what he called the "regimentation of ordinary discourse" (mathematization *in situ*). This "regimented discourse" is the conceptual language that underlies all the various symbolic representations you find in the sciences and mathematics. Quine was saying that this conceptual language is not a natural language. No one speaks it, but it is the language that undergirds the symbolic representations. Quine's philosophy of math—though not usually applied in such settings—made it feasible to apply experiential learning to teaching algebra to middle school students.

Parents noticed that the attitude of their children toward math was changing. Something seemed to be different to the Millners, the Kimbroughs, the Jameses, and others. It seemed different to Liberty Rashad, whose oldest son, Azimio, I taught in my second year at the school . . . *These kids really bonded as young people together, and they all happened to be around the same age. What was created was this very, very close-knit group of young people. They pulled me in, more so than I had ever been pulled into school before.* I was primarily talking to parents like Liberty individually. Our children were in and out of each other's homes and apartments. We were not an organization, but organized effort began to evolve out of these contacts and conversations.

One result was that in 1984–85 a group of parents decided that decisions about studying algebra in the seventh and eighth grades should not rest solely with teachers, students, and administrators. And during the spring of 1984, one of the parents, Shirley Kimbrough, sent out a letter to every parent with a child about to begin the seventh grade. *We had been meeting and discussing the academic challenges minority students face for some time. Generally, they were not doing as well as nonminority kids in math and science. Why? Bob was doing the Algebra Project with the seventh and eighth graders, but what should we expect of our children? We weren't sure. A lot of parents had not taken algebra in middle school. And then there is attitude. I remember having this conversation with one parent—a white parent who taught at another school—"I don't feel all children should take algebra," she told me. I said, "Let's find out from the parents themselves."*

Shirley's letter asked two key questions: Do you think your child should do algebra? Do you think every child should do algebra? The responses taught me a lot about attitudes toward math. All parents thought *their* child should do algebra, but not all parents thought that *every* child should do algebra. Parents could now see the contradiction between what they thought about their own children's ability and what they assumed the curriculum should offer children in general. This new awareness led the open program to invite all children entering the seventh grade in the fall of 1984 to study algebra. This invitation was extended to eighth graders as well. A Saturday morning algebra class for parents was begun, and in a letter to the Cambridge School Committee, one parent wrote: *My daughter began to overcome her fear of math and distorted perceptions of what she was capable of doing, and why it is important. I believe this was due to several factors including the climate of learning in the classroom (in part, a sense that students, teachers, and aides alike were learning together); the demystification of the subject by relating it to life experiences; and by the fact that her mother, along with other parents and community members, was simultaneously overcoming latent math panic by taking the course on Saturdays.*

In spring of 1985, the efforts of parents, teachers, and administrators succeeded in having the Algebra Project officially recognized by the Cambridge School Committee. For the next three years, the open program staff focused their regular Wednesday afternoon staff meetings on math. Under pressure from parents, "ability grouping," which unintentionally but seriously impaired the capacity of students of color and females to learn as well as they might, was replaced with individual and small group instruction. We asked students to set their own short-term and long-range goals; parents were asked to sign their child's goal statement each semester. We taught methods students could use to tackle difficult material on their own with the idea of placing much of the learning pace in student hands. Soon, students were working harder than they ever had before. Teachers met with small groups for lessons on specific concepts, and reviews. Mary Lou Mehrling found that students felt less intimidated by difficult material and more determined to master what they did not understand. *If they can go to an adult to ask a question about the materials,* when they're ready *to go to an adult, it's wholly different from being in a group, being pinpointed and put on the spot and feeling vulnerable. They're empowered, in a curious way, around materials—something I would never have even thought about.* Most Math textbooks from algebra on disempower kids. One of the real strong points of Algebra Project materials for middle school kids—the transition curriculum or the graphing calculators or computers we introduced later, for example—is their power to empower. They give students the ability to move through doing their own work, asking questions of themselves, and then approaching someone for help when they are ready. In the spring of 1986, 39 percent of the project's first full graduating class was placed in honors geometry or honors algebra in high school. Not a single graduating student was taking lower-level high school math.

As teachers, we were learning too. Mary Lou, who had little training in math at the beginning, often turned to me and asked for help in front of the students. We wanted them to understand that there was nothing wrong with not knowing something, and admitting that you did not know something could be a first step to learning. *Presenting myself as a learner, in front of my students, helped me to understand what they were experiencing, and helped them to feel comfortable asking for help. Students no longer felt threatened if they did not understand a problem or a concept, for they saw that we were all learners and that we all learn in different ways.* I was learning too, and what I was learning in my teaching was something I could not have learned in all my philosophy of mathematics courses at Harvard, because I was learning from my students. Few taught me more than Ari Cox.

Ari was fourteen years old and officially labeled "slow." During most of his schooling he had been placed in "special needs" classes. In the view of Lynne Godfrey, his sixth-grade teacher, Ari had been "written off" . . . *was significantly below grade level in three areas and he really was not getting what he needed. And then he met Bob when he entered the seventh grade and seemed to get a different message from him. One of the things Bob was doing was having what I call these "sideline" conversations with the kids outside of class—really getting to know them.* Ari told me he wanted to be able to take algebra although he couldn't multiply. But Danny Rice, his best friend, as well as my son Omo, another one of Ari's running buddies, were doing it and Ari felt he had to learn algebra too, so I began tutoring him. This dramatic change in Ari surprised many of his former teachers. Lynne told me she would never have expected Ari to embrace math. *He hated it. In sixth grade when I had him he was really turned off by fractions and didn't do anything. He was really sweet in other classes; he was cooperative and worked hard. At math, though, he was angry!*

Whatever Ari thought of me, I think part of what brought him to the work was youth culture. If your friends are doing it, sometimes it becomes important for you too. You want to be a part of it. His friends were starting algebra; he was not. When I recognized this social fact, I couldn't help wondering whether or not it was possible to find a way to build inside youth culture, even at this micro level, in such a fashion that deficits like Ari's could be overcome. So I kept working with him, and Ari stuck with me. Ari began to create an expectation for himself, and *challenged* himself to meet that expectation. Ari was reaching inside himself.

Usually, if young people like Ari haven't learned things like multiplication tables by the time they're teenagers, they're not likely to learn them. Part of the difficulty is that things that have not been learned are considered baby stuff, not what his friends, people he admires, are doing. Ari is saying to himself, "This is stuff that my kid brother who's in fourth grade is doing. I don't want to be learning what he is learning." In fact, I think at that age, if young people like Ari haven't learned something like multiplication tables, the only way to get them to feel that learning the material is worth their effort is by putting it in the context of the more advanced mathematics that their friends are doing, showing how it is necessary for the more advanced work. This is making the need to learn culturally convincing. Conviction about the need will drive demand. As a result, they are working on something because it is something they *want* to work on. Ari, for example, wanted to keep up with Danny and Omo. His friends were going on ahead; he wanted to keep up with them.

So Ari took on algebra and I tutored him every day. He gradually began to get it. "I can do this!" he shouted one afternoon. Although we had only gotten through eleven lessons in the algebra book when the school year ended, the following year he took and successfully completed Algebra 1 at the high school and then went on to geometry as a sophomore and more advanced math as a junior. He never quite caught up with Omo and Danny in school— when he was doing geometry they were doing Algebra 2—but he was always hanging in there, pushing himself, motivated. I was no longer tutoring him but would bump into him in the street and what really impressed me was that he would tell me, "Well, I go get help when I have problems." He tried to take advantage of whatever the school had set up, which is unusual for kids at the bottom levels of school groupings who are often having a very difficult time. Usually it's kids who are doing well or being pushed by their parents who seek help. A kid like Ari usually keeps silent, hoping nobody notices him or her, and more often than not falls through the cracks.

What I was gaining from Ari was a deeper insight into the mind of a student, and it occurred to me that such insight was precisely what is missing among many advocates who want to improve the math ability of students in the United States. There are a lot of well-trained curriculum experts and others who know a great deal about math, but, I began to tell myself, what is missing from their work is insight into the minds of the young people they are trying to reach. We do not have enough people with a solid enough mastery of math who are so guided by their insights into the students' ways of thinking they can reconceptualize the math in terms that allow their students to connect. In fact, the culture moves people in the opposite direction. As you become more and more accomplished in the math, you become more and more distant from the younger students. Working with Ari gave me a sense of what is going on in the mind of a student who is trying to grapple with a mathematics that is usually reserved for just a few students his age.

Ari helped open one little conceptual window to a whole approach to teaching algebra, namely, that you have to approach the child's idea of number through questions that the child has about number.

It turned out that Ari had only one question in his mind about numbers ("How many?" as in "How many fingers?"). This is the question that introduces preschoolers to counting. However, to master positive and negative numbers in algebra students need two questions: a "Which way?" as well as a "How many?"

In the meantime, Quine's insights about language and mathematics opened the door to a way to exploit the concept of experiential learning in the introduction of elementary algebra concepts. (See the Appendix for a more complete discussion of Ari, Quine, and the relationship of teaching elementary algebra to experiential learning.)

Kids have some experience that can get them to this "Which

way?" idea. They articulate some fairly sophisticated "Which way?" questions they've learned growing up: "Which way did the bus go?" "Which way did he go?" And they have answers: "Well, go down there and turn right and then, you know, go to so-and-so." These directions answer "Which way?" questions. I was thinking about this one afternoon as I went down the stairs to board the subway at Harvard Square: *How am I going to put direction in the minds of kids so that it connects to a number concept?* I still had not come up with an answer. It was not just the issue of articulating a question. I was stuck on how to get the concept of direction and numbers planted into the mind of a child so that it could take root. Then I suddenly realized that the answer was staring me right in the face, because the first thing you decide upon entering the T, or subway, in Cambridge is direction. Inbound or outbound? Which way are you going? This could provide a natural experience open to every kid living in Cambridge, putting direction together with other features of a train trip—the number of stops, the start and finish of your trip. Possibilities abounded. I decided to try out a subway trip with some students.

Six years had passed since I had started teaching at the King school when, on an icy January morning in 1988, I led an excited sixth-grade class down the stairs of the T at Central Square. I had a sixth-grade class because over the years King school teachers were insisting that the Algebra Project required an earlier start than eighth, or even seventh, grade. It was Lynne Godfrey who stepped forward to offer her sixth-grade class as a pilot. *I looked up one day and Bob was standing in my classroom doorway with these papers in his hands. He started talking about how some kids in Mary Lou's class had worked on these papers and would I be interested in looking at them. I took them home and read them but I didn't know what they were because they were really very different from the textbooks that we used. These were not computation problems. These were kids' drawings. The whole format was different. Bob wanted to know what I thought was different about this work. And he was interested in how I thought you might get certain ideas across to sixth graders. So he kept coming back to my classroom. Sometimes I could be right in the middle of class and he would say, "Okay, what time do you have a prep period?" He'd leave and show back up again. Then I started working with him. Bob would come to the house Saturday morning and sit at the kitchen table and we would do math, something like investigating the understanding of fractions. We discussed things I thought I had learned in school, but thought more about what they mean as opposed to memorizing rules. I think that Bob's persistence was appealing because it was not an "I have this neat thing that I'd like you to try out." In the open program lots of people could come in and speak to teachers like that. He was really asking me to work with him to develop something."*

Now, with Lynne's sixth graders, I was ready to put the idea of experiential learning to a test. Students had to be prepared to take algebra when they reached the eighth grade; they needed a grasp of algebraic concepts, a gateway to them. At eleven, the average age of a sixth grader, experience is the best teacher. The kids were happy to be out of the school building during school hours. We rode inbound toward downtown Boston, then outbound back past our starting point before returning to where we had boarded. I asked the kids to sketch anything that attracted their interest on the ride. I was their math teacher and I could see on their faces as well as hear some of them wondering aloud about what this trip had to do with math. I offered no explanation but I peppered them with questions that we could use later: Where are we going? What direction? How far do you think it is to Park or Alewife. What do you expect to see? On a similar trip one of Lynne Godfrey's students was what she called a "wanderer." *He just kept wandering off from the group, so I wandered with him. I asked him how many rods do you think there are and how do you know that. It started him talking and telling me that he was actually looking at the yellow panels on the ground and he figured out there were ten per panel. He was explaining his process for estimating. We walked together the length of the train station.*

Teachers learned as well, for the kids were more experienced traveling the T than they were. Teachers drove cars. Sixth-grade Cambridge kids take the T to meet their parents at work downtown, for example. When a place they want to go is too far to walk, they often take the T. Lynne told the kids they would have to pay again to get out of the station at Central Square when we returned.

Of course you don't pay again after paying to board the train. *The kids tittered, perhaps pleased as well as surprised that the teacher didn't know everything; when it came to the T, they knew better, knew more than me, the "teacher."* When we got back to the classroom I grouped the class into teams and over the next week or so they talked about the trip, settling on pictures that best portrayed important features of the trip, and finally, using magic markers, drawing a trip line on large sheets of paper.

Trips can be taken in many ways. A teacher from the rural South fashioned one entirely in the minds of her students. *We didn't have any money to pay a bus driver, and there were too many people to put in one car. And we didn't have a van. So we were going to do what the Algebra Project calls "make do." We had some discussion about stops and then we decided where we wanted to go. . . . Then we decided how we wanted to go to each of those places. You know, well, not how we wanted to go 'cause we were really on the bus in our minds, but which [place] did we want to go to first? Which did we want to go to second? How much time were we going to spend there and everything. So we created this Algebra Project trip in our minds, and we actually sat there and we did it. Students talked about what they saw and they wrote down what they saw. . . . They actually drew a trip line. And what was so good is that the students actually saw the same things at these places. As they read their stories about the trip, you'd listen to these stories and they talked about the same things.*

Not every teacher embraced our developing pedagogy. In 1986, when school officials decided to extend the Algebra Project to all sixth and seventh graders, Lynne Godfrey worked with a class while its regular teacher sat in the back of the room. *She wouldn't involve herself. She just sat back there correcting papers, and when I suggested that she get involved because that would have a positive effect on the attitudes of the students, she said, "I don't know what this is but it's not math." She wouldn't do anything. I was really upset and said so. She went to the president of the teachers' union, who told me if I spoke to her again, a grievance against me would be filed. Fortunately, the school was committed to the program. This teacher finally left and went to another school.*

We were beginning to see some results at the King school.

Teachers like Lynne helped prove that it was not only possible to make algebra enjoyable without risking a lowering of achievement, but that enjoyment boosted achievement. In 1988, scores in the open program on the citywide algebra exam were the second highest in the system. And that result changed the school system's attitude toward us. I wanted to get the program in other area schools, and at the beginning of the year we had offered our sixth-grade curriculum to three other big inner-city schools in the region. But they had turned us down. "We're traditionalists," said Steven Leonard, principal of a Dorchester middle school. He was skeptical about the merits of subway trips, and our general approach to algebra. But when the test scores came out he changed his mind. "If they can do it, we can do it," he told his teachers. We were invited to launch the project among his sixth graders. By 1992, 68 percent of the kids involved with the Algebra Project went on into ninth-grade algebra, compared with 54 percent systemwide. At Steven Leonard's school, fifty-seven sixth graders passed a difficult math proficiency test that year. In 1989, only twelve students had passed it. "That subway trip was an amazing idea," the converted principal told me.

My MacArthur fellowship had ended in 1987, but as the 1980s wound down, we had a network that linked a wide range of individuals and institutions involved with our Algebra Project: the UMass College of Public and Community Service, Freedom House, a long-established community center in Dorchester, Wheelock College, parents, teachers, and community activists. One of the groups I developed a relationship with was the Seymour Society, a small group of young Black Christians, several of whom were Harvard University students.

Somehow the generation of Black students in schools like Harvard had lost awareness of the civil rights movement. Before *Eyes on the Prize* there was almost no historical awareness—Mississippi Freedom . . . Who? What's that? You had a kind of displaced generation of Blacks wandering on these campuses. The society was named for Reverend William J. Seymour, a Black minister who founded the influential Pentecostal church movement in 1906. They were an unusual group of Black student intellectuals exploring the links among their faith, community activities, and social change in the early 1980s. Alan Shaw from this small but energetic undergraduate group asked me if I was the Bob Moses they were reading about in studying voter registration drives. He was also president of the Black Student Association. They invited me to talk with them about my southern civil rights experience.

As a graduate of Harvard myself, I knew how isolating that campus could be without real effort. It was not difficult for me to relate to the interest of Seymour Society members like Cynthia Silva. *I was an undergrad; Bob came to a Seymour Society event; he spoke at it. I don't know if he adopted us, but we adopted him, you know, as sort of a mentor. We were trying to carve out space for ourselves, linking up activism and community service with a Bible-based Christian faith.* I kept up a relationship with them, and along with Cynthia, other Seymour Society alums like the Shaws, Alan and Michelle, and Jacqueline Rivers became some of the Algebra Project's most energetic supporters in the late 1980s. The kind of help we got from Seymour Society members like Jackie led to important developments later on. *Bob needed tutors after school hours, and also help with the curriculum. Soon we had a curriculum review group meeting at my home down in Boston's South End on Sunday afternoons. Also, Alan Shaw was borrowing my car to pick up kids for tutoring sessions at school early in the morning two or three times a week. I was thinking we could make a difference in the direction these children's lives go. Of course I wanted to help.* These young people really made our preschool program work and were invaluable in helping me develop some of the project's earliest material. This was, in fact, the earliest incarnation of our "transition curriculum," which moves Algebra Project students from arithmetic to algebra and is at the heart of our program. I met with them every Sunday afternoon to go over new material I planned to use during the week. Much of this materials development was influenced by my own experience tutoring Ari and others at the King school.

It was Jackie who approached Freedom House in the spring of

1988 with the suggestion of conducting a summer algebra camp. They agreed, and the Freedom House staff were so pleased with how it went that the Algebra Project became part of their after-school program in the fall. Jackie trained and supervised a college student to continue working there with our transition curriculum after the summer. A year or so later, Freedom House hired Jackie to direct a new after-school program: Algebra Centered Enrichment (ACE).

Meanwhile, Teresa Perry, a former King open program parent who was dean of undergraduates at Wheelock College, spoke to the school's president, Dan Cheever, and I found a position there as an adjunct faculty member that gave me a small salary. I did not have a teaching position as much as I had some office space and a tax-exempt way to receive funds to continue with the Algebra Project. I worked on curriculum. A grant from the Hasbro Foundation in 1989, arranged by my old classmate from Stuyvesant High School in New York and continuing friend Alvin Poussaint, eventually enabled me to bring Jackie on to the payroll at Wheelock too, and she began developing the Boston outreach. Even before she joined me at Wheelock, Jackie and I had begun meeting with local principals. It proved an uphill slough. One school never got back to us after the first meeting. Another concluded that making the transition from the traditional approach to teaching algebra to the Algebra Project's was too difficult. At a third school, teachers insisted that the skill levels of their students were not up to algebra.

We decided on a different route to getting into the Boston schools. We went to the top. We met with the deputy superintendent for curriculum and instruction and she invited the system's mathematics coordinator to meet with us. He endorsed the project. We began planning to invite eleven schools with high percentages of minority students to participate in the project on a pilot basis. Eventually, after meetings with principals, sixth-, seventh-, and eighth-grade math teachers, and directors of instruction, this number narrowed down to three schools: the Dearborn School, the Martin Luther King, Jr., School, and the Oliver

Wendell Holmes School. We had invited all interested schools to visit our site at the King school. Only these three schools chose to visit, and in my mind it was what they saw at King that persuaded them to try the Algebra Project in their schools.

Jackie, other Algebra Project personnel, and I began meeting with teachers and administrators to discuss development of a grant proposal. Out of this came the Algebra in Middle Schools (AIMS) project. Our curriculum, and another designed by the Efficacy Institute, would be offered to sixth graders. The Efficacy curriculum was designed to teach students about the process of human development, which it defines as "building identity, character, analytical and operational capability, and self-confidence." Barney Brower, an open program administrator, introduced me to the institute's director, Jeff Howard. Traditional algebra would be offered to seventh and eighth graders. Training would be critical, for what we were proposing did not fit in any elementary school curriculum and I needed to come up with an approach that could get us inside school systems.

In October 1989, a small grant to AIMS from the Boston Foundation helped get us off the ground. The Boston school administration gave stipends for non-school-hour training to teachers in the three schools. It hired substitutes to fill in for teachers who were training during school hours. Between November 1989 and January 1990, fourteen teachers and one administrator were trained in our curriculum.

Larger grants from the Edna McConnell Clark and MacArthur Foundations that year let me bring Cynthia on board part-time, but ironically forced us off the Wheelock campus eventually; administering us had become too big a job for the institution. With these new grants Wheelock would have had to hire an accountant and set up a fairly complex system. Time for us to go off on our own, and William Crombie, who had joined me to work on curriculum development, Cynthia, my daughter Maisha, Jackie, and I began outlining the aims and rules that would govern the Algebra Project "Incorporated." Michelle Shaw, one of the Seymour Society members who, by that time, had graduated from

Harvard Law School, drew up the actual papers of incorporation and filed them in April 1990.

That MacArthur Foundation grant, which came at the beginning of 1990, as well as the support of Dorothy Strong, director of mathematics for the Chicago school system, and that of several community organizations there, also helped us extend the Algebra Project from the Boston area into Chicago. At almost the same time, the Clark money brought us into three other cities where the foundation was involved with its own projects targeted at middle schools: Louisville, Milwaukee, and Oakland. In those cities we were asked to "show our stuff" and then invited to bring the Algebra Project in. With this growth and expansion we now needed to coordinate at an entirely different level. Cynthia took over our administrative operations and the effective headquarters of the Algebra Project, Inc. was her living room. *I'm kind of a glue person, you know, hanging out with some visionary or other, nailing their feet and their ideas down to the floor, drawing blueprints . . . figuring out how many two-by-fours you need, doing a budget. I was, at the time, a single mom, and Michelle [not yet married to Alan Shaw] was my roommate. The computer was there. The printer. We got a fax machine eventually. The phone number for the Algebra Project was my home number. There were only four of us—myself, Bob, Jackie, and Bill [Crombie]—so there was enough space when we had to have a meeting.*

Our efforts converged with interest by the National Council of Teachers of Mathematics (NCTM) in "algebra for all." Throughout the country, encouraged by the NCTM, new problem-oriented math curricula were being piloted in an effort to generate more math excitement by trying something other than rote learning. A consensus had emerged to move away from tracking. And while we were, and are, part of this trend, our efforts to organize community structures to press for change and to begin to hold school systems accountable to the needs of its constituency as well as our focus on experiential learning set us apart.

The open program at King, meanwhile, had become an increasingly effective real-life poster for the project. In 1989 the program hired a permanent full-time "floating" substitute, freeing teachers to visit one another's classrooms to look at what worked and what did not work. A grant from Ellen Poss through the Kapor Family Foundation enabled Lynne Godfrey to become a lead teacher for the Algebra Project in the open program. Lynne was now hosting frequent visits from teachers who wanted to observe her teaching. The grant made it possible for Lynne to take partial leave for two years and assist other teachers with implementation of the Algebra Project. Lynne's involvement heralded the emergence of a core of teachers who would be critical to the expansion of the Algebra Project throughout the 1990s. (And every year Ellen Poss, now with her own fund, has supported the project.)

As the Algebra Project took shape, my civil rights movement experience was guiding my thinking as much as my training in mathematics. Part of understanding the movement is understanding change. Part of what happened in Mississippi was the creation of a culture of change—a change in the climate of the consciousness of Black people in that state. Part of what was involved was tapping into a consensus. People agreed that if they could get the vote it would be a good thing, and they would be better off. I felt, as I worked in the open program, that the same dynamics were at work around the issue of mathematics literacy. I think everyone agrees that if it is possible to open the door to real mathematics understanding, it would be a good thing. If *we* can do it, then *we* should. We need to uncover this consensus and develop it. Establishing this climate, and changed consciousness about mathematics, in the larger community will go a long way toward making it possible to change the culture of mathematics in Black communities, which would certainly stimulate a similar change in the larger community. I think that like the voting rights effort of the 1960s it will lead to more than just change in the teaching of mathematics.

This community organizing approach to bringing innovation into the education process differs profoundly from traditional educational intervention. At universities, scholars design interventions they theorize will result in outcomes they can predict. University researchers and consultants design convincing interventions for funding agencies, selecting neighborhoods, schools, or organizations for participation on the basis of demographics or some other quantifiable characteristic. These researchers also have intellectual roots in their own disciplines—from sociology to administration—and mainly view problems through lenses that are consistent with their disciplines.

But it is not thought that such researchers should become full-time high school and middle school math teachers, to really immerse themselves in the problem they are trying to address. Nor is it thought that high school teachers should be funded to develop curriculum on the same scale as university researchers.

In sharp contrast, working in the tradition of Ella Baker, the community organizer seeking an innovative breakthrough in education will use the principle of "cast down your bucket where you are." The organizer becomes part of the community, learning from it, becoming aware of its strengths, resources, concerns, and ways of doing business. The organizer does not have the complete answer in advance—the researcher's detailed comprehensive plans for remedying a perceived problem. The organizer wants to construct a solution with the community. He or she understands that the community's everyday concerns can be transformed into broader questions of general import. The form of these questions and the actions that follow from them are not always known in advance. I did not know that my concern for Maisha's math education would lead to the Algebra Project's raising questions about ability grouping, effective teaching for children of color, experiential learning, and community participation in educational decision making. I pulled these issues up when I cast down my bucket. Finally, unlike the researcher, the organizer helps community members air their opinions, question one another, and then build consensus, a process that usually takes a great amount of time to complete.

This is a long journey and not a linear progression. It is a journey with zigs and zags, a process of push and pull. If you are successful in some classrooms, that gives you an opening to approach the community. In order to get into all the classrooms, however—

to *all* the students—we need the community's political involvement and clout. You have to work both sides of the street at the
same time. You have to learn how to move effectively in all arenas.
I have thought of the Algebra Project as a young child who is trying to stand up and teetering and falling down a little, then getting
back up, falling down a little, and getting back up again. I hope,
indeed I think, that the project has the same kind of perseverance
that makes young children keep getting back up. And the same
kind of perseverance that eventually makes them walk. It doesn't
really matter how many times young children fall down, they keep
getting up, attempting to walk. Probably part of the reason that
happens is they have a lot of people around them who are walking.
Unfortunately, there are not a lot of projects around that are looking in this way at this issue of math literacy and how you make *systematic* change in school. The Algebra Project is still learning how
to walk.

CHAPTER 5

Pedagogy

The Experience of Teachers and Students

The most pressing consistent question students had was "What has riding the T got to do with algebra?" Though it was a struggle to not explain the idea of the train trips as the physical event on which future algebra concepts would be modeled, it was worth it. My response to the question was usually to ask another question. "What do you think the connection is?" One girl looked up at me as she was doing her math test with an "I know you won't answer this" smile and asked, "Just what did our trip have to do with algebra?" I smiled a "you're right, I'm not going to answer you" smile and said, "You're going to learn how to answer your own questions and in the days to come I'm sure *you'll* be able to answer that question."

Lynne Godfrey

I know what the kids can do if I can just get them to believe in themselves.

Johnny L. Hughes, principal, Lanier High School,
Jackson, Mississippi

By 1991 we had moved from Cynthia's home and were settled into new space in Cambridge, where we are still located. By then the first generation of Algebra Project students had graduated, or were close to graduation, from college. Many did not want to end their relationship with the project as they entered the "adult" world. Some in this group, like my daughter Maisha, who went on to Harvard University after finishing high school, had stayed connected to our work all through their college years by tutoring at

King and working with summer algebra camps. *And so then when I was a senior and I had to try to figure out what I was going to do, what work I was going to do after college, it took me a while because I really wasn't sure. I knew that I loved working with kids. And I knew that I wanted to do something I felt was working to address the problems of freedom and equality for Black people. And I felt that the Algebra Project was doing that in a way that I didn't see a lot of other types of projects doing. And so I thought about it for a while and decided I wanted to work with the Algebra Project. So I talked to my father.*

Maisha and I walked along the Charles River discussing this one afternoon. In that conversation, she also told me that she did not want to work in the Boston area. *I needed my space. I had grown up there and I spent my college years there and I just felt like I needed to have my own space. Dad was pleased that I wanted to work with the project, and there were choices.* The Algebra Project was no longer a personal experiment conducted by me in a small corner of the King school in Cambridge. Now the project was taking its first teetering steps toward becoming a national effort. In 1990 a Chicago Algebra Project had gotten under way. We also began working in Milwaukee, Oakland, and Atlanta that year. In 1991, projects were started in Indianapolis, San Francisco, and Los Angeles. That year, too, Dave Dennis, through Positive Innovations, initiated an Algebra Project "pilot" program in six Mississippi Delta schools. In 1992, a project was under way in New Orleans. A New York City project began in 1993. That year, what we were calling the Southern Initiative of the Algebra Project, under Dave's direction, reached South and North Carolina; Jackson, Mississippi; and Birmingham and Bessemer, Alabama, and Dave was getting inquiries from Arkansas and Tennessee. *We didn't go out looking. People began to call in and ask about the Algebra Project. As we expanded, I continued to have meetings that included everybody. Money from the Open Society Institute helped us have those first meetings and trainings. We would talk about operating as a region with everybody working together to give support to each other. And that's the way we try and work today. This regional approach is based on the same philosophy used in COFO. So people started defining what they wanted and the idea was, how do you pull to-*

er a structure that meets the needs? What were the needs? At first, just
achers would be saying what they needed and we would look at what re-
sources we had. The same thing happened around parents, youth, and
community. All of these components began to come together. Out of that
came the Southern Initiative; people found a source of strength in each
other, and now we ourselves are our greatest resource.

What we had learned since starting in King's open program
was beginning to take concrete form as a curriculum intervention
based on experiential learning. Both were evolving through trial
and error as well as analysis of traditional educational approaches.
I was certain now that what existed in schools wasn't working, that
traditional schooling was inadequate for equipping our students
to function in today's society. Elite private schools and elite public
schools prepared their students to become America's leaders, but
all other schools belonged to an era in which work and preparation for work were defined by factories and assembly lines. Factories and the cities they helped create became the models for
schools and their school systems, and the work in factories became
the model for schooling. Because the new technologies give rise
to computers and an ever-widening use of symbol systems and
quantitative data, we concluded that the schools and curricula we
had to struggle to design *must* put mathematical and scientific literacy on a par with reading and writing literacy. The validity of
this approach, at least as far as I am concerned, has been confirmed
in the classroom.

In my geometry class at Lanier High School in Jackson, Mississippi, the school where I now spend most of my teaching time,
we are using the TI92 graphing calculator, really a small computer. My students, like many of their generation, do not read as
much as they should. Most of what they learn they learn from
pushing buttons and seeing how images change. Their modalities
of learning have been attuned to this image-making process. If
you use these graphing calculators, you arouse their interest. The
kids will take time to try to figure out how the calculator works,
how those buttons make images come and go on the screen. They
learn something and will show you what they have learned. They

would never do that with a book. Students do not open a math book and say, "Let me show you what I know on this page," but they will show you what they know about a single button on a graphing calculator.

Therefore, I think you have got to go where the kids are. And that place is different from the place where teachers have been taught to be. Our graphing calculators completely reorganize the subject. The exercises in the chapters at the end of mathematics textbooks depend on the chapters at the beginning. With graphing calculators you can move around in innumerable ways; it's a nonlinear way of presenting information. You need teachers who are comfortable taking the subject apart and putting it back together again on the spot in response to questions of children. And this is a real difficulty. Recently, on June 3, 2000, in a radio address discussing U.S. classrooms, President Clinton said that while 95 percent of schools and 63 percent of classrooms are wired for Internet access, two out of three teachers with access to a computer say they don't feel well prepared to use it in the classroom. And the teacher-training programs that exist do not prepare teachers for this kind of work. *Worst of all, math labs in inner-city schools for the most part are used to remediate students about things the technology makes obsolete.* We need a revolution in order to get the teaching of math up to where the technology and the students are.

Our efforts in Cambridge to get schools committed to this approach to teaching rested on a foundation of consensus among parents, teachers, administrators, and community volunteers. Parents used meetings as opportunities to talk, ask questions, and join in planning. And as change began to take place in classrooms, more of the pace and scope of students' mathematical studies came under student control. Teachers began acting more as guides and coaches rather than lecturers. Even these small steps had dramatic effect as motivated students set goals. In Mary Lou's classroom, for example, *Andrea [Harvey] spoke up at one of our first meetings and said, "I'm going to do four lessons a week because I want to finish such-and-such by the seventh grade, so that I can finish the book by the eighth grade, so I can be in honors geometry in the ninth grade." This was a twelve-year-old.*

The others looked at her—this hadn't come from a teacher—and said, "Are you crazy?" She said, "That's what I'm going to do." Bob was there, and he started to frame for them why what Andrea had done was a very mature and farsighted act, and how maybe they weren't ready to do that yet. It gave Andrea a lot of support and affirmation for having said that in the group. And it changed what the others were going to say next. Everything from then on was in terms of Andrea: "Well, I'm not going to do quite what Andrea is, but . . ." (Andrea majored in music and minored in math at UMass, Amherst. She worked with YPP in 1999–2000 training math literacy workers, and in summer 2000 was certified to teach math in the Boston schools.)

Teachers were meeting in small groups for brief lessons on specific concepts, and regularly gathering for small-group review sessions. The 1986 decision that all students in the seventh and eighth grades should take algebra had lower-grade teachers questioning whether their own math curricula adequately prepared their students for algebra. We began to address this issue systematically by beginning to implement new curricula in mathematics appropriate for different age and grade levels. We knew that flexibility was key. For example, when fifth- and sixth-grade teachers tried a materials-centered approach that had worked very well at the seventh- and eighth-grade level, they found that younger children, accustomed to more teacher-centered instruction, needed more teacher-child and small-group interaction. Accordingly, these teachers modified their classroom technique while retaining the principle of encouraging greater self-reliance in finding answers to problems.

In addition to the benefits to learning attained from having the flexibility to modify the curriculum, the process gave participating teachers greater appreciation for the kind of self-reliant education efforts the project was trying to encourage in students. Teachers also gained a deeper sense of their own authority. *Bob was affirming what we were doing while he was helping us change. He didn't come in and say, "We're throwing this out, it's junk." He came in and said, "You guys are great. Wanna try something different?" When we asked, "How will it work?" he turned it around and asked, "Well, how do you*

think it should work? What do you want to have happen?" He didn't really give us a why, which admittedly was frustrating, but it also gave us
ownership around it. Bob didn't have all of the answers. At first I was really annoyed that he was making me go through this process. I kept saying,
"Bob has an agenda. Why doesn't he tell us? We're wasting so much
time!" But he knew that it had to come from us. He knew he couldn't impose, because he didn't know what would work. He wasn't a classroom
teacher. He just had the vision. If he could help us catch the vision, we
would make it work.

With elementary level teachers now wanting their students
ready for algebra in middle school, I began developing what
would become the "transition curriculum" for sixth-grade students. (We are still developing and refining this curriculum. Book
I, which is aimed at sixth graders, develops the concepts of integers, displacements, and addition and subtraction of integers.) We
say "transition" because the Algebra Project focuses on a cluster of
elementary but elemental concepts that are essential for bridging
the gap between arithmetic and algebra so that *all* middle school
students are prepared to succeed in the college preparatory mathematics sequence when they reach high school (see the Appendix).
It's a "floor." Our transition curriculum is rooted in the conviction
that intellectual development is, in part, a matter of integrating
knowledge. You want the kids to learn how to engage the in-
quiry process.

In other words, in the Algebra Project we are using a version
of experiential learning; it starts with where the children are, experiences that they share. We get them to reflect on these drawing
on their common culture, then to form abstract conceptualizations out of their reflection, and then to apply the abstraction back
on their experience. You can think of it is as a circle or clock: at
twelve noon they have an experience; quarter past they are thinking about it; half past they are doing some conceptual work
around their reflections; and at quarter to they are doing applications based on their conceptual work. In the Algebra Project this
movement from experience to abstraction takes the form of a five-
step process that introduces students to the idea that many impor-

tant concepts of elementary algebra may be accessed through ordinary experiences. Each step is designed to help students bridge the transition from real life to mathematical language and operations. Because of this connection with real life, the transition curriculum is not only experiential, but *culturally* based. The experiences must be meaningful in terms of the daily life and culture of the students. One key pedagogical problem addressed by the curriculum is that of providing an environment where the students can explore these ideas and effectively move toward their standard expression in school mathematics.

In academic language, this process can also be described as the "social construction of mathematics." Students learn that math is the creation of people—people working together and depending on one another. Interaction, cooperation, and group communication, therefore, are key components of this process. Students also help generate part of the content of instruction as well. They participate in the physical event that will generate data which becomes the vehicle for introducing mathematical concepts. Cooperation and participation in group activities, as well as personal responsibility for individual work, become important not only for the successful *functioning* of the learning group, but for the generation of instructional materials and various representations of the data as well.

There are five crucial steps in the Algebra Project curriculum process.

1. Physical Events. A trip is the central experience of the transition curriculum. The curriculum begins with a trip; this trip may be a trip on a metropolitan transit system, or it may be a bus tour or a walking tour of the students' communities. I mentioned earlier that my first trip with students was on the red line of the T in Cambridge. In the Mississippi Delta, students and teachers boarded buses. And if there is no public transportation it is always possible to walk.

2. Pictorial Representation/Modeling. In this and the next three steps, students move through a series of linked and progressively abstracted representations of the physical event. In ab-

stracting, we focus on certain aspects of an experience and ignore others. Students are first asked to draw a picture or construct a model of the event. In drawing pictures, students portray particular aspects or *features* of their experience and begin the process of abstraction. Students are free to choose whatever they believe is of interest and value to put in their pictures. In this way they exercise ownership over these visual statements.

3. Intuitive Language/"People Talk." In this third stage students are asked to discuss and write about the physical event in their own language. Their conversations and stories may be written in the language they use to negotiate their daily lives, but as with pictorial representation, the important point is that students should feel they have ownership over their descriptions. These stories provide a window to explore intuition and ideas. We tend to get two types of stories: factual reports and private, uniquely personal stories. Both need careful attention. The personal stories often conceal "data" of which the writer is not aware. On the other hand, factual reports can hide what is thematically particular and rich to the observer, and it is precisely that richness of intuitive language in writing and discussion that we want to capture at this stage.

4. Structured Language/"Feature Talk." This is not a language that the kids or anyone actually speaks. It is structured or "regimented" language aimed at explicitly selecting and encoding those features of the event that are deemed important for further study. One of its characteristics is it talks about some feature of the object (e.g., the *speed* of the car) rather than the object itself. (For a more detailed account see the Appendix.) Specifically, at this stage we isolate those features of experience around which we will build the mathematics. If students have not explicitly tagged them, the teacher introduces four fundamental and recurring mathematical features of trips: start, finish, direction, and distance, features that are present in all trips. In contrast to the mathematical reforms that followed *Sputnik* during the 1960s, when attention was focused on teaching students the vocabulary, grammar, and structure of mathematics per se, the emphasis here is

on getting students to develop mathematical models for important features of particular events. A process of mathematization. (See the Appendix.)

5. Symbolic Representation. Once students have worked through the picture making, writing, and discussion of features, they construct symbols to represent these ideas. At first, these symbols are private, holding meaning only for their creators. First in teams or groups, and then in class, students present and discuss the meaning of their symbolic representations. By sharing their meaning, the private symbols become public. The symbols are often redesigned to make it easier for the rest of the class to understand.

Even now I can remember Chad, one of my seventh-grade students years ago, looking up from reading a page in the first chapter of a traditional algebra text with a weary sigh and a puzzled expression and then saying, "It's all words." With these five steps we are trying to ward off student frustration in "the game of signs," and the misapprehension that mathematics is the manipulation of a collection of mysterious symbols. For too many young people mathematics, especially advanced mathematics, is a game of signs they are unable play. They must be helped to understand the conceptual language that is encoded in the "game of signs." When middle school students use the five-step process to construct symbolic representations of physical events—representations that they themselves make up—they forge, through direct experience, their own platform for mathematical truths. Their personally constructed symbolic representations, rooted in what they have experienced and observed, enter into a system of mathematical truth that has content and meaning.

Teachers, of course, are another part of this equation. It should be clear by now that underlying our curriculum and pedagogy is the expectation that teachers will make fundamental changes in the way they teach. They cannot simply be lecturers attempting to pour knowledge into the heads of students who sit passively like inanimate vessels. Teacher workshops and larger Algebra Project meetings, such as the periodic national conferences we hold, are usually structured around the basics of the five-step process. Through repeated experience with the model in different settings, teachers learn to work with the five steps and to understand the process as a model for designing instruction. In 1991, San Francisco sixth-grade math teacher Marion Currell participated in one of our workshops and found something that "made sense." *The Algebra Project matched how I believed in teaching—having a conversation.*

And working with Jim Burroughs from Boston's McBer Associates, we began designing what we now call our Training of Trainers program. Jim develop a Train the Trainer for the Efficacy Institute and I participated in it in 1988. Jim and I lost touch after that brief first contact. But as the 1980s wound down it was becoming clear to me that while I knew how to train teachers in our developing curriculum and pedagogy, I did not know how to train people to train teachers, a very different proposition. My movement experience in working with adults stood me in good stead when it came to working with teachers but I didn't have training concepts. I decided to look Jim up. As it happened, I bumped into Jim in a bank one day and began explaining that now that the Algebra Project was spreading to other places I needed to develop effective and systematic ways to train teachers and the trainers of teachers. Perhaps he could help.

Jim responded on the spot by saying that I should come by his house. *He did and we talked. I told Bob I would be glad to help. For me, the kind of work he was doing was close to what got me in this business in the first place. In 1990 I was spending most of my time training executives for Merrill Lynch. Although I made money, it was not very gratifying and a long way from what I intended when I started. Listening to Bob, I thought this will be a nice balance to what I'm doing and I'll feel a lot better about being tired at the end of the day.*

He was quickly drawn into our work in Chicago, where a new algebra project was beginning to take shape. There, in 1990, a group of educators and community people had identified six schools they wanted the Algebra Project to come into as soon as teachers were trained. In January 1991, I invited Jim to observe a two-week teacher training workshop in Chicago. As a result, I began holding meetings with a group of interested community people to help form a Chicago Algebra Project and to plan an approach to the MacArthur Foundation seeking money to design a training progran that would train trainers of teachers. That spring, a group that included Dr. Frank Davies of Lesley College, Dorothy Strong, director of mathematics for the Chicago Public Schools, B. J. Walker, representing the newly formed Chicago Algebra Project, and I met with the MacArthur Foundation and ultimately got funding.

Meanwhile, at the Massachusetts College of Public and Community Service (CPCS), where I had secured a part-time teaching position, William Crombie, who was teaching math and some computer science there, was also becoming involved with our project. Early in 1990 Marylyn Frankenstein who headed the math department at CPCS invited me to be part of a Boston delegation attending a meeting of the American Mathematical Society in Louisville, Kentucky. I presented a paper at the session of the Humanist Mathematics Network. Bill was also part of our delegation. Flying back to Cambridge together, we talked and I mentioned a need for help from someone with training in physics. "Well, I might be able to help," Bill said, and a group of us, including my daughter Maisha, Lynne Godfrey, and Cynthia Silva, began meeting around the curriculum, with Bill and Dan Smith, a physicist from Northeastern, contributing to issues of velocity and acceleration.

Demands for our time and energy were then coming from all parts of the country and Bill was increasingly involved in weekend workshops and training sessions with teachers. One day, while sitting in an Oakland restaurant, I asked him to consider full-time involvement with the project. He was definitely interested. *I was in a struggle with some people in the department around content. They had math one and math two—courses that were basically arithmetic and algebra. The struggle was around whether people—adults—should start at algebra rather than doing math one and math two. It was basically six months to a year before the adults got to algebra. This struggle started to break down on racial lines—the white folks in the department were basi-*

*cally the ones saying we need to keep the arithmetic. A Nigerian and my-
self were saying no.* By the fall of 1990, Bill was working with us full-
time, visiting classrooms, working with teachers.

But it wasn't just his differences with his department that attracted Bill to the project. Before he joined us, one of the first
workshops he was involved with, early in the summer of 1990,
used a grant from the Clark Foundation to bring teachers from
San Diego, Milwaukee, and Louisville to Atlanta for two weeks. *I
basically observed Bob at the workshop so it was all kind of inquiry-based,
and I thought this was cool, it was fun. The mathematics questions were
not formulated mathematically. He was pointing to the issues at the root of
every mathematics question, encouraging a kind of a general thinking
about the issue there, as if he was saying, "We can talk about that fundamental issue first and then specialize the results we get to the mathematics
formulation." In other words, for example, the mathematical idea of equiv-
alence relations—it's everyday common sense—is "make do," because
everybody makes do in one way or another. So we started with discussions
around some concepts from the general culture. One of the reasons for doing
this is so everybody has access. Everybody has something to say about it.
What all of this means is that, from the first instance, everybody has a
voice at the mathematical table.*

Movement encourages movement. In this respect also the Algebra Project was echoing the work in Mississippi and throughout
the South thirty years before. As I have tried to emphasize, the
civil rights movement of the 1960s was less about challenges and
protests against white power than feeling our way toward our own
power and possibilities—really a series of challenges by ourselves,
and our communities, to ourselves. In this new community being
shaped by the Algebra Project, Bill, along with Jackie, Cynthia,
Maisha, Lynne Godfrey, Jim Burroughs, and others took on the
task of developing methods for teachers to challenge themselves.
In Chicago, Jim, who was later joined by Bill, took the lead in designing our training effort. *We had to get into the guts of the teachers
or potential teachers. The Algebra Project needed to be internalized better.
I could see how critical it was to link data with visceral experience. This
loop was not being closed well enough. It was the Algebra Project's ability*

to make math fun that struck me. Part of it was games, part of it was the trip, and part was small group dialogue. Bill and I began writing an instruction guide for teachers—a conceptual template. This became the basis for our first Training of Trainers effort in 1992.

Because the project believes that it is essential to form a group of individuals who are committed to fostering mathematics literacy in their school *and* community, the Algebra Project has goals for teachers that reach beyond curriculum training. Teachers, we believe, have to think through and address community problems. They need to develop and hone skills that enable them to work effectively with their co-teachers and others in larger Algebra Project groups. It is ironic that in the service of this radical project, we have drawn upon corporate education methods and educator Jim Burroughs has played a key role in its design.

For many teachers our approach is a difficult shift. Some have been unimpressed or outright hostile during training sessions and often are reluctant to embrace AP methods, for our approach can seem difficult to connect to math at first. In Mississippi, for example, Marjorie Brown, almost walked away. *I was listening to Bob, I was listening to Thelma [McGee]. I was listening because there were no answers—they weren't giving answers and I was used to teachers answering questions. I got really turned off for a while. Because when you ask me to do something that I don't think makes a lot of sense, I get turned off. I was driving long miles everyday for this training. It was hot and the air-conditioning in my car wasn't working. Then we took the bus trip. We hit all those civil rights places, went to where things had happened in Greenwood. I listened to everybody's story and I was still trying to put together in my head how this connected to math. Then mileage hit me. I began to work through in my own mind ways to envision the math from this trip I was taking.*

We ask teachers to embrace change, and the pressure on teachers is not to take risks but to march whatever children they can, lockstep, toward higher standardized test scores. After a Cambridge training, one teacher told her principal she was not going to teach the Algebra Project. Other teachers were prepared and willing to go ahead and only this teacher was refusing, the school principal told Lynne Godfrey. *He found another teacher so the entire sixth grade could participate, but I thought he was letting the teacher who refused off easy. I also remembered her evaluation of the training. She was real scared about teaching this curriculum. . . . So I went by her room. She told me, "Maybe next year once I've gotten more familiar with the curriculum." And I said, "You'll get familiar with the curriculum as you do it, that's part of the process, that's how all of us start. It's like when Bob came in, I didn't know what he was doing. I didn't know what those conversations were going to be like until I started doing them." She said, "Yeah, I know you really think I can—I should go ahead and do this, I can do this, but we'll see."* The next time I came to the school she was co-facilitating an *Algebra Project* class. In the Algebra Project we have found that teachers, like students, also need nonthreatening arenas where their concerns can be articulated. While Lynne was able to have a one-on-one conversation with this teacher, the question remains as to whether something with that level of comfort can be institutionalized and become integral parts of school systems.

The crucial idea underlying our professional development and teacher training, directly connected to what we want in the classroom, is freedom to learn. Once teachers have a stake in that idea they find it liberating. And this pays off in the classroom. Visiting her once-reluctant teacher on another occasion, Lynne found her intervening with the lead teacher so that a student's voice could be heard more clearly: *The class was coming up with some [conventions] around what was meant by the four features of the trip. This kid mumbled something to the other kids at his table. This same teacher who had been so reluctant about the Algebra Project said, "Hold on a minute because I think Jonah here has something that he should bring up to the whole group." And then she said, "Jonah, why don't you go ahead and share that with the whole group. I don't mean to be disrespectful or anything," she then told the lead teacher, "but I remember before you said once we agreed to these things, these were the things we were going to use. I think Jonah's got a really interesting point; let's talk about that." Other kids started offering their take on it and Jonah's original point became an agreed-upon convention. By her giving Jonah that support it kind of leveled the playing field.* And such freedom, say teachers who stick with the program, like Marjorie Brown, or Thelma McGee who helped train her, make it possible for them to go a great distance with their students. *It was a major change not only for teachers but for the students. And I think the students were more susceptible to the idea than the teachers were initially because teachers were comfortable with the traditional way of teaching that is teacher-centered instead of student-centered. And because we did not have the Algebra Project methodology—the five steps—it held us within what I call a prison. It kept shackles on us. And when we were introduced to this methodology, this new way of teaching, it was like we were let out of prison. We were set free and you can now go beyond where you were.*

In my geometry course I ask the students to write in paragraph form and think about how they are going to incorporate their symbols into their sentences. They have to learn how to write expository English that incorporates symbolic representations about quantitative data. They must write whole sentences. The standard way of writing math—just numbers and equations—will not do. They need to come out being able to talk about these numbers. Computers like the graphing calculators are going to give them numbers and the ability to manipulate them, but what do they mean? Who is going to interpret them? My students are proud of their interpretations. They hold on to them, show them around, to their parents, to their friends, as representing something important they have learned.

Parents and citizens, of course, want to know what these kids have learned at the end of the day. They look to tests and test scores to show that the project is really working. That's a political and educational fact about today's society. But how are we going to have tests or assessments that on the one hand satisfy this *political* demand, and on the other hand genuinely help—rather than hindering or punishing—children's learning? We are in a conundrum over this question, because there is no agreement about what assessments should be like in order to do both.

The Algebra Project's approach to this complicated problem is to get the kids to take it on themselves. It is the organizer's answer:

work the demand side, the way we did in 1960s Mississippi. Kids are used to saying, "I'm going to take as little math as I can and as soon as I don't have to take any more, I'm outta here!" We're trying to reverse that. For the targeted population in the Algebra Project, the first thing we get kids to say to themselves is *I'm going to get this! I'm going to figure out where it is and I'm going after it! And if I have trouble I'm going to figure out where I can get help.* That's admittedly a lot to put on students for a subject they have traditionally walked away from, but it is at the very center of what the Algebra Project is about. Like sharecroppers demanding the right to vote forty years ago when those in power said they did not vote because they were apathetic, our students will have to demand the education from those in power who say they do not get educated because they are dysfunctional.

I'm not saying this is easy. Indeed, to work the demand side, you have to figure out how to make your way through the teenage culture. Tuning out is one of the things that defines the culture. Not all the kids do it, but many in our target population do. They cling to that part of the teenage culture that says "I'm not going to let you teach me." Generally with these kids it does not take destructive forms—socially destructive activity. It's more like preoccupation, a habit of losing attention or not being able to maintain and sustain attention. You can spot them in a class. I've often said that if the sixth graders can count and we can get their attention we can introduce them to important algebra concepts. The question is, Can we learn to get their attention?

Sometimes resistance to being taught has to do with anger. I've seen some kids—I've had some kids—who are just too angry to learn. There the issue is breaking through, finding a way to penetrate into that anger and hostility. Their stance at that level, "I'm not going to let you teach me!," can take the form of direct anger and hostility, disruption, or it can take the form of evasion. And this evasion is not just inattention; it is tuning out. When you open your mouth you're tuned out by them. This is where even the most conscientious teacher needs help because if you have a full class and you are seeing eighty or ninety kids across the day, you don't need that. You're trying to prepare for class, and you have to be in and out with the counselors, talking to parents.

And then you have some kids who take the stance "I'm not saying that you can't teach me, that I refuse to let you teach me, but I'm not cooperating in this either." It's their response to the structures they encounter and the educational system as they perceive it. For all of the kids, there are huge chunks of their lives that we just don't see, that many teachers do not want to see. Sometimes the debris of it rains down on us as if from a sudden thunderstorm. That some kids even keep coming to school instead of being lost to the streets suggests some remarkable reserve of strength, some hope for something better that we are obligated to meet. If the kids can find their voice, the door to change begins to open much wider. That's what I mean by working the demand side of the problem.

Take James, one of my students at Lanier. One day he walked up to me with a request, a request that surprised me. "April and I . . . uh, would you take us to get somethin' to eat?" James asked. I was surprised because James was saying he wanted to do something. This was very unusual for James to reach out in any way and to ask for anything—I don't ever remember him asking for anything. So I ageed. James called his mother and April called hers. Then we went to get some pizza. And talked. James and April on one side of the table, me on the other side.

One of the things I said to James was that in the classroom I always had to sort of draw him out, that he never volunteered to say anything and there was always the tone that made it seem that he was saying, "I'm not going to show that I am interested even if I am." Why is that? I wanted to know, and asked him, "Do you really have that attitude?" "I behave that way in all of my classes," James answered. He hinted at some anger, telling me that his father was murdered by a woman who was the mother of a brother he had never seen. She was back out on the streets of Jackson, Mississippi.

For three years before this conversation—since he was a seventh grader—James and I had been working together. But only now was he feeling safe enough to begin revealing himself in this way. With this opening, as he and April ate their pizza, I pushed some, encouraging James to change how he behaved in class. "You can get ahead of the game," I said. In class we were using TI92 graphing calculators, brand-new at the time. "You're the only kids in Jackson schools using them," I told them. "You can make yourselves expert," I said, pointing out, moreover, that becoming expert required taking what they were doing to another level. They would have to think about it in a different way and then push the calculator, discovering what it could do. Explore its possibilities, I urged them; use the calculator as opposed to just sitting back and waiting to see what someone else can do.

James didn't respond, didn't tell me right there on the spot that he would do this, but he was listening. He and April finished the pizza and I drove them home. I dropped James off first; April lives near me. "Do you think James will change?" I asked her. "I think he will," she predicted. And the next day in the classroom James began to pursue me. My class is open. Kids get up and walk around. James had his calculator and he was working on a problem. He came up and asked me, "Did I do this—am I doing it right? I'm having trouble here." After school he came to the math lab and we began to work on a problem. I asked him to get it ready so he could present it to the kids in class next time. He agreed to this.

Three days later, I asked James to go up to the overhead projector and we started in on the exercise. He would state the issue and I would repeat it. "Good," I thought as we began. One of the issues I had been talking to James about was being willing to step forward in the class and taking a lead in helping the class move along. But he had to be comfortable with himself to do that. It looked like he was. We went through the whole exercise and that afternoon he came back to the lab and we began tackling another problem. We were trying to have two measures on a circle—a central angle and the arc, and an animated point moving around the circle. The problem was to get the calculator to document the change in the central angle and the arc at the same time. James had to figure out how to do this. I had never done it and I didn't try then. James kept coming back and showing me what he had done and I'd say, "Well, it's not quite what we want. You've got to keep working on it."

So he worked on it for a week after class and he got it. He showed it to me and he'd gotten Shemeka, another student, interested. She'd been working on a line segment problem and now she said, "Tomorrow, I want to work on what James is working on." So I said, "Okay, if you finish up your work tomorrow in class early, then you can work with what James is working on." She did, and the next day after class I sent a whole section of the class as well to work with James. I had decided that James was now ready to run a group by himself without my help. Having a student like James working with kids who need to catch up on a specific topic is central to the Algebra Project and we have found it to be extremely effective.

With James there was a deep level of satisfaction for me. Yet even now I sometimes remind myself, "Bob, there are levels of this work that are not completely in your control." Take James; I still do not exactly know what triggered James into coming around, although I recognize that I am a part of whatever it was. Even James isn't completely clear. *Mr. Moses said he knew I could do better and that I needed to come out of myself. You wanna hear but at the same time you're sayin', "Why you talkin' to me?" Then it started clickin' in my brain. I am smart. I can do things! And the next day I started to do more stuff.*

How will the Algebra Project grow its young people? This is a central and not completely settled question for us. Part of the answer is that you need older people who are in constant enough contact with a small group of young people that you can develop a real relationship—a relationship that can move young people, penetrate their cultural barriers, and become a relationship that can help them grow. In our targeted population, this requires contact over time and contact outside of school. Trust has to anchor these relationships, the belief that a grown-up person is not going to disappear in one way or the other—a kid like James might put it as a kind of security in the knowledge that "you will be there when I need to reach out."

I think generating this kind of security is critical to populations of young people who have been hurt in different ways in their basic relationships with adults. And clearly this is not something that is achieved by building up a central bureaucratic staff. So, I ask myself, how do you create these kinds of niches within the project? How does the project develop a critical mass, a critical network of such relationships?

CHAPTER 6

South Again

> In the middle of our meeting there was a fire in Shirley's home and she had to leave. The next day, she was back, explaining that her kitchen had been completely destroyed. So why was she back here? There was nothing she could do about her kitchen right then, she said, so she had come back to the training session "because I don't want to miss any part of it. It's too important." This is a whole other level of commitment, I thought to myself.
>
> Dave Dennis

Mississippi has changed in many ways since the 1960s. African-American voter registration is routine, and Mississippi has more Black elected officials than any state in the country. The White Citizens Council has disappeared (although white power has not). A Black person can walk into almost any roadside restaurant or rest room without risking assault and jail. There are Martin Luther King Streets, Medgar Evers Avenues, and Fannie Lou Hamer Libraries. But there is also one constant from the old days. Mississippi remains at the bottom when it comes to education. And Black schools remain at the bottom in the state.

The civil rights movement ended the doctrine of "separate but equal," and gained African Americans access to public schools that were once "white only." But these schools quickly became "Black" as whites fled to private "academies" for their education. Reflecting on what had changed and what had not changed in the state, Mae Bertha Carter, who lived all of her life in Sunflower County and fought for school desegregation in the 1970s and 1980s, noted shortly before she passed away in 1999 that *the way to*

control Black people or anybody is to keep them dumb. You keep them
dumb and you can control them. Back in slave time they catch you reading
and they would whip you. Education, that's the goal. Getting knowledge
and understanding. If you are uneducated you don't know nothing. You
don't know what's going on around you. . . . So what they're doin' is
handicapping kids. These school systems ain't doin' nothing but handicap-
ping these children. Indeed, only 38 percent of Mississippi's eighth
graders scored at or above the *lowest* level of math proficiency. A
third of Mississippi's population has not even finished high school,
with that number leaping to 50 percent in Mrs. Carter's home-
land—the Delta—where almost a third of the population has not
even attended high school. And it was in the Delta that the Algebra Project took its first steps in Mississippi.

The Delta is a fertile rural floodplain in the northwest corner
of the state. Cotton and railroads opened it up in the nineteenth
century. Today its economy is driven by catfish, soybeans, and rice
as well as cotton. In 1950 there were a hundred and ten thousand
agricultural jobs in the Delta; by 1980 there were only seventeen
thousand. Today the Delta is mostly small strapped towns and villages. The Delta's poverty rate is triple the national rate. Greenville, with a population of forty-five thousand, is its largest city
and a two-hour drive from Jackson, a Mississippi metropolis with
its population of two hundred thousand.

When the movie *Mississippi Burning* was released in 1988, Ron
Baily, then a history professor at the University of Mississippi, decided that he was going to do a workshop around the film and invited movement people down. It was at this gathering, which in
many ways was a protest over how movement history is presented,
that I reconnected with Dave Dennis after being out of touch with
him for more than two decades. At this time I was also traveling to
Chicago, Cleveland, and Atlanta; their school systems were consulting with me about middle school math as a result of an out-of-
court settlement between the EEOC and the Ford Motor Company requiring that some $10 million be spent looking for ways to
increase the pool of Black engineers. At this point history inter-
vened again in Atlanta, where apart from my consulting we were

also trying to begin developing an Algebra Project. There I reestablished contact with the Southern Regional Council (SRC), an organization set up over eighty years ago to tackle issues of race and democracy in the South. It had administered the Voter Education Project money we received in the 1960s. Although the voting drives had long ended, the SRC had continued its involvement in the Delta, spending almost half its annual budget in this most impoverished section of Mississippi trying to tackle issues of political and economic access. Assisting schools had become an important part of its work and it was interested in what the Algebra Project might offer.

During that two-week training of teachers from Louisville, San Diego, and Milwaukee in Atlanta, which had so interested Bill Crombie, SRC executive director Steve Suitts contacted me and asked me to conduct an Algebra Project workshop for his staff. They were impressed, and when not long after that session they received Ford Foundation money to research "appropriate" education projects in Black belt areas of the South, they asked us to do the research in the Mississippi Delta. Steve also decided to help us put through a separate proposal to the SRC to begin a pilot program of the Algebra Project in the Delta. By early 1990 we actually had the money in hand and I turned to Dave, with whom I had been maintaining a dialogue since our 1989 poolside conversations in Mississippi, and asked him if he would lead the organizing of that program. A historical moment had brought us together in the 1960s, and now that we had gotten back in touch with each other again some force larger than the two of us seemed determined that we should stay connected. Around this time the civil rights museum in Memphis had its grand opening and both Dave and I went there together as invitees. And when we left Memphis I accompanied him back to Lafayette, Louisiana, where he was still living and practicing law.

By this time a pretty clear idea had taken shape in my mind: *we have a tool here for organizing*—math is a tool for organizing around the issue of access in the economic arena. We were already working in Chicago with school reformers and community organizing groups who were looking at education as an organizing tool. Charles Payne, the historian, now on our board, invited me to come in. So, with the SRC's interest and my own interest, I began thinking about how to go about doing this in Mississippi. One thing that my experience has made clear is that doing anything would require somebody that I could really count on, and Dave came immediately to mind. Dave told me that he had just formed and incorporated a company called Positive Innovations and was thinking about doing a history of Louisiana, doing something around that with kids and schools. *The documentary piece is what I really had in mind. There are pieces of the movement story I don't want forgotten by history. With money film director Phil Alden Robinson got from Universal Studios, Bob, Phil, and I wound up researching a movement story built around McComb's 1961 student movement. (On February 27, 2000, this story premiered on television as a film called* Freedom Song *starring Danny Glover.) We set up the Mississippi Community Foundation with a board of movement people and began meetings and interviews with local folks in southwest Mississippi—really acting as consultants for the film. At the same time, Bob was still talking to me about the Algebra Project and I was beginning to listen more.* I suggested that Dave go up to Chicago and participate in a training session we were conducting there before making a final decision about staying on to do Algebra Project work with us in Mississippi. I think he was shocked by what he saw in the Chicago schools he visited and it was another shove that pushed him toward committing to our work. *Nobody seemed to be learning, but just surviving. In Chicago I finally recognized the need Bob was talking about. And though I wasn't prepared to tackle Chicago I was ready to go into the Delta.*

Dave began organizing small meetings throughout the Delta in which we talked about the Algebra Project. Starting with SRC contacts, Dave slowly organized a group, at this point mostly administrators, superintendents from Delta counties, some teachers, and community representatives. *Everyone agrees the project or something like it is needed. A network would be a base of strength and I knew I could not operate in isolation if the Algebra Project was going to work.*

Although math teachers especially were interested in our approach, superintendents, for the most part untrained in math, had some doubts—not mathematical doubts but political ones. Both Dave and I were known in the Delta, but not as educators, and one administrator remembers there was an undercurrent of suspicion that we were coming back into Mississippi to reestablish ourselves as civil rights leaders. *"Bob Moses. Come on, what's his real intent? What's his motive?" Mostly coming from white school superintendents. And Bob never did say anything. He'd sit out there as we [administrators] argued, and wait all day.* The attitude of administrators was going to lead to some difficulties down the road, but at this point we were paying for everything and administrators like county school superintendents were eager for any help they could get. As with voter registration almost four decades before, SRC efforts notwithstanding, no one was paying much attention to education needs in the Delta. For a moment we largely had the field to ourselves.

At a meeting in February 1992 attended by about eighty people, mainly from the Delta, organized and hosted by Dave and his wife, Carolyn, I introduced the concept of the project to a group gathered at Mississippi Valley State University. I told them that if they wanted the Algebra Project they would have to set up a group that was going to be responsible for implementing the project. We reached a decision to implement the project in six schools in the Mississippi and Arkansas Delta—five school districts. A planning group was organized: the Delta Algebra Project Planning and Coordinating Group. Though the Delta Algebra Project (DAP) was open to anyone in the community with a stake or interest in schools—parents or community groups—it was dominated by school administrators. Teachers were represented as well, but from the beginning relationships were strained; administrators were not comfortable with either the math or the pedagogy. Teachers were hardly going to buck their more dubious superiors even when they agreed with us. In any case, the form of the meetings DAP was conducting did not allow for this kind of challenge. But it was a starting point. Later that year Dave and his family moved from Lafayette to Jackson. *I was really in this project because of Bob. I was still growing into it. I'm saying, "This sounds right, it looks right, but let me see."*

Our philosophy called for grassroots involvement and developing it was at once easy and very difficult. The education system operates very much in a top-down way. Local folks at the grassroots did not see themselves involved in decision making about math education. Moreover, there is an institutional assumption that filters into the consciousness of local people, that kids are unable to do this work, will fail to gain the kind of math literacy we aim for. Perhaps a few can, the system says, but not everyone. Dave and I could not help but see parallels with the 1960s when voting was considered "white folks' business" by many. Dave especially heard echoes of what we used to hear "back in the day." *People would talk in 1990 about opening the door for the future but they weren't saying "we can do this." They didn't think they were educated enough. They thought math was for some special group of people. I began to realize that we had to change the culture that breeds this attitude about education in the community.* That's the difficult part. On the other hand, across the Delta there were teachers committed to finding a better way for their students, waiting—like trees, as the old song goes, "planted by the water."

Initial contacts in the Delta provided by the Southern Regional Council led us to the campus of Mississippi Valley State University. And there we met, and involved, Constance Bland. After getting a master's degree in computer science with a minor in math, the Clarksdale, Mississippi, native and mother of two began teaching at the university. How she became involved is illustrative of teacher involvement wherever the Algebra Project has begun work. *I was kind of curious and I started going to meetings. Still, I wasn't committed. I hadn't seen a curriculum. I liked the idea of math based on a student's experience and I also wanted to meet teachers in the system. After all, my kids were going to get to the sixth grade one day. It wasn't until I was well into a training session and realized how intuitive answers to math questions became with the Algebra Project approach—thinking about answering a question rather than doing arithmetic—that it really began to sink in just how valuable this project was or could be.*

In the Delta, teachers became a crucial driving force for the project, in some ways our first organizers. Some, after initial reluctance, found themselves committing to our program to their own surprise. Shirley Connor, a mother of three and a math teacher for twenty-four years at Simmons High School in Hollandale, Mississippi, first met with Dave and me at a small workshop we held at her school early in 1992. Almost immediately she threw a question at me: "Where's the book? Give me the book?" *I didn't know anything about the project and it was just another workshop to me. I was sure there had to be some kind of book and thought if Bob would just give it to me I could study it, get what I needed from it, and find some more useful way to spend my time. I didn't understand him when he said he didn't have a book for me. Bob said, "No book." I said, "Forget it."* But others above her had some say-so too. Shortly afterward, the school principal made Shirley coordinator of the Algebra Project in Hollandale without telling her. *A girlfriend told me about the appointment. I cornered my principal and said it would be nice if you ask people if they want to do things and not just tell them. "I don't like that!" I said. He said, "Well, we picked the best person for the job." I said, "I don't want to hear it," and walked away, heading out of the office. The superintendent of schools was coming through the door. He stopped me and told me the same thing. "You're the best. You have a master's degree in math. You know more about it than anyone else." And so I started going to Dave's meetings, getting involved, and in the end looking forward to the training. I've been with the project ever since.*

Shirley became key and presently is a primary leader in the development of teacher development programs in the Southern Initiative of the Algebra Project and she was essential as we wrestled with working out an effective way to get the Algebra Project rooted in Mississippi. In the Delta we faced some issues that didn't come up in an urban area like Cambridge. For instance, how would we provide support in a network of widely scattered towns and villages? How would teachers and kids take trips when buses were difficult to find and secure and the distances too far for walking? Like Constance Bland, Shirley credits as a primary reason for her attraction to the Algebra Project its use of experience. *The project modeled for me the process of letting students learn from their own experience.*

Getting back into the Delta also brought race to the fore in a more visceral way than it had in Cambridge. Although a majority of the students in Delta public school systems are Black, a majority of the teachers are white. One of the biggest problems we had was getting Black teachers to speak up. At our first two-week training in Greenwood, white teachers sat at tables together and Black teachers sat together at others. Finally one day, Cleeta Ryles, an Algebra Project facilitator from Chicago, proclaimed, "I'll change this," and, accompanied by a professor from Northeastern, sat at a table with white teachers. At the barbecue that ended the session, white and black teachers were comfortably sharing space under magnolia and live oak trees.

During the 1992–93 school year Dave and I continued holding community meetings modeled on the meetings we used to have in the sixties. In Sunflower County, a county once among the most hostile to civil rights, we found significant support for our efforts in another teacher, Thelma McGee, who was teaching mathematics at Meritt Middle School in Indianola. *Bob did his presentation and I was very, very impressed. So impressed that I came back and I did a workshop with the math department and shared the ideas and sold them on the idea of trying this because we hadn't had anything else really work with our students. In Mississippi, the bottom line is test scores. If your test scores aren't up, you're on probation, you're in trouble. That following summer I went through a two-week training, and in September implemented the Algebra Project. The students were excited because it was the first time they were not demanded to sit in straight rows "with your faces facing me, no talking." You know, the way we've always taught. I came in with a "new" concept. "Okay, you don't have to sit in your chairs. I want you to all get into groups." If you have to get on the floor, get on the floor. Truly, they were excited about it. But, the bottom line is that the very first year, the math scores were stable. We didn't lose any ground in Indianola in math scores. But the amazing thing is that in reading the test scores went up because they were doing reading and writing in math. The following year they both continued to go up. Other teachers who were not*

Algebra Project teachers began to come by the classroom to see what was going on. They liked the idea of cooperative learning, so they started to implement that in their classrooms and began to look at some of the techniques that we were using. The whole school was excited.

Shirley and Thelma are good examples of how teachers as well as students change. In the beginning neither said much at meetings or questioned much, especially if there were whites or administrators present. But one-on-one, in working groups with parents and the kids, they were excellent. Shirley especially has blossomed with her involvement in the Algebra Project. Dave kept putting her in situations where she could not be silent. He made her facilitate meetings—threw her in the water, so to speak. Dave believes that's a good way to teach people to swim if you have confidence that they can, and are prepared to make sure they don't sink. Thelma, really speaking for the both of them, recalled learning how to swim recently. *I remember during a training session right when I was beginning I asked a question of a group of teachers. There were two very different opinions within the group and it really got out of hand. I was trying to get them to see the math in it. I wanted both the groups to see the math. I guess because I taught math it was so easy for me to see. I was really, really frustrated because I felt they should have been able to see that right off the bat. I don't even remember what it was now. It got to be a one-on-one thing between one person here and one person here. You looked around at the other groups, and they had shut down. I was really angry at myself because the words couldn't, wouldn't come to me—you know—how to handle this, how to pull them back together. That I had allowed it to go on too long and to get too out of hand. Too heated. I think it was Jessie Cooper from New Orleans who said, "Oh what the heck, it was the end of the day and they were just tired or frustrated anyway," that it could have happened to anybody. But it didn't. It happened to me. I was thinking that evening, that night, What can I do to bring them back together? I talked with Jessie. And that next morning when we started off I sort of summarized the things that we had gone over, that we had talked about, and brought them up to where we had left off. I gave them a different way to look at it and then somebody said, "You know, you're right, this will work;*

I can see this now." Then the other person in the other group said, "Yes, I can see it too." I could feel my face lighting up.

By the spring of 1993 more than 125 educators and community organizers from around the country gathered at Delta State University in Cleveland, Mississippi—Amzie Moore's hometown, and I wished he could have been there to see this. It was our first national conference. And frankly, no one believed that such a conference could be successful in a place like Cleveland, where the nearest airport is in Memphis, Tennessee. We were meeting to share ideas, concerns, and goals for the Algebra Project. Also attending this meeting were about two hundred Mississippi middle school students who gathered to talk about what they had been learning using Algebra Project methods over the school year. As this conference wrestled with difficult issues—curriculum and teacher training, the role of the national office and national organization, the purpose of community organizing, civil rights and education—it raised as many questions as it answered. But that has always been a quality of the Algebra Project. Answers are finally found in the work.

I was at this point visiting the Meritt Middle School in Indianola twice a week to work with sixth and seventh graders in the classroom. Some afternoons students bused in for workshops from as far away as West Tallahatchie County. Thelma McGee had a key to Meritt Middle School and kept it open. *We had busloads of people by 1994—kids coming from Shelby. We had a busload of kids coming from Hollandale. We had kids coming from West Tallahatchie. Bob and his son Taba were teaching the games. And parents were coming out. They were very supportive.*

We are beginning to see what is possible. The efforts of teachers as well as project staff take place both inside and outside of the classroom. Where student, parent, community, teachers, and school administration have come together as in West Tallahatchie County, Mississippi, progress can be dramatic. In that county 94 percent of the students are African American and 96 percent receive free or reduced lunch. In 1995, a year after we began working there, district students taking the standardized Algebra 1, U.S. history, and functional literacy tests for the first time reached and/ or surpassed state benchmarks. In 1998, the district was removed from the state's Department of Education list of probationary schools. Change is reflected in more than test scores, say teachers like Harvey Smith. *Before the Algebra Project, there was little communication or association among the teachers, especially from school to school. The AP has brought us together as a team. There is no more "us and them," just all of us for the students.*

But teacher interest and community excitement notwithstanding, we still had the cautious attitude of school system administrators to deal with. The sort of freedom that excited the students and teachers like Shirley and Thelma made some school officials uncomfortable. And under pressure from state authorities to bring up test scores, they were not inclined toward "experiments." Nor was the idea of empowerment in the classroom for teachers and students eagerly embraced. Adding to their discomfort, parental involvement meant questions in a system that traditionally did not welcome questions. As Hollandale school superintendent Harold Sanders remembers: *When we first considered the Algebra Project we thought it was going to be practical math. Once we got in and began to find out with the training more about Bob's ideas, some of the superintendents began to wonder whether or not it was going to be a 1990s civil rights issue or whether it was going to be about teaching children algebra. We did not have mathematicians in our group and we wanted something that was going to deal on day one with algebra—algebra content. Bob was trying to build up that fifth and sixth grader by using things that were relevant to him like the railroad track—everyday activities. The transition curriculum is not organized the way your standard math book is.*

Sunflower County also illustrates how quickly the ground can shift beneath your feet. At the start of the 1990s a local movement in Indianola put a Black superintendent in charge of the school system; he was the city's first. Railroad tracks divide Indianola. North of the tracks there is a predominately white public elementary school with a white principal. Debbie Murphy, a teacher who had undergone Algebra Project training, taught there. South of the tracks the elementary school is Black with a Black principal. Thelma McGee taught there. There was a "transition" school for seventh and eighth graders that we thought would receive students from both schools. Then the superintendent, who had gained his office in part through local protests and organizing, and who was instrumental in bringing in the Algebra Project, was transferred. I had been hoping to follow students from Debbie's and Thelma's classes to the transition school. This was where we'll really be able to do something, I thought. But there was no interest from the central school administration now. The transition school was scheduled to be made into a public technical school, freeing whites from the burden of the cost of private "academies" while opening its doors to middle-class Blacks as well. It felt as if the Algebra Project and I were now unwanted and unwelcome.

I had worried about the need to bring the community into what had traditionally been the preserve of school administrators but the burden of wrestling with this fell on Dave's shoulders. He was organizing. My involvement with the Delta had pretty much been confined to the classroom. Dave and I discussed the superintendents' conflict of interest and we recognized that because the school system was *theirs,* any real deep and forceful criticism of the system reflected on them. As Dave recalled of Shirley Connor recently: *Once after Shirley spoke at a meeting a superintendent walked up and told her, "If you were working in my school district, I'd fire you now."* We needed a body with some autonomy from the system. Dave began reconsidering his approach. *By late 1994, DAP stopped inviting Bob and myself to its meetings. Parents and other community folks stopped attending DAP meetings too and it was pretty much an organization of school system administrators. The final insult came when they hired this white guy to administer the organization, skipping over trained and capable teachers like Constance or Shirley, or Debbie or Thelma. He knew nothing about the Algebra Project; I mean, this guy wouldn't have known the Algebra Project if it walked up and kicked him. It was back to the drawing board. The key, I knew now, was to keep the kids in focus. Organize around them. Organize teachers, parents, and other community folk around student needs. Of course you have to figure out what those needs are. And you can't do that unless the young people have a voice and you are willing to listen. After that I began to involve the youth in all aspects of decision making. All community meetings had to have young people at the table. They not only became participants in the meetings but also became the key to organizing and facilitating community meetings and in some areas became part of the decision-making process. They began to attend school board meetings and organize after-school programs with support from parents and a cross section of the community. They were beginning to demand that the community see and hear them.* Experience helped teach. Dave kept getting burned by trying to operate at a level that is akin to other established groups like university coalitions, the Southern Regional Council or Department of Education coalitions, where you are trying to, as positive innovations, negotiate and hold people like that accountable to what they say they are going to do. In the end, however, you have no power. The power that we have is with our target population—the kids and their parents—and unless that is organized, it's voiceless.

The importance of this became clear in the summer of 1995. With the help of Southern Echo, a community organization founded by SNCC veteran Hollis Watkins, a math games league had been developed in Indianola. At tournaments students competed in games built around factoring numbers, writing equations, and other calculations. Parents participated as scorekeepers. In August the league was told by the superintendent of schools that it could no longer use the middle school without his permission. Letters were written and ignored. But when parents got the backing of the local steelworkers union, the superintendent backed down. Recognizing their power, parents now pressed him on why science labs were not available at the middle school.

For a time I did a lot of the initial organizing as we spread across the north. When the southern opportunity opened up I really had no inclination and didn't think that I could continue to do that work and increasingly got out of organizing work at the site level. Dave Dennis has picked up that entire burden. I have over the years stayed focused—and gratefully so—on what we are going to teach and how we are going to teach it. It is an area that has remained neglected, especially at the high school level. Teachers don't have a strong math background and mathematicians don't know what to do with their math skills when it comes to teaching young people. By 1995 I was tinkering with clusters of math concepts. One cluster, visible in the first book of our transition curriculum, deals with addition and subtraction and related concepts. We're still working on multiplication and division and the concepts related to them. Part of what we are trying to do is lay out concepts that assist the transition from arithmetic into higher forms of mathematics.

Constance, Shirley, Thelma, Debbie, and Ann Braswell, from Greenwood, went to Nantucket, Massachusetts, for two weeks of training with Jim Burroughs two months after the Cleveland conference. A core group of teacher/organizers was starting to emerge. And they too challenged themselves as well as the system, and bonded. Dave well remembers how trying to select who would go to the Nantucket conference made that clear. *In the summer of 1993 the national office of the Algebra Project sent down Jim Burroughs to interview five of our key teachers with the idea of selecting two of them for teacher training in Massachusetts. Shirley, Thelma, and Constance were among the five, and two white teachers, Debbie Murphy from Indianola and Ann Braswell from Greenwood. Who is this Jim Burroughs? they wanted to know. Why are we being interviewed? I couldn't give them good answers because beyond selecting a couple of teachers, the purpose of the interview wasn't very clear to me either. I hardly knew Jim myself. How could someone not familiar with our "culture" and needs down here come down, interview us, and claim to be doing any sort of meaningful analysis? the teachers asked. What kind of decision making was this? A couple of teachers would be selected for training; the others would not. It wasn't as if the teachers themselves were making that decision; the decision was in Jim Burroughs's hands and they did not like it.*

They pressed this issue with Bob and myself, pointing out that a couple of them had not taken summer jobs as they usually did in order to work with the Algebra Project. We tried to explain that the decision on who would go to the training was up to Jim. The teachers went into a back room to hold a discussion among themselves. They came back out and told us they had decided that if they all couldn't go, no one would go. I could have jumped up and kissed them.

Almost immediately upon returning these teachers began working with me at a two-week training of teachers in the Delta and then went to Jackson to begin training small groups of teachers there. One of the teachers attending that first Jackson training was Lynn Moss, a young teacher of Lebanese background who had come to Jackson in 1991 "almost burned out" after teaching amid corruption and lack of services in her hometown of Laurel, Mississippi. Middle school reform had been the talk in Jackson but it was slow in occurring. Tearfully, Lynn told Ken Acton, her principal at Brinkley Middle School, that she was going to flee the frustrations of teaching for an office job in the state's Department of Education. But a colleague, Victoria Byrd, had encountered the Algebra Project in California and had been pressing Acton to bring it into Brinkley. He was eager to keep Lynn and sent her to one of our pretraining orientation sessions at Northwestern Middle School. *And all I remember is Dave Dennis getting up and being so . . . fiery. He was talking about how we were not educating our Black children. I remember him asking, "Who do you think the jails are being built for?" He talked about how we had closed the door for our Black students to take algebra. Then Bob got up and in his quiet way began to talk about the project. I was just blown away. I think their advocacy triggered my interest. I was a longtime advocate of education. When I first started teaching in 1975 we did not have a school lunch program. We did not have kindergartens. We did not have a compulsory education law. All the basic things most states had, we did not have in place until about 1982 with education reform, and we had fought long and hard for that. Listening to Dave I thought, My God! That man is just like I am! When I got back to school I said I definitely wanted the training.*

Lynn and her colleague Victoria Byrd began working with young people like James, then a sixth grader in her class. To James and most of the kids, suddenly math seemed like something to enjoy; they hardly realized they were learning. *I remember the trip. It was a day out of school, something fun to do.* That trip, which included stops at civil rights sites, generated excitement among the teachers first, and more dramatically than in Cambridge you could see how they connected it to teaching the kids. *We traveled in three buses— we had a huge group of kids. One teacher's daddy was the coach at Ole Miss when James Meredith was trying to get in and when we walked into the civil rights room of the [state] capitol they were running black-and-white newsreels from then. There was a car on fire in one of them and this teacher said, "That's my car! That's my family's car! That's what hap-pened to my daddy's car!" She forgot that there were children there and kept saying, "I can't believe this!" Finally she called out, "Boys and girls, come here; let me tell you about this. When I was a little girl. . . ." And another teacher was a Black lady who had wanted to be involved in the movement. But she lived in this rural Mississippi county and her grandad kept saying, "Why do you want to do that?" And she remembers wanting to join the freedom riders when they came through. This all started dia-logue among us teachers and the children became engaged. They didn't have the background we had but they were picking up on our excitement and we could use both the excitement and the actual trip to explain and talk. It helped us understand the importance of cultural experience and the need to teach to the culture of the children. We [teachers] began to meet at my house, my apartment, and plan and work.*

Mississippi drives home the complexity of grappling with and changing "a system that does not lend itself to your needs." In this state, where I have been concentrating much of my energy for the last five years, it has been a seesaw struggle every year. Frequently, the system works to dampen demand or, if possible, to cut it out. In 1997 when some 120 seventh-grade students we were working with at Brinkley Middle School sought to take Algebra 1 as eighth graders, the school administration said it was going to limit Alge-bra 1 to two classes, which of course effectively eliminated more than half of our kids. I questioned this and that resulted in a large meeting at the school. The kids came to it with their parents and when it was my turn to speak I asked all the kids to move to the front. I had decided to speak directly to them. "I can't make you take algebra," I began. "But this is why we want you to. Algebra opens the door to college preparation. You may not go to college but if you don't go it should not be because you haven't prepared yourself to go. Society is already prepared to write you off the way sharecroppers up in the Delta have been written off. They say you don't want to learn. You can change that and *you* have to decide whether or not *you* want to do it. I can't do that for you." I talked to them about the computer, and what it means—the issue it raises about literacy and being able to gain access to jobs.

After this meeting instead of having two classes we got five. The kids were given a sign-up sheet with the understanding that any kid who requested algebra could take it. But then a few days later some of the math teachers said to the kids, "We want you to take a test and after you take the test, decide again whether or not you think you should take algebra." And some kids decided against taking algebra, or perhaps their parents decided for them. We lost two classes. In the end we got three classes, one more than the original two but fewer than there could have been before interest was targeted for reduction.

I was deeply disappointed but the issue of demand was taking clearer shape in my mind. We need the young people and the students to make a demand and then follow up the further issue of getting teachers and administrators to translate this demand up into a policy change so they can't or don't dampen the demand and so protect some perception—whatever the rationale is—about what is "best" for the kids. Because they do not say that what they are doing is going to hurt the kids, instead they say what is at play is their understanding of where the kids are at and what might be best for them.

We saw something like this in New York when we first went into that city. The superintendent asked, "Is there a demand for the Algebra Project?" Our people said, "Let's try and see what the demand is." They organized workshops and the superintendent wrote letters to all of his fifth graders and their parents inviting them to these workshops. By the time he got a couple of hundred responses, he said, "I've got too many letters; I can't meet this demand." And he stopped the process instead of trying to translate the demand into the next step by saying, "Look, I've got a thousand parents here who want their kids to take algebra and what I need are more resources and people to accommodate the demand." And all those community folk who were just getting started with the Algebra Project didn't know how to leverage their demand to create more demand, how to effectively mobilize the community and get people out to meetings exerting pressure. So the demand collapsed. Even in Mississippi there were several instances when the system came down on Dave and his operation when he thought he was at the table and actually they were just waiting to yank the chair away as he started to sit down.

So what we are on in some senses is a learning curve. If we are going to be successful in the broadest sense there is an organizing job out here, because the only ones who can really demand the kind of education they need and the kind of changes needed to get it are the students, their parents, and their community, which largely remains silent on issues like this. It was what we saw as Brinkley eighth graders demanded algebra and brought their parents into the discussion. We, as their advocates, do not have the kind of traditional power base from which to advocate to the people who hold power to force them to respond and change their ways to accommodate this demand. This is similar to what happened to the MFDP. They went up to Atlantic City and the system reacted to their demand just as at Brinkley the system responded. In both cases the system does not meet all of your demands but gives you something if only to keep you quiet. It is never everything that you want. And then you've got to decide what you are going to do in response. We are beginning to see this capacity to respond emerge in other areas of the South where we are working.

Weldon, North Carolina

The Spirit of Ella Baker

> In . . . the period of struggling to be accepted, there were certain goals, concepts, and values such as the drive for the "Talented Tenth." That, of course, was the concept that proposed that through the process of education black people would be accepted in the American culture and they would be accorded their rights in proportion to the degree to which they qualified as being persons of learning and culture. . . .
>
> [There was] an assumption that those who were trained were not trained to be part of the community, but to be *leaders* of the community. This carried with it another false assumption that being a leader meant you were separate and apart from the masses, and to a large extent people were to look up to you, and that your responsibility to the people was to *represent* them. This means that the people were never given a sense of their own values.
>
> Ella Baker, 1969

> Now why is it that children at a young age have all this WHY? Then when they get older, they don't have any WHYs? What happened? What are the schools doing to get rid of the WHY? If you take away the WHY, then there is no potential.
>
> Valerie Whitaker, teacher, Weldon Middle School

Weldon, North Carolina, is a rural town located in the Roanoke River Valley in the northeastern corner of the state. As a child Ella Baker lived nearby in the neighboring town of Littleton after moving there from the rough port city of Norfolk, Virginia, where she was born. Miss Baker's mother pushed for the move. She wanted to go back to her family's homestead in North Carolina, where she felt life was more "cultured" than in Norfolk. The river made the land in this valley rich, and hardworking independent Black farmers were among those who worked it—strong people like Miss Baker's grandfather, who paid his former master five dollars an acre for land on the plantation where he was once enslaved. From early in this century until the 1950s Weldon thrived and there were busy stores and shops on its streets. The Seaboard and Atlantic Railroad stopped there picking up peanuts and cotton grown in surrounding farmland. Today, however, there's hardly any traffic on the streets of the town's business district; many storefronts are vacant. Businesses have moved across Interstate 85 to the city of Roanoke Rapids. The train depot has shut down. So has the bus station and the town's two movie theaters.

There are a little over a thousand students in the Weldon City School District. Ninety-eight percent of them are African American. Almost half of these kids are being raised in single-parent homes and almost two thirds receive Aid for Dependent Children (AFDC). Poverty of income and education has defined the town for half a century now. Although 74 percent of the mothers are working, per capita income is only $12,650. In 1994 Weldon ranked at the very bottom of North Carolina's 119 school systems.

In rural systems like this, under the best of circumstances, it is difficult to keep teachers. The pay is low and amenities are few. It is easy to feel lost and forgotten in what seems to be, and often is, an educational backwater. Consequently, teacher turnover is high in places like Weldon. There is an especially high turnover of math teachers, with schools everywhere short of them, in urban areas as well as rural areas.

Increasingly, scores on standardized tests have become the barometers by which schools are judged. In the fall of 1995 North Carolina began implementing a new standard course of study and a new accountability model, what is called "ABC"—Accountability, Basics, and Community Involvement—which set goals in the core areas of math, science, social studies, and language arts. Schools were to be judged by end-of-grade standardized tests. If a school fell below a certain level—the fiftieth percentile—the state was empowered to parachute in "assistance teams," state Board of Education people with powers that superseded the local school administration. In 1997 a state team arrived in Weldon. The middle school was in transition. For years Weldon's middle school grades had been split between three different schools. In 1992 it was proposed that both the sixth and seventh grades move to Weldon High School, where the eighth grade was already located, giving these students access to the gym, the library, and computers. This triggered much argument. Teachers at the high school did not want to give up space. Parents were afraid of the influence of older students on younger students. The students themselves were upset at all the uncertainty.

In January 1996 the move was finally made and Weldon Middle School was officially established. Lydia Harding Elder was named the new principal and almost immediately the state told her that Weldon's middle school grades were under scrutiny. With state assistance she was expected to pull the school up to satisfaction by the following year or the school would be removed from local control. As an assistant principal before becoming principal, Miss Elder had worked hard from the start to gain parental support and involvement in the new middle school . . . *and when the assistance team came in, parents were very paranoid, they were feeling very uncomfortable, and the word was out—it was a state "takeover." The team was focused on getting the kids to [state] standards. They don't understand that there are just some things that have to take place when you are in a community like ours and community involvement is a major piece. That has to be nourished. By the time we were ready to get what the state said they wanted together, they were here.* Such pressure, where teachers and schools are rated on how their students perform on standard tests, makes them reluctant to do anything that in their minds is not related to the official North Carolina course of study. And here we were, just arrived in Weldon the year before with our Algebra Project ways.

A number of things were converging to help generate an atmosphere open to change and experiment. In addition to Lydia Harding's dynamic principalship, a new and committed superintendent of schools—Dr. Jerry Congleton—had come in. Community involvement in schools was growing. The father of one of the project's most active students, Ernest Banks, was assistant superintendent. A strong youth group based primarily in the sixth and seventh grades was emerging. And there was Valerie.

An interested teacher who becomes committed is almost always an important starting point. So it was in Weldon. It is impossible to talk about our work there without talking about Valerie Whitaker. We do not have a way of predicting the emergence of these dynamic teachers: Shirley Connor of Hollandale, Jessie Cooper out of New Orleans, Lynne Godfrey in Cambridge, and others, except to note as was true in the sixties, such leadership emerges with the movement that emerges. Valerie was interested in us before we even arrived. As a sixth-grade teacher at Weldon Middle School she liked keeping abreast of what was new. So one day early in 1993 while she was perusing some professional literature while at the library, an article on the Algebra Project caught her eye. *This sounds really good, I thought. I saved the article and told myself, "If I ever see anything about the Algebra Project around here I'm going to sign up for it." Well, about two years later, Deborah Lanham, the assistant superintendent of schools, asked me about the project. There was going to be a training session held at the Holiday Inn on the edge of town as part of the Roanoke River Valley Consortium. This was something I wanted to be in! Some of the other teachers were kind of cautious. They kept waiting to do the "X" "Y" or the "X to the 3rd power, minus 3 to the 2nd power, the square root . . ." Some were like, "My kids will not be able to do this. I can't get them calm enough to do this cooperative learning stuff." Me, I'd been dreaming about doing this. It changed my perspective from doing math to understanding math.*

The Roanoke River Consortium, which had put together this training, consisted of five school districts in the Roanoke River Valley. The Z. Smith Reynolds Foundation had funded a proposal by Dr. Doris Williams, then director of the Office of School Services at North Carolina Central University, to implement the Algebra Project in Durham and the five consortium school districts. Doris was also chairing the board of education in Warren County, one of the consortium school systems. *My job here at the university was to do partnerships between the university and low-performing school systems. And I said, "Aha! Here's my opportunity."*

Right away, however, despite initial enthusiasm for our project, we faced an issue that continues to surface and is arguably one of the largest roadblocks to getting the project off the ground in many places: alignment. Your program sounds fine, administrators of school systems say, but we have expectations of what our students are to learn in any given semester or year. "Show us how your program gets them there; we can't see it in your material. It does not seem to cover all the objectives we have in the standard course of study." What is meant from this point of view is if the standard course says "include fractions," you should be able to go to a textbook and find a chapter on fractions. Or if the standard course of study says "include some probability," there needs to be a chapter or section of a chapter in the textbook that says "this is probability." As soon as we got started teachers in particular pointed out that in our curriculum there is nothing that says "now we are going to discuss fractions." Even our table of contents does not say "this chapter discusses this particular topic." "Your stuff is nice but we have to cover all of this basic material," teachers told us. "We have to make sure we've got this material covered before the end-of-grade tests and we don't see this in your AP book." Indeed, the AP curriculum is an integrated curriculum. A particular chapter will cover several different topics. Somehow we had to convince teachers and administrators that every objective in the standard course of study is covered in the AP curriculum. Dave tackled this problem by drawing on *regional* resources he had organized through the Southern Initiative. The key people who worked through this model of alignment were Maisha, Sharon Spencer, Laura Smith, Nancy Ledford, and Valerie Whitaker. This process actually began in Warren County and was completed in the teacher training in Roanoke Rapids, North Carolina, in

1996. This was based on a process first developed by Bill Crombie and teachers from Marlboro County, South Carolina, under the leadership of Julia Cain and Nancy Ledford in 1994–95.

We began meeting with teachers monthly after classes, bringing with us both *The North Carolina Standard Course of Study List of Objectives—Goals and Objectives* and the AP curriculum. Dr. Laura Smith from North Carolina Central took the lead in this effort. *We worked through our curriculum with them. If the students are supposed to learn how to divide and have remainders, then we could show how our "winding game," which is based on the Chinese zodiac and a base-12 system, is used. There are twelve signs in the zodiac. For playing the winding game there are twelve chairs, twelve spots. They are placed in a circle. The individual player will walk around them a given number of times. Each time is a multiple of twelve. Then that player will walk a predetermined number of chairs beyond a set multiple. For instance, if that player walks seven chairs beyond, if the player circles those chairs three times and then walks to seven more chairs, then that is thirty-six plus seven, which is forty-three. Now, everybody watching will say, okay, the player walked past thirty-six chairs and then seven more so he walked past forty-three chairs. Each time he wound those chairs—made a winding around those chairs—that was twelve chairs. So twelve into forty-three will go three times with a remainder of seven. We could tell the teachers, "Okay, so this is division, division with remainders. If you want to you can incorporate decimals here—instead of saying, 'Remainder seven,' you can go ahead and use decimals. So now, you're covering division, you're covering some form of decimals." We use units in our book, so on the state objectives list we literally wrote in Unit so-and-so, say, Unit two beside whatever the objective was. Usually that would be more than one place in our curriculum. Each objective in the North Carolina course of study could have many units and lessons from the AP curriculum. When we were finished they were able to see that every objective in the North Carolina curriculum was really covered. There might have been one or two gaps but then we wrote extensions to cover those that were not covered.* Of course Laura Smith didn't do this all by herself. Sharon Spencer, also of North Carolina Central, joined her in the effort. And my daughter Maisha was involved as well as teachers from Marlboro County, South

Carolina, where we had begun working before starting in North Carolina. This project within the project was being worked through with teachers because it was the teachers who had to see the relationship of our curriculum to the state objectives they were obligated to meet. We did not want to just tell them, "This is what you do." They had to have ownership of the process, be in possession of it in their own minds, so they could believe it could be done if we were to go any further in North Carolina.

They saw the correlation. But were they convinced to take a chance with us? No, for in addition to end-of-grade tests there are nine-week tests. At the end of each reporting period students take a cumulative test on what they've learned during that period. What they are supposed to be taught is mandated by the state too. So now, teachers said, "We've got to concentrate on integers here. We can't go on to decimals and probabilities." Priorities were being structured by a tight time frame with little give. And even though the transition curriculum covered everything the state required over the year, the short-term timing was wrong. Most of the consortium tried to finesse us in response to this pressure. Our visiting schedule had been set up at the beginning of the year. Teachers knew when we would arrive. We discovered that on the days we were scheduled to come to their classrooms they would do the Algebra Project curriculum on that day. They would prepare the students the day before. Then, after we left, they would go back to their textbooks.

In Warren County, for instance, next door to Halifax County where Weldon is located, we did the alignment and visited the county for two years. The teachers were not implementing the curriculum. Every time we went there we were confronted with a new set of complaints why they could not implement the Algebra Project. Finally Dave said he'd had enough and pulled out of the classroom. *The reason that I decided to pull out was because the teachers refused to do the project although the school district had embraced the project. The school district was confronted with the choice of either strongly reprimanding or firing the teachers. But if they fired the teachers, or the teachers quit in anger, the district would not have had any teachers to replace them. This is a problem throughout rural areas, where it is always difficult to find and keep teachers. What was underlying the resistance to us was fear. The middle school teachers were having a difficult time with the math content and the technology. The district had purchased graphing calculators; the teachers refused to use them. They were in closets along with our curriculum.* After school work still goes on but our curriculum is not being used in the classroom. (When writer Charlie Cobb walked into one Warren County Middle School classroom, unused Algebra Project transition curriculum books were still sitting in boxes in a closet. "I really think the program is fine," the teacher told him, "but with the kind of pressure we have on us, my classes and my students need more structure and discipline. We just can't have all that back and forth in here and get anything done.") Of Warren County teachers, says school board chair Doris Williams, *It became really clear that they were seeing the Algebra Project curriculum and the standard course of study curriculum as two separate curricula, and they were not willing to do both. And if they had to choose, they were going to go for the standard course of study.* It's a kind of fear, Valerie says, deeply embedded in the system. *They feel like, "If I do something different, it may not work." And "I have seen some success with the traditional way, so I'm going to stay on this traditional path and maybe I'll see some more."* Yet whatever answers I do not have about what to do, I know that if we're talking about getting math literacy to all instead of an elite that catches on right away, what we have been doing traditionally is not working. In Weldon, though, we have begun to find a way that works.

I think several factors came into play enabling the AP to sink roots in Weldon. And this is where the real lessons are, not in the obstacles we have yet to overcome. There was Valerie, of course. And there was also a school administration led by a new superintendent, Jerry Congleton, that was willing to stick with us. The system provided "release time" enabling teachers like Valerie to undergo training and participate in workshops. And importantly, there was the community itself. Doris makes the point that Weldon has about a third of the schoolkids that Warrenton does so, *in Weldon there seems to be much more hunger for help to overcome the prob-*

lems they have in that community. Almost everybody coming to help is welcomed with open arms. For a long time there had been tension and bad feeling between the community and school administration, so in some ways in 1995 the project played a bridging role coming in at the same time as a new school administration. Our presence offered a nonthreatening context for administration and community to talk with each other instead of fighting with each other because students were at the center of both our concerns. Nelson Edwards, a parent and chair of our community organization, says *the superintendent would come to our meetings, the principal too. And the principal was happy because there was some kind of program trying to help, trying to help the kids. They were going to support it because of that and to my knowledge that's where cooperation really started.* There were other sources of support from the community: Miss Dora Smith prepared food for meetings; there was actually a hospitality committee. Miss Mason got on the phone to get people out to meetings. Miss Joyce Harris who has served as our youth coordinator. Almost from the beginning Melinda Clark has been planning meetings as community development facilitator. And Mr. Edwards, whose daughter Quanda has emerged as a dynamic youth leader, was especially energetic, organizing in a way that I remembered myself doing years ago. *I would go out to kids' houses and try to persuade them to come to our meetings, to get involved. And to bring one more individual with them, their neighbor, their cousin, aunt, or somebody. And the majority of people would say, "For what? You know they gonna do what they want to do anyway." I'd try to tell them that this is separate from the school system. The school system doesn't have control. But it's kinda hard to do when you have a title saying Algebra. When you say "algebra" people automatically see "school." And I don't care if you sit there and talk, they will sit there and listen but they're thinking "school system."* In 1997 the school administration even donated an old unused building for us to use as a community resource center.

Nonetheless it was hard for Valerie that first year. She split her class into two groups. One group did the trip in November, the other in December. Bad weather closed the school often. She was able to get through only the first unit of our curriculum and finally returned to the standard course of study, although she participated in the curriculum alignment work. She was by herself. There are only three middle school math teachers, one for each grade. The other two were new and not trained in the Algebra Project approach. Teachers leave. Teachers get sick. Teachers are reluctant to try something new. And what she recognized was that the kids were where the program needed to anchor itself. *You could say I'm cloning myself in them because it is difficult to maintain teachers—they get up and leave. So I'm looking at reaching through the children, getting the children committed to the project and letting them be teachers for students. Students look to each other, you know.*

Those sixth graders she started with are ninth graders now. As eighth graders their commitment was going to be a test for them and the Algebra Project.

When the 1998 school year began, twenty-two of the fifty-seven eighth graders who would be starting high school the following year thought they were ready for algebra and planned to take it. The problem was, these "rising ninth graders" who had taken a prealgebra course the year before had no algebra teacher and now found themselves in a math limbo instead. Furthermore, the school was short of algebra textbooks. Their eighth-grade math teacher, brand-new to the school, complained to Mrs. Harding Elder that there were not enough Algebra 1 books, and there was also no teacher manual. "Neither is critical," the principal replied. "Good teaching is the key; what you're teaching and how is what is important," she said in response to the teacher's complaint. You must want us to eat and sleep this job, the teacher continued with her objection, and stated that she would not do that. She also told the twenty-two students that she really didn't believe them capable of algebra. The test scores show you're not capable of doing algebra, she said to them before quitting a month later. The students were not at all unhappy when she left. It was like she had a chip on her shoulder about us, many thought. Now a substitute was brought in but the substitute returned to the prealgebra textbook. For the twenty-two desiring to take algebra this was ground they had already covered. In an effort to meet their demands another teacher was asked to take on teaching the algebra class. He didn't like it and thought that the principal, a former algebra teacher, should block out time to teach the class herself. "This is not in my job description," he declared.

The school then hired a soft-spoken young woman working at a Roanoke Rapids Radio Shack electronics store who had a chemistry degree. She had actually applied to fill an opening to teach science at the school but another kind of pressure was on the school. A standard math test for eighth graders is one of the tests the state uses to judge a school. The school *needed* a math teacher. This teacher was not a math teacher but was hired as one, and to the students appeared unsure of herself as she undoubtedly was. She whines too much, some said, and we need to learn. She can't teach it. Valerie Whitaker, a sixth-grade math teacher and involved with the Algebra Project since its start in Weldon, is more understanding of inexperience; it made this teacher timid but . . . *With these students, when you have a point you better know how to make it with them. They are not timid and like to see strength in people who are teaching them.*

By November frustrated students like fourteen-year-old Quanda Edwards were complaining aloud. *At the regular community meeting we held at the school we were saying we can't continue with this kind of confusion. We have this teacher today, this teacher tomorrow. How can we learn? But the parents were siding with the school, jumping all over our case. I remember one of them standing up and saying, "All that glitters is not gold," for whatever reason. And we were saying, "You all just don't understand how it is. If things continue like this we're not going to be ready for the algebra test in the spring."*

Dave Dennis had come over from Mississippi by then. *We had a meeting and the adults started to get on the kids, telling them things like "it takes time" and to "be patient." The kids were defiant, though; they didn't know any other way to be heard. Quanda stood up at one point and said, "I don't have time to be patient about my education." It was the first time I saw our kids standing on their own feet to make a demand for the education they wanted. We didn't prompt them. Positive Innovations hadn't organized their protest. They did. In the end we were able to reach agreement on how to deal with both the regular math and the algebra. The kids agreed to after-school and weekend study. We got Professor Laura Smith at North Carolina Central in Durham to agree to come over and work with the kids after school once or twice a week, and Freddie David drove up from Bennettsville, South Carolina, to work with them on weekends. I was seeing commitment.* By March, community meetings were centered on student issues with participants asked to come up with strategies and solutions to problems they believed were in their power to accomplish. It's not that all problems were resolved, but a collaborative approach had taken root.

This is not so much a story about algebra, although I will conclude this tale of testing in Weldon by reporting that despite having eight teachers over the year all but four of the twenty-two students who took the state's algebra 1 test scored at or above the fiftieth percentile—the state's standard for proficiency. Freddie David, whose four-hour commute from Bennettsville to Weldon to tutor three weekends every month from January to April can only be called heroic, was surprised. *Frankly, I was expecting for about half to prove proficient and hoping for 65 percent of them. It was very rewarding seeing 85 percent.* The commitment Dave talks about was at the root of this success. The principal did wind up teaching algebra. A science and math class was combined and the ninety minutes of shared time was largely devoted to math. Freddie adds community to commitment. It was hard for the kids, Freddie notes, and sometimes he even found doubt creeping into his own thinking, *and there were times when I said to myself, "I just don't see this happening." Factoring gave them a lot of trouble. And we had a lot of information to get across in a short period of time. But then they got graphing quadratic equations almost right away. Basically, these kids were hungry for learning and I think they felt they couldn't let the school or the principal, or their families or the community down on these tests. There were times when they wanted to give up; they rebelled against giving up time for things they enjoyed in order to study. They were spending three hours a day studying math in school plus studying on weekends. But finally they were determined to prove themselves. What they lacked in math skills was more than made up by being so good at critical thinking. They knew how to ask questions that would give meaningful answers.*

For all the difficulty surrounding this test it is best viewed as confirmation of three years of work, the beginning, I like to think, of establishing a culture of learning. They were demanding to learn as sharecroppers demanded the right to vote. We had teenagers committed to after-school and weekend study at the expense of their regular pleasures. And in emphasizing this I do not mean to minimize our academic success. Even the state had recognized our work. In August, a few weeks before the start of school, and the start of the teacher difficulties, the state's Board of Education had given our kids an award for moving the school from being one of the poorest in the state to an "exemplary" status. School officials like Assistant Superintendent Lanham credited the Algebra Project. *In 1994, that was the year the Algebra Project was introduced, only 34.2 percent of our students were rated as proficient in math by the state's Department of Public Education. In that first year math scores for grades three through eight increased to 42.7 percent. In 1996 they increased to 47.5 percent proficiency. And last year they increased to 54.4 percent proficiency. The state goal is for at least 50 percent of your students to be proficient. So from 1993, a year before the project began, to 1997, they've gone from 37.9 percent proficiency to 54.4 percent proficiency.*

I want to stay with this idea of community, for it is community that goes a long way in explaining the achievement of the Weldon students. But let's backtrack for a moment. The consortium that opened the door to our entrance into Weldon, the steady expansion of the Southern Initiative, and Dave's conscious effort to build regional interaction and cooperation all undergird this community. This is a southwide effort. Presently the Southern Initiative reaches into schools in five states and we have trained over five hundred teachers since our Mississippi beginnings in 1992. And we can certainly document our academic effect. West Tallahatchie County, Mississippi, has traditionally been one of the state's poorest-performing school districts. In 1993 two sixth-grade teachers, Bessie Campbell and Harvey Smith, reluctantly underwent our training. By the 1996–97 school year when ninety-one students, thirty-one of whom were Algebra Project students, took the state algebra 1 test, the district reached or surpassed state benchmarks.

We began working in Bessemer, Alabama, in the fall of 1993. The steel industry has suffered a dramatic decline and 73 percent of the students in this city just twelve miles from Birmingham receive free lunches. When Michael Russel became director of instruction in 1995 he decided to do a comparison study of the city's five elementary schools, using three of them as an experimental group and the two others as a control group. The experimental group would receive instruction using the Algebra Project pedagogy. The control group would receive traditional instruction. Mike decided that the experiment would last for three years. *One of the faults that I had found with our own school system was that we would implement a program, stay with it for about a year, and, if no results were seen in a year, it was trashed. I decided we were going to commit to something, we were going to be committed to it for a long haul, and look at the results and see how it is going.* Predominantly white West Hills, one of Bessemer's top elementary schools, was a control school. It was paired with Abrams, a school whose students come from poorer segments of the Black community. Its makeup—useful for comparison—is similar to Hart, one of the schools in the experimental group that is predominantly black with a large proportion of its students drawn from a poorer economic strata of Bessemer as well. The first year of the study Hart did about five points better than Abrams on standardized math tests. It was twenty points behind West Hills. The next year Hart stayed about in the same place, Abrams did better than usual and West Hills dropped fourteen points. By 1998, West Hills was back up to its usual range of fifty-nine points, but Hart now had the best total mathematics score in the city—sixty-two points. *Here the kids from the lowest socioeconomic group were outperforming our middle-class kids and our upper-echelon kids at our flagship school. This proved to me that I needed to put my money where my mouth was and push this program.* Mike now expects that within three years our transition curriculum will be taught, starting in the fifth grade, to all of Bessemer's elementary school children.

Frankly, it is rare to have a school system as committed as Bessemer's has been under Mike's leadership. In 1991 Dave went to Bennettsville, South Carolina, with high hopes. This is the hometown of Marian Wright Edelman of the Children's Defense Fund (CDF) and an old colleague of both Dave and myself during the 1960s in Mississippi. The CDF had a summer program and although its emphasis was on reading skills we had been invited to introduce the Algebra Project. The following year we began training teachers in Bennettsville and Marlboro County. Soon we had a core group that included Julia Cain and Nancy Ledford as well as Freddie David. Both Julia and Nancy were teachers in the gifted-students program. Also involved was Brenda Dixon, math coordinator for the county. Interestingly, many in this group were related by blood. Freddie and Julia are brother and sister. Brenda Dixon is a cousin. "There are a lot of us in the county," Julia said once.

The Marlboro County program was one of the more successful programs until after the 1996–97 school year. There was a strong youth group, many of whom have now graduated and gone on to college. Blenheim Middle School had the greatest number of AP-trained teachers and was the highest-rated school in the district. Its principal credited the Algebra Project as instrumental in their success. But suddenly, administrators decided they no longer wanted the project. They never explained why to us. And seventeen-year-old Shannon Lawson's analysis seems as good as any. *We should have the Algebra Project here but although the school board doesn't want to admit it, they're kind of scared. Because when you talk about algebra, a lot of people are not good in math. And here we are saying we want it in middle school. In the middle schools down here, only if you're in advanced math in eighth grade will you take Algebra I—no pre-algebra. And we want it introduced in sixth and seventh grade. They say, "Why bother?" It's not going to be on any of the tests and that's all they're looking at, I guess.* School doors were closed to us but students with the support of teachers like Julia Cain, Freddie David, and Nancy Ledford work outside of the classrooms after school. Ironically, as Dave has noted several times, it is Marlboro County that partly explains our success in Weldon. *Even though trainers Julia, Freddie, and Nancy were not allowed to continue the implementation of the project in the Marlboro County School District, they were credited by other school districts—Weldon especially—with helping the progress of their students and teachers. Young people from Marlboro County who had been trained in Algebra Project summer camps were used to help train Weldon students.*

Each site was building on the other. In Bessemer and Birmingham, Alabama, we relied on the skills of Shirley Connor and Constance Bland from Mississippi as well as my daughter Maisha for teacher training. Many in that first group of teachers who were trained in Birmingham and Bessemer left the system but our work in Mississippi had already created space for more teachers from the district to be trained. During the 1993–94 school year we developed a teacher support program directed by Bill Crombie. Bill and the Positive Innovations staff, which now included Shirley and Jessie, conducted monthly classroom visits to Birmingham, Bessemer, and Marlboro County followed by workshops with teachers implementing the Algebra Project. Teachers were identified for further training with Bill and Jim Burroughs. And underneath all of this Dave continually moved around the South—encouraging cooperation to foster a broader identity and organizing a regional development approach. *Well, we started off in small pockets here and there. And then we got some funding that came from OSI which allowed us to bring people together from all the sites. And we decided to bring them together to decide what to do with the money that was available for the sites. What do you want to use the money for? was the question. At that meeting, which we held at a conference center in Olive Branch, Mississippi, in the summer of 1996, we agreed to take the COFO approach, a regional approach. And one of the things they decided was to pool part of their money and put it into a budget based upon needs they agreed on. That meant they would have to meet on a regular basis. One of the questions I was trying to raise with them was, What can you do by yourself and what requires unity?*

We are, however, faced with how to sustain what we have begun. When Valerie's students move on to other classes, the teachers *in other subject areas accept the program, see its effectiveness, and have a high regard for it. But a lot of them, when the children move to another class, may not be as yielding as to let them express their views. The [students] feel like they're supposed to talk it out and you're supposed to serve as mediator. The teachers are like, "Ain't gonna be no mediating. It's going to be what I say and that's it. Sit down and be quiet!"* Changing this kind of relationship rests with the students. They are just beginning to think about how to organize themselves.

CHAPTER 8

Shaping Demand

The Young People's Project

The 1960s movement in Mississippi and across the country was driven by the young people. I was seventeen years old when I first became involved directly with the NAACP in Shreveport, and twenty years old when I joined the New Orleans Chapter of CORE. I was twenty-one when I joined the freedom riders. The sit-ins and most of the direct action activities were driven by the young people, supported by adults who helped to give us a place to stand and the space we needed in which to move. We learned to speak and to organize. The sharecroppers responded to this and made the demand that changed the culture. Today, in the demand of equal access to education, the Algebra Project brings to the fore-front the fact that again young people are driving and making the demand for changes that give them greater control over the things that affect their lives. They pull us in as well as themselves.

Dave Dennis

I speak as future roots. It all seem true
Who am I?
a young Black brother
Raised with one mother and three brothers.
I'm trying to survive the world AND
make history.
But before I go I want to know the lost
artifacts and unsolved mysteries.
Sometimes all I see is what the white man
teaches is always true.
Now it all comes to my senses and sticks to my brain

like glue.
Never heard of a freedom ride or a sit-in,
Would I sacrifice my life or get my chest beat in?
Sacrifice my life?
I do, what I do
'cause I do what I do.
Don't judge me on the color of my flesh,
Judge me as a citizen with equal color
And pray to Lord Bless.

Quinton, 15, Weldon, North Carolina

The schools of this nation confront a massive problem. Most people recognize this even if they do not agree what the problem is. We are faced with the challenge of devising a solution that is up to dealing with it. You cannot even approach dealing with the huge problem we have in the schools, using skeletal, weak solutions. I believe you cannot approach solving this problem unless you have the ability to grow the solutions from within schools and communities themselves, with increasing strength. We really need an approach to this problem that has the capacity to evolve from within and to match its dimensions. But how?

The stories in this book—the narratives of organizing both in the South in the 1960s and then in schools with the Algebra Project—contain this message: this is what organizing looks like on the ground; this is how it works, in all its messy detail. This is how folks get convinced to register to vote; this is how you convince a school to take a chance on a program that is trying to change the system. I believe that the kind of organizing we have been doing for years in the Algebra Project represents a radically different and new approach to the problem of how to create systemic change of our schools. Indeed, I think the idea of *systemic* change of our schools is itself a radical idea. And some of the most important lessons for how to continue this effort lie in the history of those remarkable years of Black civil rights transformation.

In the final analysis, as we've seen, the story of the voter registration drive in the South in the decade of the 1960s is a story of people struggling for greater control over the decision making that affects their lives, of people who learn to step forward to make a demand on society in their own voices. Ultimately, this is what must happen with our young people today, especially young people of color and young people from the poorest of our communities.

So, as I try to envision the future of the Algebra Project, one of the crucial issues in my mind is whether this generation of young people will begin to demand the literacy in mathematics it is assumed they do not want, demand this tool that is so essential for meaningful citizenship today. Do they have a consciousness about what is necessary? Can they create a culture in which they begin to make a demand on themselves and then on the larger society?

Our history points toward some possible directions. But the specific question about young people and the Algebra Project raises larger questions about how we should organize today. History can help, but can we as a people begin to really take some kind of hold of our history and use it effectively? We have not done that very well so far, and some of the most useful lessons contained in our history remain obscured. Much of our history does not exist in classroom teaching. The civil rights movement is more often than not discussed as a series of protest marches. The people who really made change and the ways they effected change are not recorded in the official canon of "civil rights history." As a consequence, it is difficult for ordinary people to see themselves as being central to making change.

In suggesting powerful and useful links between the past and present, I am not indulging in some romantic longing for the past. I know that we cannot build a culture of change in exactly the same way young people in the 1960s did. For one thing, our kids today are more conscious of obstacles. They buy into the status quo, which still stamps them as inferior, in ways that young people could not buy into racial segregation and discrimination four decades ago. If you are a kid, for example, it can be great to go into a classroom and not be required to do any work, a relief not having anything, or not having very much, expected of you. Complaining about *that* is too often not part of students' conversation; nor is it something most students bring to their parents or that they make into a community issue as students made lunch counter segregation an issue in 1960.

Many poor and minority kids know how far behind they are; it is part of what frightens them. But their response is not to organize for change, or to make plans for direct action. Some of this has to do with the time we are living in. It is difficult to think in terms of community. Ironically, the very victories of the civil rights movement have in some respects drained the community of human resources. Power seems unassailable, invulnerable when faced with challenge.

Kids in the 1960s were more conscious of being in a struggle for change. They did not say, when faced with obstacles, "How are we going to do this? Maybe we should think about whether we can or not." In the movement young people said, "It's a part of our struggle; let's do it!" We *first* decided what it was we wanted to do and then figured out a way, or ways, to do it. That is a very different mind-set from what you find inside classrooms today. This is not merely an age difference. Although the young people of SNCC and CORE were in their late teens and twenties, many of the movement's young people were in high school or even middle school. Rather, I think part of what defines the difference in times is that what young people are up against today is less clear than the raw racism of segregation laws and the Ku Klux Klan. The obstacles to young people taking charge today and shaping a movement in a quest for intellectual or cultural rather than political emancipation are more insidious than old segregation laws. The racist message of intellectual inferiority makes the goal seem beyond reach. And one of the valuable lessons to be drawn from the southern civil rights movement is that you have to shake free of other people's definitions of who you are and what you are able and willing to do.

In this regard, the emergence of the Young People's Project (which the kids typically call the YPP) is one of the most important developments in the Algebra Project. The Young People's Project begins to open up a way for our young people to continue with *us* as they move into college, then graduate and enter graduate school or the working world.

I can't help thinking of my own children in this respect, and more broadly of that whole group of young people in Cambridge where the project first took root. When Maisha was at Harvard, she and a group of these kids were doing volunteer work at the King school. She organized some of her classmates. Later on, my sons and their friends did the same, bringing in other students with their work. And finally, my youngest, Malaika, did this after enrolling in Spelman College in Atlanta. It is not difficult to envisage, at college campuses around the country, nuclei of students who are graduates of the project who help develop an expanding network of college kids committed to working with the project—young people who catch a consciousness that for their generation math literacy can become as important an organizing tool for education and economic access as the right to vote was for political access for Blacks in the 1960s.

Is the institution of autonomous groups of young people, operating within the schools and in the community and linked to other young people's groups around the country, all concerned with this same issue, empowering enough to foster meaningful change? I think so, and my vision of the Algebra Project's future even depends on it. If "student power" can take root, nurture itself, receive critical support, evolve, and grow over the next fifty or seventy-five years, as "high" technology increasingly defines work and citizenship, the YPP and other such networks defined by young people can become important in establishing a culture of math literacy in the targeted population. Even as kids pass through school, the community remains, as does the need for educating each successive generation of young people. The work of the Algebra Project can become institutionalized through the kids who come back and take our work into the community. And you don't need all of them coming back. All you need is a critical network, a few, three or four out of a hundred who decide, "I'm going to take up this work," who come back and organize, or fit fostering math literacy into whatever they do.

This dynamic, which is actually playing out inside project sites in Cambridge, Massachusetts, Weldon, North Carolina, Mississippi, and other parts of the South, is similar in some ways to the way young people pulled each other into the movement in the 1960s. Which raises the question: Can the YPP, now developing a network of young people committed to math literacy work, foster and give form to something that can properly be called a movement? All of the elements that will have to come together for this cannot be predicted. Movements don't come from any single place.

If you look carefully at the 1960s, you will realize we didn't create the civil rights movement we were part of and helped to shape. You can't say that any single person actually put that movement together. What we did then was create a network that helped sustain and advance the movement. Our specific network grew out of the sit-ins. And although we weren't well educated in it for the most part, history was somehow present, and there was a consciousness that the "movement" wasn't just our little network. Movement history came into existence when the first African walked off the first slave ship in chains. It shaped events long before our involvement as young people in the 1960s. Rooted in history's soil, there were movement branches that spread across terrain we were not traversing as we freedom rode or sat in or did our organizing work in Mississippi and other places in the South.

Now we have put together what might be called an Algebra Project network. There may be a "movement" starting or reflected in this if all over the place little groups of people begin to spring up, deciding that "hey, we're going to master math literacy." But that does not exist yet around the country. It is difficult. And slow. It may turn out, however, that the young people in the Algebra Project will tap something that generates that kind of power.

I think cultural identification is part of what is going on. Even though this was Mississippi and there's a different culture from mine in Cambridge it's really one and the same, a basic spin-off of the hip-hop culture that I grew up with. All of the things I was seeing the Mississippi kids doing or talking about—even though the language was a little different—it was what I had experienced growing up, hanging out.

Omo Moses

The kids talked to me about my accent, told me I sounded funny. They'd tell me I sounded like I was Jamaican and that was funny to me. We'd talk. After class we'd sit down and talk about whatever. I'd shoot dice with them for marbles or something. I'd just play. If we weren't doing anything I'd act like I was some kid that they knew from the neighborhood. If we were teaching, I would teach, but then some of what we talked about, or what we did when we weren't teaching, would come into the teaching.

Taba Moses

In 1992, my youngest son, Tabasuri, entered Tufts University. He stayed there only for a year before dropping out. Taba, schools, and authority—including mine—had been rubbing uneasily against one another for several years. There had been run-ins with police. By the time he started college, Taba's best friend in high school was in jail. Before going to college Taba had taken a stab at a Connecticut prep school and did well academically, but he was expelled after trying to get repayment from a student who ran up a huge bill on his phone card. The school accused Taba of extortion when he tried to get his money back. College really didn't work for him either. It wasn't really on his mind; he had no real motivation.

So I decided he should accompany me as I began working in Mississippi. Some of this was just my feeling as a father that I needed to be physically close to Taba, that he needed to see what I was doing and how I went about my daily routine. I have always felt, too, that the Algebra Project should encourage families to work together; that the project should be a place where kids who don't quite fit into traditional systems have some way of moving with opportunity. So in my mind, part of the reason to have Taba traveling with me was the thought that he could with a certain degree of safety experiment with his life, try out some things for himself.

And that is what Taba began to do. Traveling with me he began assisting teachers in the Delta and in Jackson, learning to get up and talk to them as a young adult. *At first I was always doing this with my father, and then one day while he was in Cambridge he needed a root canal or something. Anyway, he called Dave Dennis to say he wasn't coming down although he was expected to do a workshop. I was in Mississippi and since Dave still wanted to do the workshop he said I had to do it with him. There must have been two hundred kids there; it was the first time I really did one on my own. I was nineteen.*

Taba's style of working with kids connected meaningfully to their youth culture. He was a part of it: *We were going up into the Delta. We'd go there every week. My father used to go in one classroom, and I would do the same stuff he was doing, but in my own way, in another classroom. This was in 1993. And it was like a situation where I'd make mistakes, but then I learned to turn my mistakes into something positive. I might be working on frequency distribution charts. And I'd set it up or put out the wrong combinations or something that the kids would catch. Or I'd catch them two minutes later. I'd be doing something and I'd be like, "Oh, man, this won't work." I'd say, "Oh, I messed up," and they would start laughing. And then we would go all the way back, just go over it. And that made it easier for them once they realized that, well, if I could make a mistake—if Taba from Cambridge could make a mistake—it's not a big deal, we can make mistakes too. . . . I go into the classroom with the attitude that I don't expect people to give me respect that I don't deserve. And I think a lot of teachers are in positions of power with their kids. So they automatically assume that because of who they are the kids have to respect them. And they demand it. And I look at it as though, even if I was teaching them, the kids should have no reason to respect me unless I give them a reason to. And if you don't, then they won't, they won't respect you. And a lot of times you won't get anything done. Instead, you end up in a power struggle with kids over who rules the classroom.*

Later on, my son Omo and other young people connected to the Algebra Project in Cambridge, like London Hardy and Dacco Garcia, were coming down to Mississippi, working with students and schools, providing a model for kids younger than they were to think about. Watching the response to them, I could almost see a critical idea taking seed in the minds of young students like Sammie Myers whom they worked with: "Hey, I can be like these guys; it would be cool to be like these guys when I get out of school." *Taba would say like, "Hey, little man, come here. What you doing?" Like that. I'm just trying to talk all cool to him. Since the sixth grade Taba and Omo have been like big brothers to me.*

It came into sharp focus at an Indianola workshop on the graphing calculator that mathematician Leo Edwards conducted for us. It was our first workshop on the calculator. And originally it was just going to be for about thirty teachers and trainers. But I thought it might be good to involve some of the Jackson kids as well. We brought up nine of the middle school kids that Khari and Taba had been working with for a few months.

Dave set it up. *In the Southern Initiative we weren't using the calculators then and a lot of the adults were skeptical about using them. They were resistant to the technology. But the kids weren't. For the first time, I think, we were putting their culture on the table . . . Nintendo, pushing buttons, computer stuff. That was the language they spoke even if they didn't know anything about the more sophisticated graphing calculator. In any case, the Cambridge kids knew how to use them. So, although this was Leo's workshop, the Mississippi kids could be taught in part by their own generation and learned more easily than the older generation being taught in the same workshop. When the kids left the workshop they were trying to figure out ways to use the calculator more. The adult teachers weren't.* Observed Leo of his experience with the teachers here and elsewhere, *At workshops teachers often learn what you tell them but don't know enough math to answer any student's question that comes from out of the box.*

The Indianola workshop was my first real glimpse into the possibility that we were on to something with the kids we had been working with in Mississippi. We were all staying in a motel;

the kids were in the pool playing, splashing, and horsing around generally. But a couple of them came up to me and said something like, "When I grow up I'm going to be just like Basonge, or Khari, or Karimu, and the other guys who were down for the workshop. I'm going to work for the Algebra Project." I realized that these young people could do what Leo or I could not, for all our training in mathematics. *Our* young people could make algebra "cool," a hip thing for other young people. Interacting with a crew not much older than themselves who had been in the Algebra Project made becoming math literacy workers—although the phrase hadn't come into use yet—something that the kids could see themselves doing. I remember asking one of my seventh-grade students, Melvin, when we were working on structures with gumdrops and toothpicks, if he thought he could do this and stay with the Algebra Project. He looked up at me and he said, "I don't know." And he didn't know. But a year later he came up to that Indianola workshop. And he's still involved with the project, getting ready to go to college.

London Hardy, director of the Cambridge YPP, offers an even clearer example of how young people connecting to young people shapes the Algebra Project. He'd grown up in our neighborhood, had been coming in and out of our home since childhood, but was never really deeply involved with the project as it evolved in Cambridge while he was in public school. In 1990 he began attending Wilberforce University. *While I was going to school it was basically friends keeping in contact by telephone. We had scattered from the old neighborhood but still wanted to keep up with each other—"What are you doing now? How are you doing?" Taba was telling me about the traveling he was doing with his father, working on the Algebra Project. I didn't talk about the Algebra Project much with Omo; he was away at school playing ball.*

Coming home for vacations, London (and he is really standing here for several in the circle of boys who grew up with Omo and Taba) became more involved with the project as he continued his dialogue with Taba. And after graduating in 1995 he began tutoring. He even went through an Algebra Project training program along with Dacco and Omo; all three of them—the youngest barely out of boyhood, really—in a group of adult teachers. *We were asking ourselves, how can we build and develop young people in Cambridge the way they were beginning to do in Mississippi? Although kids here were taking the Algebra Project curriculum, they weren't organized. "What do we have to do to get an organization for young people?" we kept asking as we talked back and forth. There was a group of us, and we said we should start by working in Algebra Project classrooms. And the teachers really went for this kind of help. Soon I was working with sixth and seventh graders in four or five schools. We had a huge workshop at the AP office and got some more youths involved.*

There is a way that young people reach young people, are able to touch each other, that in my view is central to the future shape of the Algebra Project. London wasn't "sold" a program idea. Understanding the Algebra Project was simply part of a long and broad relationship that connected Omo, Taba, and others in the neighborhood. They "sold" each other on the work. Also, the younger Cambridge kids they had begun to work with wanted to hang out with London and this Algebra Project crew—these older guys—as young guys always want to do. And this hanging out didn't have to be on a street corner. *For instance, I'm a little kid, sixth grader maybe, and Dacco is a support person in the classroom. I say, "Can I hang out with you after school? What are you doing after school?" Boom, boom, boom. What's really coming out of his mouth, even if he doesn't use the words, is "after-school program," and that's basically how the after-school program happened. We had the idea, but at the same time it was an idea that came from the kids.*

Taba credits Omo for doing much of the groundwork that enabled this multilayered interest in the project to find concrete expression. *My brother had done a lot of the prework. Just setting up the first meetings with London and Lynn, and dealing with the Cambridge Algebra Project. And so, London works full-time, Dacco, part-time. We set up an office at home. We got some computers. And we got two kids, Antoine in the ninth grade, and Jakeem in the eleventh grade. They work part-time. Eventually when the after-school program gets going in a local youth center, we've got about fifteen kids who know how to do graphing calculator workshops. They also make decisions around who goes to national meetings.*

London followed Omo and Taba into Mississippi. He came down that fall of 1996, the first of the Cambridge YPP group to arrive. There was some trepidation, for the Deep South's image as a land dangerous to Black people still lingers. *I'm in the "dirty South" now and I get off the plane thinking, they gonna know I'm different, from the North. And I'm expecting every white person to either lynch me or don't say nothing to me. Taba met me and he had a dog with him. An old white man came up and asked, "What kind of dog is that?" and we started having a discussion about the dogs. That just kinda threw me off. From then on, I told myself, let's be open-minded. Of course I know the racism is there too.* I think this North–South connection is as important as the generational link that ties these young people together. The tightly knit Mississippi group did not know very much about the older Cambridge group. *One of the first things that Taba and Omo said was have a relationship* with *them before you just grab them and say, "Let's do this." Talk to them and see what they're all about. Hang out with them and do what've you've got to do with them. I did that; we went to a couple of movies, played some ball, talked a lot. And I was saying to myself, "Wow! These kids are really tuned in, pumped up, involved." They were asking, "When we gonna do our next workshop, where we gonna travel, and when we gonna do this or that?"*

As in the earlier movement, exposure helps fuel effort and change. The closeness in age and the willingness of the Cambridge folks like London, my own children, Dacco, and others helped the Mississippi kids begin to think that this was something they could do. And I don't have any doubt that if we are able to stabilize the resources and the funding, that we'll be able to institutionalize this and get trained kids who come back to work in the community.

The key is that the young people have to figure out how to organize themselves. Math literacy, like voter registration, provides them with a tool for such work. We are not really trying to develop an organization as much as develop the idea in the kids that it is largely their work to get the training, to master difficult mathematical literacy concepts to the point where they can explain them to other people. And they have to translate this into entrepreneurial-type activities, to figure out how they can use this intellectual capital to really generate income and resources necessary for survival over the long haul. This is the issue of the change in the technology from technology around physical work to a technology around mental thought, where a lot of the capital is intellectual capital. They have to understand that part of their function is to marshal their intellectual capital and put it to work for themselves if they are to avoid getting into a situation where they are just posturing, believing that what is important is holding office, or just being in an office, as opposed to really doing work.

> Being in the Algebra Project I sometimes get from other kids, "You make me sick, you're such a nerd, you think you're smarter than everybody else." Or I get the "You're in the smart class and you think you know everything more than everybody else." Now, I'm just a straightforward person and if you say something like that to me, I say, "Well it's not my fault, because as smart as I am, you can be as smart as I am too if you just put forth the effort." And they are like, "Well, you just think you're so smart." I say, "I think I'm smart and there's no reason why I shouldn't, but, you know, you shouldn't be jealous over something like that. If anything, you should be working harder for yourself to get where I'm at or higher."
>
> Quanda, 14, Weldon, North Carolina

> My friends question me a lot about what I do. I don't think they understand when I tell them I leave school and go to work at the math lab. They say, "What do you mean, you're going to work? That's not working. You're just going over there and with those computers." Working is McDonald's or Jitney Jungle, to them. They feel like I'm just learning, you know. And most people don't put work and learning together.
>
> Heather, 16, Jackson, Mississippi

In working toward developing an effective network of literacy workers, we have to work through different layers of demands. The first layer is the hardest in some respects. And it is the most important. The target population, the kids we are working with, have to make the demand on themselves. They have to commit to going after real mathematical competence, and they have to begin to see themselves as a driving wedge in creation of a culture of mathematical literacy.

It has got to be real. What made voter registration organizing real was that in the end adults who weren't you had to make a decision that they were going to go down to the courthouse and try to register, at grave risk in many cases to either themselves or their family, their livelihood, or something. That act of courage and commitment made it real, made it something the organizer could not do himself or herself. And this is one of the salient distinctions between leading and organizing. You're in an organizing mode when you are working with some other people to get them to do something that you cannot do yourself. You can't go down to register—you could go sit in, yes, but you can't go down to register for these other people. And that reality puts you in a different mode, because you've got the problem of convincing other people—whether in voter registration or in education—that the idea of challenging yourself and the system that defines your life is an idea to be embraced.

So that's the task the YPP and other young people in the Algebra Project have taken on. The problem of convincing other young people that mathematical literacy is something they need, that acquiring it is work they should commit to, and that spreading it wherever they can is also their challenge. We want them to make the first demand on themselves. We want them to make the transition into thinking that they have to put energy and time into literacy, their own literacy.

This primary level of demand—the demand kids make on themselves—accelerated with the involvement of the first Algebra Project graduates, the kids who came along with my kids. All of them are in their twenties now. They up the ante and get young people to do what they do, stand up in front of their peers and by doing so make algebra, learning it and teaching it, all right—hip, cool, or whatever. This was something I could not convince Omo and Taba to do, although they were used to me standing up in front of them. We were not able to get anybody young to stand up in front of other young people when I first started. The attitude was "explain something in front of everybody?" Grown-ups did that, for *their* reasons—sometimes for the *wrong* reasons. So, it really put a different spin on the matter when Omo, Taba, Maisha, Malika, Kharri, London, Karimu, Basonge, and others began to do this.

Their interventions frequently make a dramatic difference. Once I was working on a classroom presentation with a student, Sammie Myers. He had the math but I was trying to stress that language was important too. Sammie and I were going over and over the words he needed to use for his presentation. I stopped him four times and asked him to begin again. My daughter Maisha, who was now assisting me in the classroom, saw Sammie tightening up, shutting down. *Each time he tried to do it, my father told him, "No, you have to say it like this." The presentation had to do with traveling from Brinkley Middle School to Johnson Elementary School. As Sammie moves toward Johnson the distance is decreasing and there was a way that Dad wanted him to say it. Sammie kept saying it his way and my father was making him start over. I could see what Sammie was feeling. He starts mumbling; his voice gets softer. His body starts to slouch like the tone in his voice. He's trying to do what Dad is telling him to, but is really saying, "I don't really want to say it like this, it's just that you're sitting here making me do it." Dad finally says, "Okay, you need to practice some more." Sammie was ready to leave. He's thinking, I'm outta here, gone; I'm not doing this anymore. I could see exactly where he was coming from. I pulled him aside. "What's going on?" I asked. "I'm not doing it," he said. "Bob's picking on me. Other people get up there and they do it, but he has something to say about every little thing that I say, you know. So I'm not going to do it." I told Sammie that I would work with him. I explained that it can take a while to learn something but I could help him. Finally he goes back in. Before he did, I also told him that when I was growing up Dad did the same thing to me, always pressing me to say things precisely; that's just learning the language of mathematics. Sammie said, "I'm not trying to be a scientist and be all precise." I said something like, "Well, that's just the format. It's not that you don't understand but you have to take your understanding and do the hard job of embedding words in your brain that are consistent. And to use these words takes practice, constant practice." And that's what we finally did.*

I think an important part of what has made Maisha and the others want to do this work is simply the long years of being around it, which began when they were small. When they got bigger, all those years the project had been in their life helped them think of themselves as still being a part of it. They went out and did various other things. Went to college. This. That. They come out of college and the project is still going on and they say, "Yes, I'm part of this; I was part of its beginning." So, there is some sense that really wasn't obvious from watching them when they were younger, that they had internalized being tied to the Algebra Project even during years when they were not actively engaged in its work.

The emergence of this first group, over a period of eighteen years has really put us into a different level now. It has become clear that the young people could do what we could not. We couldn't model for them the process of young people standing up in front of young people. Maybe we could have preached to them, but we couldn't model it for them. They can, on the other hand, be models for each other, and they can attract other young people; they *do* attract young people, particularly in the South. It becomes something young people begin to create a culture around. So, there is another level of demand, which is the demand of the young people on each other to create an association that is uniquely theirs.

> Young people in the Algebra Project have embraced the slogan "Each One Teach One." Students who are part of the Algebra Project become math literacy workers once they begin to teach others what they have learned. Indeed, math literacy workers began growing under our noses from the very start of the Algebra Project. . . .
>
> In order for the Algebra Project to fulfill its mission it must produce thousands of mathematically literate students. Already there is a

core group of young people who have gone through the Algebra
Project. They represent the first fruits of a growing math literacy tree.
Even as we move, from sixth grade to seventh grade to eighth grade
and on to high school and college, we reach back to help develop
math skills in those coming behind us. The roots of this tree grow
stronger each time we look back to help develop a new math literacy worker.

from the statement drafted at the 1st National
Algebra Project Youth Conference, May 3, 1998

After the Indianola workshop the students began to really think
about organizing themselves. They bonded on this trip, and it laid
the foundation for a real commitment to the work, Omo told me,
confirming my own assessment. *I think something about traveling together is either going to tear you apart or bring you together. We hadn't really known what to expect, although we had prepared for the workshop a
lot, done a lot of work, and gotten a lot of materials together. Afterward,
you're sharing experiences, and you have something real positive to look
back on. We made a real good connection with other students while we
were up in the Delta. We had always been saying that we can teach other
students and they will identify but that was the first time we made a connection with those other students.* Furthermore, they had gotten paid
for their week of work in the Delta, and liked that too.

Still, among these Mississippi youngsters, nothing much that
was concrete emerged immediately after Indianola. Dave was doing a little work with them and they were using the Positive Innovations office in Jackson for meetings, *charting up every idea because
we had decided to become this group, even before we had a name,* recalls
one of those young people, Java Jackson. They kicked around a
few names. Other young people who had been involved with the
project in Cambridge were also becoming involved with the Mississippi kids.

The summer after the Indianola workshop with Leo Edwards,
the students were back in the Delta. This time they were now running their own workshops on the graphing calculator under
Omo's direction (Omo, who graduated from George Washington

University, where he majored in math and creative writing, came down and spent the 1996–97 school year at Brinkley Middle School.)

Omo was also making frequent trips back to Cambridge. This was when he, London, and Dacco underwent training with teachers and they began working in schools. The idea of a young people's organization within the Algebra Project, long germinating in conversations Omo, Taba, London, Dacco, and a few others had been having, finally sprouted a name. *I remember sitting in the car with Taba one night, talking about the work we'd been doing, and the students, and Taba said, "You know, the young people's project . . . " And, I think in some ways, just that conversation and just saying the name kind of put a lot of clarity on it for me. Ever since then I have known what it was we were building around. Before then I was unsure; we were just together.*

From Cambridge, the YPP idea was not only carried south, but actually took formal shape there too. Omo began pushing Dave to get the YPP incorporated, which he did in September 1996. YPP is a Mississippi company that I hope will take possession of the games and math tools we have designed. There are number theory games that have developed within the project and I think the young people can and should market them.

As with the sit-ins, the link between North and South has developed quickly. Its first link was forged with the young voice of Omo speaking to young Mississippians unsure of just who this new crew coming out of the North was. *I remember Demetrica Gordon asking, "Who's London?" and "Who's Dacco? Who are these people? And what's this money doing next to their names? What's this about computers and how come we need computers? And . . . " I was trying to explain that there was a YPP in Cambridge and they were saying, "What are you talking about?"*

Similarities of age and culture quickly overrode differences of geography or place of origin. *Taba was young, so that caught everybody's attention,* recalls Java Jackson, who had just graduated from high school and became involved with the Algebra Project as a sixth grader. *He was handsome, and he was active, full of energy. He talked to us like he was one of us, for one thing. "Yo, Shorty!" You didn't feel uncomfortable getting the wrong answer with him.* And lest you think Java is just reflecting the attitude of young girls toward a slightly older guy they find attractive, Sammie Myers, another one of those sixth graders, remembers that *Taba talked to us with kind of an East Coast attitude, like "Well, yo, dog. You need to do your work, you know what I'm saying, before I smack you. You know what I'm saying." After school, most of the stuff went on with the boys. He might pick us up after practice and we might go to the mall. Just kicking with us. Hanging out. We might go over to the hotel where he was staying. Just kicking with him.* More analytically, Java notes *Taba did things they couldn't do. You can look at that in two different ways. Some people may say that maybe that was a bad influence, but then again, you could say it was a good influence on you. He could do what he wanted to because of his education.*

When we began working in Marlboro County, Warrenton, and Weldon, Dave began trying to work with a group of about thirty or so high school and middle school kids. *I was not communicating. I called Maisha and asked her to begin working with me. She did and I saw her establish a relationship with them that I could not.*

The lessons learned—as when a group from Mississippi came to Cambridge in the summer of 1999 to work with younger students there—are not necessarily great lessons. Indeed, more often than not they tend to be simple. Still they contribute, small step by small step, to a wider understanding of the world that surrounds them. For instance, one of the students up from Mississippi who came to Cambridge for this summer project said he'd always thought of northern cities as huge, so he was surprised that you could walk to places the way they did in the South. The informal learning exchanges that happen *within* the Algebra Project are an important part of the process, as it was with the civil rights movement.

In a formal organized sense there are only two official YPP sites: Cambridge and Mississippi. But the YPP has passed some major hurdles that will be important to its future growth. From the beginning, it has insisted on respect, and its own budget, which it puts together and is responsible for executing. However, let me add, for it is important to understanding the complex process of growth and development among young people in the Algebra Project, that the stance of the Young People's Project is not yet the general stance of the young population we target. The AP on one level is working in schools and has thousands of kids making demands on themselves, with various levels of intensity, to negotiate the college prep math sequence. But most of those kids are not making any demands that they should associate with each other to promote math literacy, or to promote a youth culture where math literacy is a very important driving force.

It has become clear, however, that from within this broad population you can attract a network of kids to make such a demand. This second level of demand on each other is a collective demand, a more political one. I think the strongest political idea embedded in this work is the idea that if you can really bring about any kind of change at the bottom it is going to change everything. The world looks very different standing at the bottom. And if the people who are standing there, looking up, get themselves positioned in different ways to make this demand, then that's political. The first demand that kids make on themselves must be real in order for the second level of demand, where they are associating with each other, to take root.

A network, a tradition like this involving teachers, students, schools, and community, is not established in one fell swoop. You go around it and around it, and you keep going around it and deepening it. You keep returning to it until all the implications of what you are doing become clear and sink in.

> Most Black kids want to do something with their life.
>
> Darren, 16, Weldon, North Carolina

> We're still fighting now, but it's not a physical battle the way it was then; it's a mental thing.
>
> Quanda, 15, Weldon, North Carolina

History demonstrates that taking responsibility for one's own life, one's own learning, can change a person. I consider Fannie Lou

Hamer a symbol of that philosophy, and it is an important part of the Algebra Project. Simply put, mathematics must be seen as relevant to gaining control over your life, as connected to change for the better. If math has no relevance to a student's life, that student will not learn it. And this is what makes young people talking to and pulling in other young people so central to our efforts.

It's just a beginning. The kids do not really have a trained person's grasp or understanding of what they are asking, although their potential to force change is enormous if they can only discover it and tap into it. This does not happen all at once. Let's go back to April 1997 when, with the reluctant support of school authorities (see Chapter 6), a large number of Brinkley Middle School students in Jackson, Mississippi, took the statewide algebra test. To prepare for it, they began a series of Saturday workshops. Those workshops were built around the graphing calculator, a tool students are permitted to use on this test.

Students attending the workshops were divided into groups and in them, with the help of student facilitators, went over a selected set of problems from a practice test that was similar to the actual test they would be taking. These workshops made a difference in two related ways: they prepared students for the pending algebra test, and, just as important for organizing around math literacy in the long run, the workshops gave students a way to help prepare other students unable to attend them—effectively creating a core of student tutors. These workshops are some of the roots from which grew young people like Cedric Johnson who now call themselves "math literacy workers" in the Algebra Project. He was one of those eighth graders. *I felt prepared for the test because I had experience with the calculator, and in the Saturday workshops I was able to finish work I had not completed in class, along with extra work that I would be able to take back to the classroom and explain to my classmates who did not attend.* . . . And in Sumner, Mississippi, up in the Delta, a tiny town straddling Highway 49, which I remember as notorious for its hostility to civil rights—Emmett Till's body was found nearby in the Tallahatchie River—sixteen-year-old Martin Saulsberry says, *I'm learning to be a leader, so I can come back and help my community. And lots of kids are doing this in different ways. My way is the Algebra Project.* As in Weldon, North Carolina, and Bessemer, Alabama, strong backing from the school administration has helped us gain gradual but steady improvement in math.

Martin had become involved with the program as a sixth grader. *In "normal" math classes they taught that math requires you to think of everything in a certain way. You have to do a problem in a certain way. There's a formula for equations and you follow that formula to get the equation. In the Algebra Project, it was the way you thought that counted. I remember once we were trying to figure out how to show the six routes of a train with unifix cubes that only went in four directions. Finally after thinking about it I said, "Why don't we put two more routes on top of two of the routes?" Some of the group I was in objected. "They didn't say we could do that." But I convinced them. "They didn't say we couldn't either."* For Martin, the project has meant discovery that he could lead. By the eighth grade, *if I was put into a group of kids, I would help them out. I would sort of be the leader of a small group. But I never thought of being a leader of a community. Then when I was in the ninth grade the YPP was formed and Omo and Maisha started getting me to meetings and conferences.*

We have had our ups and downs with school administrations, but student networking has been a constant driving force in the project. As far back as 1995 Dave and Doris Williams organized a "Youth Math Summit" in Durham, North Carolina. About 125 middle and high school students were bused in from Weldon, Warrenton, and the Marlboro County school district. Maisha, Omo, and students from Jackson came in to teach some of the AP games. During a discussion one of the young people from Marlboro County said it would be good if what they were experiencing in Durham could happen every summer, and Dave committed to supporting that idea: *if they were prepared to take responsibility for organizing and implementing it. The young people then selected members of a planning committee that resulted in the development of Algebra Project youth camps in the Carolinas. The presence of kids from Jackson was a key part of this because the kids from the Carolinas wanted to be like the kids from Jackson, and because of the kids from Jackson, felt they could do this work. We used the YPP to help develop, manage, and facilitate the camps which have been held for five summers straight.*

Not long ago I was watching some of the kids I had as seventh graders preparing themselves for a workshop in Mississippi, at Lanier High School, where they would make a presentation using fraction bars. One of the students, Jonathan, got into a discussion of the feature talk that led him into a discussion about the length of a fraction bar. When he began talking about area, there came a realization on his part that he was committing line segments to having area. So the question was, Do line segments have area? It was a good discussion. Even though in some sense he knew that line segments don't have area. At another level Jonathan was rediscovering what he knew, making it more his own. It has taken a while from the starting point of the games we played when students like Jonathan were sixth and seventh graders for them to see that we were really doing math. They began to see what they could really do in high school and that too is some of the power driving the YPP.

We don't listen to kids enough. Really listen. It is a difficult thing for grown-ups to do—listen and actually pay serious attention to what young people are saying. In the Algebra Project we are still learning how to do this also. It is the voices of the young people I hear every day, more than anything, that gives me hope.

> APRIL: Boys get more peer pressure than girls, that's why I think it's really good when they're on the honor roll.
>
> ANGELA: Yeah, when they make good grades everybody wants to talk about them. You know how they be hearing that young Black men are always being in jail and stuff, and I be happy to see a young Black man—you know—doing something positive, getting his life together.
>
> JONATHAN: That's true, the boys have—a hard image.
>
> APRIL: And their—sorry—egos.
>
> JONATHAN: Boys can only do one thing, play sports. This is the way people see. Be smart or be tough.
>
> APRIL: The ones that are all three are nice.

JONATHAN: I think you can get respect . . .

APRIL: If you got that image.

ANGELA: So the bigger boys don't come picking on you.

APRIL: Kiki got respect and he's little. If you walk around acting, sulking all the time, like you hurting or whatever, like you want to cry, you gonna get picked on.

ANGELA: You can't go to school and just walk around—"They gonna talk about me today," and be cryin'.

JONATHAN: Self-respect. People respect you if you respect yourself.

I think a math literacy worker is dedicated. You've got to have responsibility if you tutor somebody your own age. They gonna want to play. You've got to keep them on track.

Andrea, 14, Weldon, North Carolina

I like trying to teach other folks, kid to kid, teenager to teenager. And teenagers can explain something to teenagers. They're not going to look at grown-ups like they'll look at somebody just like them. I ain't saying all grown-ups are slow, but if a grown-up says something to you, they might say it, like, in a grown-up way—a longer way.

I'm a math literacy worker. I speak math. I do math. I work with math.

David, 13, Weldon, North Carolina

We should have the Algebra Project here but although the school board doesn't want to admit it, they're kind of scared. Because when you talk about algebra, a lot of people are not good in math. And here we are saying we want it in middle school. In the middle schools down here, only if you're in advanced math in eighth grade will you take Algebra 1—no pre-algebra. And we want it introduced in sixth and seventh grade. They say, "Why bother? It's not going to be on any of the tests," and that's all they're looking at, I guess.

Shannon, 17, Bennettsville, South Carolina

They're probably thinking, "If this doesn't work, then it's going to be our fault because we let this come into the school system. So we're not going to take any chances. We're not going to let it into our curriculum."

Stargell, 18, Bennettsville, South Carolina

Slavery does not happen when one group believes themselves to be superior. Slavery happens when the other group believes themselves to be inferior.

Martin, 16, Sumner, Mississippi

Movement emerges from Movement. Little did we understand in starting out as organizers that the movement in Mississippi to get the right to vote would set in motion fundamental changes in U.S. politics—would lead in fact to a complete recasting of Democratic and Republican Party politics. I think the Algebra Project as it prods school systems, connects young people to a math literacy network, and commits communities to the idea of change can have the same unpredictable, transformative impact. As we come to a stopping place, Ella Baker's words are worth repeating.

> *In order for us as poor and oppressed people to become a part of a society that is meaningful, the system under which we now exist has to be radically changed. This means that we are going to have to learn to think in radical terms. I use the term* radical *in its original meaning—getting down to and understanding the root cause. It means facing a system that does not lend itself to your needs and devising means by which you change that system. That is easier said than done. But one of the things that has to be faced is, in the process of wanting to change that system, how much have we got to do to find out who we are, where we have come from and where we are going. . . . I am saying as you must say, too, that in order to see where we are going, we not only must* remember *where we have been, but we must* understand *where we have been.*

My oldest son, Omo, entered Mary Lou Mehrling's King open program class in September 1984 with two of his buddies, Danny Rice and Ari Cox. I taught algebra to Omo and Danny, but not to Ari, who didn't know his multiplication facts. However, when Ari entered the eighth grade in September 1985, he wanted to be in algebra with his buddies, and Mary Lou and I agreed to let him try. We were still using Saxon's *Algebra 1,* and by keeping a close watch on Ari, we moved carefully through the text, one problem at a time. When we began addition of integers on the number line, Ari kept getting a wrong answer. His method was to ignore the signs of the integers and calculate an arithmetic answer. Thus, in Ari's mind, "$5 + -7$" was converted to "$5 + 7$" and the answer was 12. It finally dawned on me that Ari had only one question in his mind about his numbers: "How much?" or "How many?" as in "How many fingers do you have?" or "How many toes?" Not the kind of question Saxon had in mind with his number line addition problems. That was *Ari's* problem.

It took a while, but I finally had the insight that I needed to put another question in Ari's mind about his numbers. To make a successful transition from arithmetic to algebra, Ari would need at least two kinds of questions about number joined together in his mind. He had only one kind, the kind he learned before he came to school, the kind his parents, relatives, and friends had taught him, the "how many" questions: "How many fingers?"; "How many toes?" But what was the other kind of question? And when we settled on it, how would we get it into Ari's mind together with the "How many" questions around his number concept? That was *my* problem. Looking back, it is clear that the answer to my problem evolved over the next three years into the transition curriculum of the Algebra Project.

Early in the '84–85 school year, we got word at King Open that a parent had written a letter to the Cambridge school board to inquire about its policy on who could take algebra and when. The school board referred the issue to the superintendent, Robert Peterkin, who asked the math coordinator, Paul Lyons, to investigate. Paul routinely advocated screening prospective Algebra 1 students with the "Orleans-Hanna" test. However, his mandate as math coordinator did not allow him to *require* schools to adopt this policy and the discussions at King Open did not reach any consensus. In the meantime a small group of Black high school teachers were investigating the lack of representation of Black students in the advanced math and science classes at the high school and issued their report to the school board in the spring of '86. A group of us at King Open, Sandra Darling, program administrator, Mary Lou Mehrling, Lena James, parent liason, Shirley Harvey, parent, and myself went to participate. We decided to raise the question of who takes algebra and when? as a matter that impacts who enters advanced math and science courses in high school. One school committee member remembered the note to the superintendent about just this issue and asked for a review of the Algebra Project at King Open. The subsequent meetings with the school board member, school system administrators, and representatives from King Open credentialized the King Open Algebra Project within the Cambridge Public School System. As soon as this happened the K-6 teachers at King Open began discussing how to better prepare their students for algebra in the seventh and eighth grades and Sandra Darling submitted a proposal to the Massachusetts State Department of Education to organize a series of workshops for the next school year on teaching algebra. The proposal was funded and every month across the '86–87 school year all the teachers at King Open participated in a workshop with some expert on the teaching of algebra. One result was to raise the teaching of math to as central a concern for the entire staff as the teaching of reading, writing, and language arts. At the close of these workshops, Lynne Godfrey, the sixth-grade math teacher, offered her class to pilot materials that I might develop. In the meantime I had settled on the other kind of question to put in Ari's mind: "Which way?" Ari, and everyone else, already has this kind of question, but Ari had not put it together with the "how many" question around his concept of number. How to do that? Inspiration came one day while entering the T, the mass transit system serving the Boston metropolitan area. The sign over the entrance said "inbound," an answer to a "which way" question. By the '88–89 school year we would be walking Lynne's students to Central Square for a trip on the T, but first I had to develop the materials.

I spent the '87–88 school year doing this with the help of a group of Black Harvard undergraduates, members of the Azuza Christian Society. We met every Sunday afternoon at the apartment of Eugene and Jackie Rivers. Jackie coordinated the participation of the Society members and one of them, Alan Shaw, who had just graduated from Harvard and was enrolled in a master's degree program at the Media Lab of MIT, got up early every school day, driving to pick up that day's Azuza participants and get them to the King school by 7 A.M. The daily presence of the Azuza members made the morning sessions exciting for a group of forty or so sixth and seventh graders from the King Open that Lena, the parent liaison, helped to recruit. Every Sunday I presented material to the Azuza members and we would try them on the King Open students during the week. We did this for the whole '87–88 school year.

It was during the '87–88 school year and the subsequent two years in Lynne's classroom that the concept of a five-step curricular process took shape. My doctoral topic had been an examination of the history and insights of W. V. O. Quine's philosophy of math, and one of Quine's insights turned out to be of direct relevance and importance to the teaching of school mathematics. Quine insisted that elementary arithmetic, elementary logic, and elementary set theory get started by what he called the "regimentation of ordinary discourse, mathematization *in situ*." To which list we should now add elementary algebra. Scientists, Quine said, put a straitjacket on natural languages.

Students at the King Open were very much into using their experiences as a springboard to and a grounding for ideas to investigate. King Open teachers of the 1-2, 2-3, and 3-4 classes had access to Wheelock College, which used the theories of Dewey and Piaget and others to train K-6 teachers. But while the experiential learning continued into the 5-6, 7-8 classes for other disciplines, it came to an abrupt halt in math by the fourth grade when students began to divide with two- and three-digit divisors (so called "long division"). Quine's insight turned out to be a bible upon which the marriage of experiential learning and mathematics could be more than a passing affair. Experiential learning theory is grounded in the countless cyclical experiences in which people try something, then think about what they did, then make improvements, then practice their improvements. It would seem that we learn most of what we know, from language to cooking to building shelters to live in, by applications of this process. One model for experiential learning is often presented as shown below:

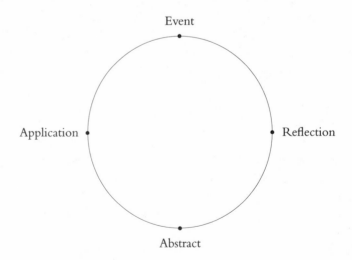

In this model at noon there is an event *(we try something)*, then at quarter past there is reflection on the event *(we think about what we did)*, then at half past there is an abstract conceptualization of the reflection *(we make improvements)*, then there is an application of the conceptualization *(we practice our improvements)*. Quine's insight provided the final link in the answer to our previous question, *"How to do that?"*: How to put (for Ari) his *"which way"* questions together with his *"how many"* questions around his concept of number.

The event would be trips on the T. We took our first trip with Lynne's sixth-grade math class in the fall of '88. When the students returned we had them draw pictures, write stories, and talk with one another about their trip, mediums in which the students reflected on the event. We thought of all these mediums as the students' "ordinary language descriptions" of the event and came to call all of it their *"people talk."* Next we looked in their representations of their *"people talk"* for features of the event that we were going to mathematize: the trip had a start *(Central Square Station);* it had a finish *(Park Street Station);* it went 3 stops and it traveled inbound *(see diagram 1).*

DIAGRAM 1   *Representation of a trip from Central Square to Park Street.*

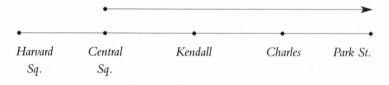

| Harvard Sq. | Central Sq. | Kendall | Charles | Park St. |

Students drew a version of diagram 1 as part of their *"people talk."*

When we returned we got off at *Harvard Square* which gave rise to diagram 2:

DIAGRAM 2   *Representation of a trip from Park Street to Harvard Square.*

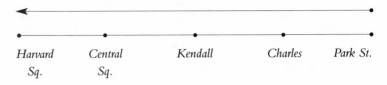

Harvard   Central   Kendall   Charles   Park St.
  Sq.   Sq.

This and similar events have provided thousands of sixth graders over the past thirteen years with a natural context for connecting two kinds of questions, *"Which way?"* and *"How many?"*, around their number concept. These diagrams illustrate *(in people talk)* that the *Park Street* Station is 3 stops inbound from *Central Square* (Diagram 1), and that *Harvard Square* is 4 stops outbound from *Park Street* (Diagram 2).

From these statements we can frame questions:

- In what direction and how many stops is *Park Street Station* from *Central Square?*
- In what direction and how many stops is *Harvard Square* from *Park Street Station?*

Both questions ask about the position of one station relative to another. Both answers are displacements: 3 stops inbound; 4 stops outbound. Both answers contain a "which way" as well as a "how many" component. Such quantities emerge in countless situations in which two measurements are compared relative to one another, and it stands to reason that scientists and mathematicians would invent some way to represent such quantities. (See Hoffman, *About Vectors.*)

As a prelude to mathematizing the answers to questions 1 and 2, we introduce a simpler context in which two students, Coast-to-Coast (*CTC*) and Watch Me (*WME*) are asked to stand up and compare heights.

If we simply ask, *"Which student is taller?"* we usually get an answer like:

1. *CTC* is taller than *WME*.

If we now ask what *feature* of *CTC* and *WME* we are talking about, the answer will come back, *"Their height."* We then ask (I have done this with numerous audiences of all ages and backgrounds) the students to construct a sentence that makes this same comparison but begins with "The height of *CTC* [H(*CTC*)]." We invariably get back the answer: The height of *CTC* is greater than the height of *WME*.

2. H(*CTC*) is greater than H(*WME*).

We now ask, "Where is the information about height encoded in sentences 1 and 2? In 1, the feature *"height"* is explicit in the linking phrase *"is taller than."* In 2, it is explicit in the name phrases H(*CTC*) and H(*WME*) having been completely erased from the linking phrase *"is greater than."* Never have I heard student or adult offer 2 as a response to the straightforward question *"Who is taller, A or B?"* The answer will come back "A," as the case may be, and then when prodded for a more elaborate answer, *"A is taller than B."* But never, *"The height of A,"* which makes no sense, or *"The height of A is greater than the height of B,"* which makes sense but sounds stilted. But this is Quine's insight: the symbolic representations in all of mathematics and science are representations of a conceptual language that no people on earth speak as a natural tongue. We came, in time, to call 2 *"feature talk,"* an example of what Quine calls *"regimented language."*

The above analysis takes us part of the way in showing how Quine's insight helps answer the "how to do that" question. We take students' *"people talk"* (their writings, pictures, verbal exchanges, etc.) and identify the relevant mathematical features, develop symbols for these, and construct questions (if we can) that will elicit appropriate *"feature talk."* This is the hard conceptual work without which the abstract mathematical symbols fly away from all but a small percentage of students.

If we go on to ask how much taller is *CTC* than *WME*, we might get the response:

> 3. *CTC* is 6″ taller than *WME,*
which leads students to:
> 4. H(*CTC*) is 6″ greater than H(*WME*).

Taken together 1–4 illustrate general tendencies of *"people talk"* for the simple comparative situations we are investigating: English piles information into the *"linking phrase." "Feature talk"* requires that "6″" be relocated to a name position.

But the "6″" is not a feature of *CTC* or *WME* in the way that height is, rather "6″" is a feature that quantifies the height comparison, makes it more specific. To mathematize this common, and deceptively uninteresting statement, requires two unanticipated moves. First, an "operation" of comparison *(c/t)* is explicitly introduced, yielding a sentence such as:

> H(*CTC*) compared to H(*WME*) is 6″ greater
> 5. H(*CTC*) *c/t* H(*WME*) is 6″ greater

Second, the directional component in the linking phrase "is 6″ greater" is explicitly attached to the quantity 6″ *("Which way?"* is connected to *"How many?")* and the identity predicate "is equal to" is introduced and made explicit:

("=" *for "is equal to"*)
> 6. H(*CTC*) *c/t* H(*WME*) = +6″   (*Statement 6 may be read the same as 5.*)

If we ask "How much shorter is WME than CTC?" we get the following sequence:

> 7. *WME* is 6″ shorter than *CTC*
> 8. H(*WME*) is 6″ less than H(*CTC*)
> 9. H(*WME*) *c/t* H(*CTC*) is 6″ less
> 10. H(*WME*) *c/t* H(*CTC*) = −6″

If we now know that CTC is 6½ ft. tall, then we may extract the following two subtraction statements:

> 11. H(*CTC*) *c/t* H(*WME*) = +6″
>   78″   −   72″   = +6″
>
> 12. H(*WME*) *c/t* H(*CTC*) = −6″
>   72″   −   78″   = −6″

Statements 11 and 12 represent a sea change in students' metaphor for subtraction, which, in algebra, is now assigned the all-important task of keeping track of the position of two measurements relative to one another. We are interested in *WME's* height relative to that of *CTC* and vice versa. Currently, they are left to figure all this out on their own, 90 percent never do. How could they when their textbooks don't address it.

We return now to our trip on the T and our questions that inquire about the relative position of two station stops on our trip. The feature of the stations that concerns us is much more subtle than the feature that we worked with *CTC* and *WME*. We are interested in the *location* of one station relative to the *location* of the other. Obviously everything worth somebody's time and attention has a location, if only for that person, but less obviously everything has a location only relative to something else. As far as we know, there is no absolute location in the whole universe.

For diagram 1 we have the following sequences of statements.

13. *Park Street* Station is 3 stops inbound from *Central Square.*

14. Location of *Park Street* Station is 3 stops inbound from the location of *Central Square.*

15. L(*PK*) is 3 stops inbound from L(*CSQ*)

16. L(*PK*) *c/t* L(*CSQ*) is 3 stops inbound

17. L(*PK*) *c/t* L(*CSQ*) = +3

   (*17 may be read as 16*)

For diagram 2, we have:

18. *Harvard Square* is 4 stops outbound from *Park Street* Station.

19. L(*HSQ*) is 4 stops outbound from L(*PK*)

20. L(*HSQ*) *c/t* L(*PK*) is 4 stops outbound

21. L(*HSQ*) *c/t* L(*PK*) = −4   (*21 may be read as 20*)

Note both the height comparisons and the location comparisons yield displacements as answers: positive and negative numbers wed direction *(which way?)* to quantity *(how many?)* to create the numbers algebra requires.

Students draw trip lines (variations of diagrams 1 and 2) as part of their "people talk" about the trip, then to generate subtraction equations for 17 and 21 we need a way of assigning numbers to the various locations on the trip line. To do this, we ask students to choose one station as their benchmark station, their point of reference, the station from which they observe the train passing by. Different students choose different benchmarks. Each student assigns zero to his/her benchmark. The results are tables 1 and 2.

TABLE 1 *This table mathematizes answers to the question: In what direction and how many stops is Park Street Station from Central Square?*

"L(PK)" means "the location of Park Street"

Student	Benchmark	Coordinate System	Symbolic Representation Integer Equation
A	Harvard Square L(HSQ)=0	CSQ PK •——————▶ •——•——•——•——• 0 +1 +2 +3 +4	L(PK) c/t L(CSQ) = +3 +4 - +1 = +3
B	Central Square L(CSQ)=0	CSQ PK •——————▶ •——•——•——•——• -1 0 +1 +2 +3	L(PK) c/t L(CSQ) = +3 +3 - 0 = +3
C	Kendall L(K)=0	CSQ PK •——————▶ •——•——•——•——• -2 -1 0 +1 +2	L(PK) c/t L(CSQ) = +3 +2 - (-1) = +3
D	Charles Street L(CH)=0	CSQ PK •——————▶ •——•——•——•——• -3 -2 -1 0 +1	L(PK) c/t L(CSQ) = +3 +1 - (-2) = +3
E	Park Street L(PK)=0	CSQ PK •——————▶ •——•——•——•——• -4 -3 -2 -1 0	L(PK) c/t L(CSQ) = +3 0 - (-3) = +3

TABLE 2   *This table mathematizes answers to the question: In what direction and how many stops is Harvard Square from Park Street?*

Student	Benchmark	Coordinate System	Symbolic Representation Integer Equation
A	*Harvard Square* L(HSQ)=0	HSQ ← → PK 0 +1 +2 +3 +4	L(HSQ) c/t L(PK) = -4 0 - (+4) = -4
B	*Central Square* L(CSQ)=0	HSQ ← → PK -1 0 +1 +2 +3	L(HSQ) c/t L(PK) = -4 -1 - (+3) = -4
C	*Kendall* L(K)=0	HSQ ← → PK -2 -1 0 +1 +2	L(HSQ) c/t L(PK) = -4 -2 - (+2) = -4
D	*Charles Street* L(CH)=0	HSQ ← → PK -3 -2 -1 0 +1	L(HSQ) c/t L(PK) = -4 -3 - (+1) = -4
E	*Park Street* L(PK)=0	HSQ ← → PK -4 -3 -2 -1 0	L(HSQ) c/t L(PK) = -4 -4 - 0 = -4

Tables 1 and 2 show that Quine's thesis, mathematics *in situ,* the regimentation of ordinary discourse, provides a way to effect a stable relationship between mathematics and/or science and experiential learning, one that could last beyond third grade and could be extended into high school and college. The process levels the playing field, brings in issues of language and symbolic representations, and opens up a mathematical landscape in which concepts central to all of scientific thought are introduced without fanfare to all beginning algebra students (e.g., "objectivization" and *"relativization,"* cf. Born, *Einstein's Theory of Relativity,* p. 2). Just as we assign measure numbers to *CTC* and *WME* to represent their height relative to some arbitrary unit of measure: H(*CTC*) = 78″ and H(*WME*) = 72″, we assign location numbers (coordinates) to trip points to represent their location relative to some arbitrary benchmark station: If L(*CSQ*) = 0, then L(*HSQ*) = −1, and L(*CH*) = +2. In this context we may interpret the integer equation +2 − (−1) = +3 to mean that L(*CH*) is 3 stops inbound from L(*HSQ*). By this means, the transportation system becomes available as a means of verifying the truth or falsity of subtraction equations directly, without reference to addition. Equations such as (−2) − (+2) = −4 and (−1) − (−4) = +3 may be checked in an appropriate *"transportation system"* to see if they are true or false.

The transition curriculum has acquired a life of its own. Hundreds of teachers have been trained in it, educators in graduate schools study it, and a small group of mathematicians, trainers, and teachers in the Southern Initiative of the Algebra Project work to reshape and refine it to meet the needs of particular teachers and students. Equally important, students in the Algebra Project who have founded the Young People's Project (YPP) have adapted the math games in the curriculum as their own and invented new ones, and are currently using them and other math activities to create a new culture around math literacy among their peers in after-school, Saturday, and summer programs.

During the years 1992–95 I assisted the seventh- and eighth-grade Algebra Project teachers at Brinkley Middle School in Jackson, Mississippi. Then in the '96–97 school year, I followed students from Brinkley who had completed Algebra 1 as eighth graders into Lanier High School and taught them a geometry course driven by the T192, a handheld computer. In '97–98, I was asked to teach a full load, six geometry courses, but for the next two years I had four geometry and two algebra courses. The algebra courses have given me a chance to revisit the central concepts of the transition curriculum. Revisiting the elemental concepts of algebra, it came to me that students construct representations of addition and subtraction in arithmetic in which the concept of direction *(Which way?)* is assigned to the operations. *For example the equation "4 + 3 = 7" may be represented like so:*

DIAGRAM 3

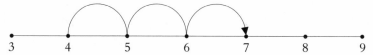

In this representation, called "adding on," it is addition, not the number 3, that carries the instruction to "hop" to the *right;* the "3" tells the students how many spaces to hop, not which way to hop. However, when students transition to algebra they must learn to think of "+" as giving an instruction simply to move and look to the displacement that follows to inform them both which way and how far to move. Using the transportation system as a physical model for such representations, we get the following diagrams and sentences:

DIAGRAM 4 *If I start at Kendall Station and travel two stops inbound, at what station do I arrive?*

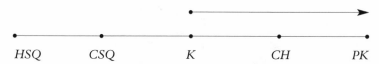

For diagram 4, we have the following sequence of statements:
    22. Start at *Kendall,* move two stops inbound, arrive at *Park.*
    23. $L(K)$ move two stops inbound arrive $L(PK)$
    24. $L(K) + (+2) = L(PK)$

DIAGRAM 5 *If I start at Kendall and travel two stops outbound, at what station do I arrive?*

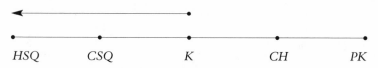

For diagram 5 we have the following sequence statements:

25. Start at *Kendall,* move two stops outbound, arrive at *Harvard Square.*

26. L(K) move two stops outbound arrive L(HSQ)

27. L(K) + −2 = L(HSQ)

As before, students choose different benchmark stations and assign integer coordinates to the points on their trip lines and generate simple addition equations to represent the two diagrams. See tables 3 and 4.

TABLE 3 *This table mathematizes the answers to the question: If I start at Kendall Station and move two stops inbound, at what station do I arrive?*

Student	Benchmark	Trip Line End Coordinate System	Symbolic Representation Integer Equation
A	*Harvard Square* (*HSQ*)	K PK 0 +1 +2 +3 +4	L(K) move +2 = L(PK) +2 + (+2) = +4
B	*Central Square* (*CSQ*)	K PK -1 0 +1 +2 +3	L(K) move +2 = L(PK) +1 + (+2) = +3
C	*Kendall* (*K*)	K PK -2 -1 0 +1 +2	L(K) move +2 = L(PK) 0 + (+2) = +2
D	*Charles Street* (*CH*)	K PK -3 -2 -1 0 +1	L(K) move +2 = L(PK) -1 + (+2) = +1
E	*Park Street* (*PK*)	K PK -4 -3 -2 -1 0	L(K) move +2 = L(PK) -2 + (+2) = 0

TABLE 4 *This table mathematizes the answers to the question: If I start at Kendall and move two stops outbound, at what station do I arrive?*

Student	Benchmark	Trip Line End Coordinate System	Symbolic Representation Integer Equation
A	Harvard Square (HSQ)	HSQ K 0 +1 +2 +3 +4	$L(K)$ move -2 = $L(HSQ)$ $+2 + (-2) = 0$
B	Central Square (CSQ)	HSQ K -1 0 +1 +2 +3	$L(K)$ move -2 = $L(HSQ)$ $+1 + (-2) = -1$
C	Kendall (K)	HSQ K -2 -1 0 +1 +2	$L(K)$ move -2 = $L(HSQ)$ $0 + (-2) = -2$
D	Charles Street (CH)	HSQ K -3 -2 -1 0 +1	$L(K)$ move -2 = $L(HSQ)$ $-1 + (-2) = -3$
E	Park Street (PK)	HSQ K -4 -3 -2 -1 0	$L(K)$ move -2 = $L(HSQ)$ $-2 + (-2) = -4$

(NOTE: This treatment of addition is not present in the transition curriculum but evolved as indicated above when I returned to teaching Algebra I at Lanier and further reflected on the "Which way?" and "How many?" questions. The transition curriculum adopts the approach to addition in which all the numbers are represented by directed line segments (arrows). The physical system for these representations is a type of relay race in which the passing of the baton is represented by addition, so that addition has the interpretation of "followed by" and the direction and movement are assigned solely to the displacements. [See Hoffmann, *About Vectors*, p. 1.] In textbooks, this treatment of displacements is presented in two dimensions whereas the relay race takes place along a line.)

There is a sense in which representations presented above for addition in algebra are extensions and generalizations of arithmetic representations; unfortunately, the same is not true of the subtraction representations. Third- and fourth-grade students who observe that one pencil is left when three pencils are taken away from a group of four pencils, might represent this as "4 − 3 = 1" and draw the following diagram:

DIAGRAM 6   *Representation of "4 − 3 = 1" as an arithmetic subtraction problem.*

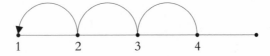

However, in the analysis given above for subtraction in algebra the equation "4 − 3 = 1" will be represented in a diagram as shown:

DIAGRAM 7   *Representation of "4 − 3 = 1" as an algebra subtraction problem.*

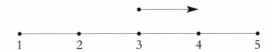

Here the subtraction sign serves to compare the location of 4 relative to 3. In the comparison model for subtraction, the equation "4 − 3 = 1" tells us that 4 is located 1 unit to the right of 3.

Moreover, in the analysis given above for subtraction in algebra diagram 6 will be represented by the diagram and equation show below:

DIAGRAM 8   *Representation of diagram 6 as an algebra subtraction problem* ($1 - 4 = -3$).

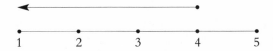

In our comparison model for subtraction diagram 8 tells us that 1 is located three units to the left of 4. This is represented by the equation "$1 - 4 = -3$," which compares the location of 1 to that of 4. Diagrams 9, 10, 11, and 12 below lay down a foundation for parallel diagrams that are representations for central concepts of subtraction and addition in algebra.

Diagrams 9 and 10 are for east/west trip lines; diagrams 11 and 12 are for north/south trip lines.

DIAGRAM 9   *The displacement moves east.*

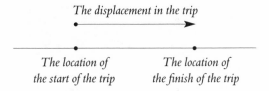

The displacement in the trip

The location of
the start of the trip

The location of
the finish of the trip

DIAGRAM 10   *The displacement moves west.*

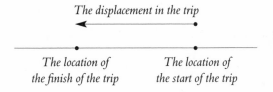

The displacement in the trip

The location of
the finish of the trip

The location of
the start of the trip

DIAGRAM 11
The displacement moves south.

DIAGRAM 12
The displacement moves north.

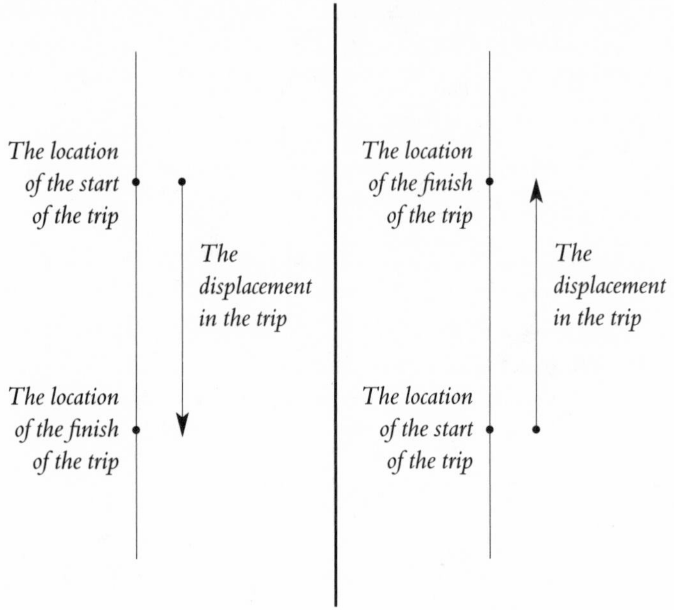

In each of diagrams 9, 10, 11, 12, the displacement provides an answer to the following questions:

- How far and in what direction is the finish of the trip from the start?
- What is the position of the finish of the trip relative to *(compared to)* the position of the start?

These diagrams capture two important relationships, which may be expressed in the following sentences. Each sentence applies to each of the diagrams 9, 10, 11, and 12.

- Sentence *(passive voice):* The location of the finish of a trip relative to *(compared to)* the location of the trip's start is given by the displacement.
- Sentence *(active voice):* From the start of a trip, move according to the displacement, arrive at the finish of the trip.

We look at both sentences with a shrug and say, *"So what's new?"* That's a point that Quine struggled with as much as anyone, namely the role of the "obvious" in the discipline of mathematics.

To construct symbolic representation for the above two sentences we need symbols for the following features and expressions. One possible set of nonstandard symbols is given in table 5 below.

TABLE 5

Feature and Expressions	Nonstandard Symbols
The location of the start of a trip	*ts*
The location of the finish of a trip	*tf*
Displacement in the trip	*td*
Relative to (*compared to*)	*c/t*
move	$\longrightarrow$
is given by, arrive	EQ

In table 6 we give a symbolic representation for each sentence using the above symbols. To read the symbolic representation, just read the sentence it represents.

TABLE 6

Sentence (*Passive voice*)	*The location of the finish of a trip relative to (compared to) the location of the trip's start is given by the displacement.*
Symbolic Representation	*tf* *c/t* *ts* EQ *td*
Sentence (*Active voice*)	*From the start of the trip, move according to the displacement, arrive at the finish of the trip.*
Symbolic Representation	*ts* $\longrightarrow$ *td* EQ *tf*

Once introduced, coordinates fix the locations of the start and finish of a trip and enable us to quantify the displacement in the trip. Table 7 introduces standard symbols used around the globe as placeholders for such coordinates. It also gives the standard symbols for the other *"expressions."*

TABLE 7

Feature and Expressions	Nonstandard Symbols	Standard Symbols
The location of the start of a trip	*ts*	$x1, y1$
The location of the finish of a trip	*tf*	$x2, y2$
Displacement in the trip	*td*	$\Delta x, \Delta y$ *Read "Delta x,"* *"Delta y"*
Relative to (*compared to*)	*c/t*	—
move	⟶	+
is given by, arrive	*EQ*	=

Notice that the subscripts "1" and "2" are used to distinguish the location of the start of a trip from that of the finish. On the other hand *"x"* and *"y"* tell us whether the trip is on an *east/west* line (*diagrams 13 & 14*) or a *north/south* line (*diagrams 15 & 16*).

DIAGRAM 13   *The displacement (Δx) moves east.*

DIAGRAM 14   *The displacement (Δx) moves west.*

DIAGRAM 15
The displacement (Δy) moves south.

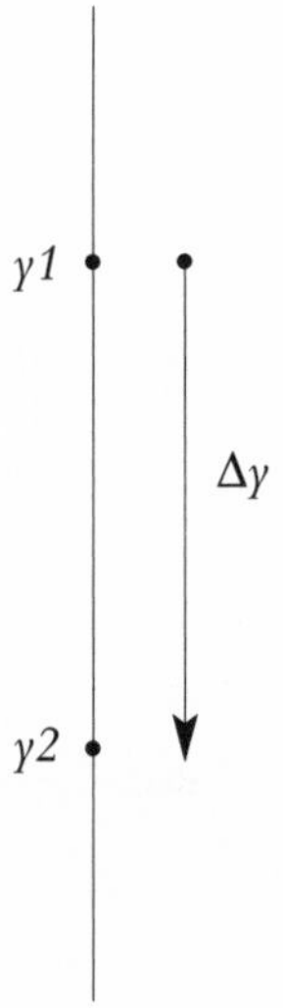

DIAGRAM 16
The displacement (Δy) moves north.

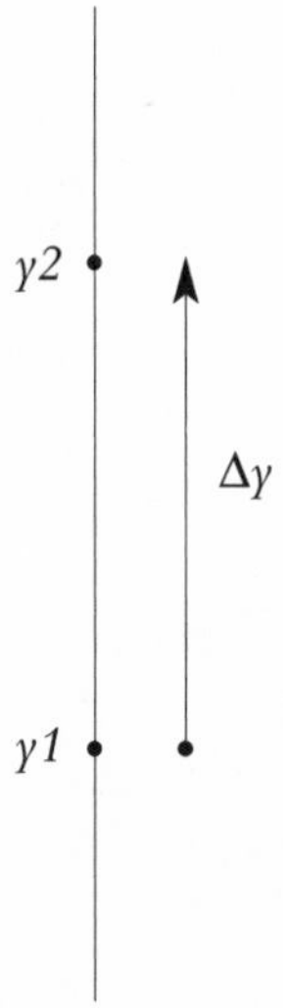

The equations for diagrams 13 and 14 use *"x."* Think of x as a point that starts at location *x1* and moves a displacement Δx to arrive at the finish location *x2:*

$$x1 + \Delta x = x2$$

In the equation below, Δx, the displacement, tells us the location of the finish, *x2*, relative to the start, *x1*.

$$x2 - x1 = \Delta x$$

In standard notation "Δx" represents displacements to the *east* or *west*, while "Δy" represents displacements to the *north* or *south*, so that the equations for diagrams 15 and 16 are as follows:

$$y1 + \Delta y = y2$$
$$y2 - y1 = \Delta y$$

The Constant of Main Street

The following diagram shows the intersection of *East* and *South Streets* at *Benchmark Plaza*. *East Street,* runs east and west while *South Street* runs north and south. *Walmart* and *McDonald's* are on *East Street,* east of *Benchmark Plaza,* while *Comp U.S.A.* and *Office Depot* are on *South Street,* north of the plaza. *Main Street* runs southeast, crossing *South Street* to the north of *Comp U.S.A.* and *East Street* to the east of *McDonald's. Main Street* is under construction from the location of *Books-A-Million* (which is on *Main Street* due east of *Comp U.S.A.* and due north of *Walmart*) to *Jitney Jungle* (also on *Main Street* but due east of *Office Depot* and due north of *McDonald's*). The city has established a detour on *Main Street* from *Books-A-Million* to *Jitney Jungle.* Traffic is first displaced due south until it reaches a street (running east-west) that connects *Office Depot* with *Jitney Jungle.* At that point traffic is routed by a displacement due east, where it gets back on *Main St.* at *Jitney Jungle.*

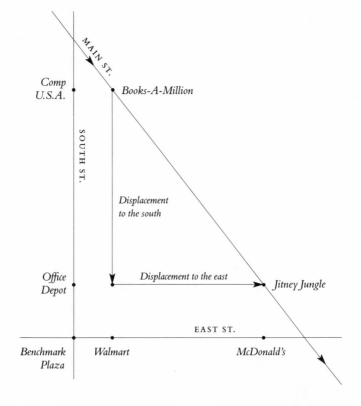

We represent the displacement in the first leg of the detour by "Δy." The diagram shows that Δy is the same as the displacement in a trip from *Comp U.S.A.* to *Office Depot*. This gives rise to the following sequence of statements:

28. The displacement in the trip from *Comp U.S.A.* to *Office Depot* is given by Δy.

29. *Office Depot*'s location compared to that of *Comp U.S.A.* is given by Δy.

30. L(*Office Depot*) c/t L(*Comp U.S.A.*) $= \Delta y$.

If we assign $y2$ as the location of *Office Depot* and $y1$ as the location of *Comp U.S.A.*, both on *South Street,* then we can represent 30 as:

31. $y2 - y1 = \Delta y$

(Note that Δy, a displacement, does not have a location.)

On the other hand we represent the detour that travels due east by "Δx."

The diagram shows that Δx is the same as the displacement from *Walmart* to *McDonald's:*

32. The displacement in the trip from *Walmart* to *McDonald's* is given by Δx.

33. The location of *McDonald's* compared to that of *Walmart* is given by Δx.

34. L(*McDonald's*) c/t L(*Walmart*) $= \Delta x$.

We now assign $x1$ and $x2$ as the locations of *Walmart* and *McDonald's,* respectively, which gives the equation:

35. $x2 - x1 = \Delta x$

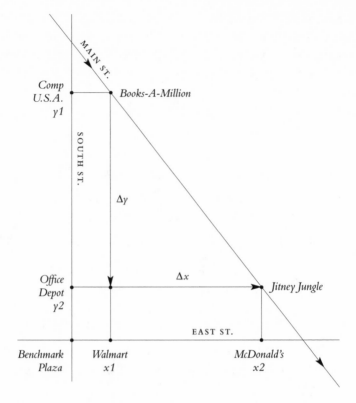

Main Street is a one-way street. Detours on *Main Street* always follow this pattern: Start at some initial location (such as *Books-A-Million*) on *Main*, travel due *south*, turn and travel due *east* to reach some final location (such as *Jitney Jungle*) on *Main Street*. In this case Δy always represents the first leg of the detour (travel to the *south*), and Δx the second leg (travel to the *east*). Now it is a fact that no matter where the city establishes the initial location and the final location of a detour, the ratio of Δy to Δx is always the same number: it never changes; it remains constant; the townspeople call it the *constant of Main Street*.

$$\frac{\Delta y}{\Delta x} = \frac{y_2 - y_1}{x_2 - x_1} = a\ constant$$

Students of Algebra 1 are asked to master the concept of a linear equation and its graph, a straight line. But at the very core of these concepts is the *constant of Main Street,* the ratio of two displacements. We can always take a ruler and draw a line through two points on a piece of paper. Then relative to some system of coordinates with some benchmark point *(the Origin)* we will have a ratio:

$$\frac{\Delta y}{\Delta x} = \frac{y_2 - y_1}{x_2 - x_1} = a\ constant$$

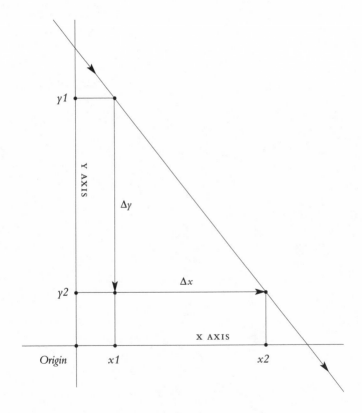

The idea is that as long as the start and the finish of a *"detour"* are distinct points on the line it doesn't matter what their locations are relative to each other; the ratio of Δy to Δx will remain constant. Mathematicians call this constant the slope of the line and label it *m*. In terms of the physical system described above the constant gives information about the inclination of *Main Street* relative to *West* and *South Streets*. At its core are several key concepts of elementary algebra and subsequent mathematics. We have discussed at least one of these in some detail: the concept that subtraction in elementary algebra is assigned the task of keeping track of the position of two measurements and/or locations relative to each other.

This last discussion should discourage any thought that the concepts treated in the transition curriculum are not of the utmost importance, requiring detailed and careful attention in some treatment or other if we, the adult community of educators, are to be responsible in our all-consuming movement to see the student community meet our standards in learning elementary algebra.

ACKNOWLEDGMENTS

First, to a giant in the Mississippi struggle, Mrs. Annie Devine, who crossed over as the last sentence of this book was being typed. Her strength and commitment, and the strength and commitment of people like her, transformed the nation.

To Zora Cobb, nine now and who I know felt far too much of her father's time over the last two years was spent with this book. But I also know that deep down she likes the idea of this book. And thanks to her big brother, Kenn, always present, easing any worry about my being away so much.

To Ann, wife and friend, with enough love to tolerate the upstairs hall being a yearlong clutter of files, books, boxes of documents, transcripts, and regular promises that it would all be cleaned up "soon." The book could not have been done without her support.

The kids, especially those from Weldon, Jackson, and Bennettsville, for whom a northern writer's ways were strange and puzzling. Yet they were generous with their time and eager to offer their thoughts. Once again they remind us of how much we owe to Black struggle in the South.

Thanks to Shae Goodman Robinson, principal of Brinkley Middle School in Jackson, Mississippi; Johnny L. Hughes, principal of Lanier High School, also in Jackson; and Lydia Harding Elder, principal of Weldon Middle School in Weldon, North Carolina, for granting access and thoughtful insights into the schools they administer.

Shirley, Jessie, Merle, Thelma, Constance, Freddie, Julia, Nancy, Lynne, Lynn, Doris, Valerie, Marjorie, Marion, Miss

Byrd, Miss Wilma Morris, and Howard Saunders, educators all, remind us how much commitment counts.

Special thanks to the folks at Positive Innovations and the Algebra Project, Inc. While doing their regular work, both organizations gave me help in innumerable ways. Without their assistance this book would undoubtedly still be in draft form.

I thank, too, Beacon editor Andy Hrycyna, for both his patience and consistently good advice.

There are some sources of material other than my own interviews and Algebra Project material that should be acknowledged. The quote from Ella Baker that opens chapter 1 and reappears at the end of the book is from Joanne Grant's essential *Ella Baker: Freedom Bound,* published by John Wiley and Sons, Inc. Miss Baker's quotes on leadership in chapter 2 are from Charles M. Payne's important work on the Mississippi movement, *I've Got the Light of Freedom,* published by the University of California Press. The Amzie Moore epigraph in chapter 2 is from Howell Raines's *My Soul Is Rested,* published by Putnam's Sons; the 1977 quote is from an interview that is part of the University of Southern Mississippi Civil Rights Movement in Mississippi oral history project. And hovering over every one of these pages are all the SNCCs and local folks from Mississippi (especially Joe and Rebecca McDonald of Ruleville) who took me in some forty years ago and, in teaching me, changed me forever.

And lastly, heartfelt thanks to Mary Ridley, who got the tape transcriptions done, thereby removing a great burden from my shoulders by making the actual work of writing far easier than it would have been struggling through a mountain of audiotapes.

—C.C.

This story has been unfolding for the past forty years, but it took Charlie to get it told. I wonder who else was there as it unfolded and could tell it? In any case, Charlie has it told and we're all grateful, especially me.

On the movement side of this story are my "fundis" (my elders, my teachers, my mentors): Ella Baker, Amzie Moore, C. C.

Bryant, Imogene Bryant, Webb Owens, Alleyene Quinn, E. W. Steptoe, "Sing" Steptoe, "Old man" Saunders, Mrs. Pilcher, Fannie Lou Hamer, Hartman Turnbow. They saw to it that I had places to sleep, meals to eat, change to keep; they strode the path ahead of me, watched my back, aimed a weapon; they took my life into their stories and my story into their Lives.

On the family side of this story are my father, Gregory H. Moses (Pop), and his brother, William Moses (Uncle Bill). They taught me to look through the lenses of the "common person" at the life all around me. On the family side also is my mother, Louise Parris Moses. She showed me how to live silence, quietly. Her passing on early, in 1958, released me to do what was coming, the movement.

The hands of the young held the reins of the movement. Young Black students in the South started the movement with their silent "sit-ins" at lunch counters in February of 1960. The sit-in movement gave rise to the Student Nonviolent Coordinating Committee (SNCC) in April 1960 and by August 1960 I was traveling to Cleveland, Mississippi, to meet Amzie. We name a fraction of the young people of SNCC in this book; here we acknowledge and thank them all.

From 1960 through May of 1976 my wife, Janet Jemmott, and I lived in Tanzania, where we established our family: Maisha, Omowale, Tabasuri, and Malaika. Bill Sutherland introduced us to Julius Nyerere, who secured positions for Janet and I as teachers in the Ministry of Education. We worked at Samé Secondary School, where I taught math and Janet taught English as a second language. I wish to extend my deep thanks on behalf of Janet and our family, to Bill, president Nyerere, the staff and students at Samé, Baba and Mama Modenge, and the people of the WaParé community who welcomed us and provided space for our family to take root and flourish. During the years when Maisha, Omowale, and Tabasuri were born, Janet's mother, Jessie Jemmott (Bibi), came and spent six months for each of her "grands." Our family owes a lot to Bibi. Then there was Mzee Omari, who stepped up to take care of the children, and finally Hamisi Abdalah, a young elementary school student who adopted our family. We thank them all. During those years we were part of a small circle of "Wa Negro" (Blacks from the United States) who shared community together and we thank them all, especially Vida Gaynor.

In the years from 1976 to 1982 our family was supported by a grant from a program the Ford Foundation established to help minorities gain Ph.D.s and we thank them. During those years Janet decided to pursue a career in medicine and when, out of the blue, I received a MacArthur Fellowship in 1982, "a way out of no way" was opened.

In the years from 1982 to the present, Janet completed medical school and began her practice of pediatrics at M.I.T., our children transitioned through their teenage years and into their mid- and late twenties and we started the Algebra Project.

From 1982 to 1987 the Algebra Project was incubating at the open program of the Martin Luther King school in Cambridge. The sole financial support during these years was the MacArthur Fellowship and I thank them. I thank Mary Lou Mehrling, who invited me to teach algebra to students in her 7-8 class and to Lynne Godfrey who piloted the Algebra Project's "Transition to Curriculum" in her sixth-grade class. I also thank the members of the Seymour Society, African-American undergraduates at Harvard, who helped launch that material. Also many thanks to Sandra Darling and Lena James, King Open administrators.

When the MacArthur Fellowship ended, Teressa Perry, dean of students at Wheelock College, introduced me to its then president, Don Cheever, who secured a position for me at the college that enabled me to continue working to develop the Algebra Project. Many thanks to Teressa, Dan, and other Wheelock faculty.

As the project began to reach out from its base at the King Open I was joined by Cynthia Silva, Jackie Rivers, and Bill Crombie and I thank them. During these years the project picked up support from the Hasbro Foundation, the Edna McConnell Clarke Foundation, and the Boston Foundation. Special thanks to Anna Faith Jones and Wendy Puerifoy (now with PEFNET), who have remained staunch believers in and supporters of the project from those years to the present. Many thanks to Jeff Howard of the Efficacy Institute for introducing me to the culture of training trainers and to Jim Burroughs, who established the Algebra Project's Training of Trainers program.

During the nineties the project established small efforts in urban school systems across the country and a sizable effort in the rural areas of the South. Many thanks to the project's participants (students, parents, teachers, administrators, and community activists) across the country. This work expanded with the help of major grants from the MacArthur and Lilly Foundations, the National Science Foundation, and particularly the Open Society Institute.

—R.M.

INDEX